LOCAL
AUTHOR

A Cry for Justice

A Cry
for
Justice

*Daniel Rudd
and His Life in
Black Catholicism,
Journalism,
and Activism,
1854–1933*

GARY B. AGEE

The University of
Arkansas Press

Fayetteville

2011

ISBN-10: 1-55728-975-1
ISBN-13: 978-1-55728-975-9

15   14   13   12   11   5   4   3   2   1

Designed by Liz Lester

⊗ The paper used in this publication meets the minimum requirements
of the American National Standard for Permanence of Paper for Printed
Library Materials Z39.48–1984.

LIBRARY OF CONGRESS
CATALOGING-IN-PUBLICATION DATA

Agee, Gary Bruce, 1965–
     A cry for justice : Daniel Rudd and his life in Black Catholicism, journalism,
and activism, 1854–1933 / Gary B. Agee.
          p.   cm.
     Includes bibliographical references and index.
     ISBN-13: 978-1-55728-975-9 (cloth : alk. paper)
     ISBN-10: 1-55728-975-1 (cloth : alk. paper)
          1. Rudd, Dan. A. (Daniel Arthur), b. 1854. 2. African Americans—Biography.
3. African American Catholics—Biography. 4. African American journalists—
Biography. 5. American Catholic tribune—History. 6. African American political
activists—Biography. 7. African Americans—Civil rights—History. 8. Civil
rights—Religious aspects—Catholic Church—History. 9. Social justice—United
States—History. 10. United States—Race relations—History. I. Title.
     E185.97.R83A43 2011
     282.092—dc23
     [B]

                                                        2011034110

We think we will live long enough to see a black man president of this Republic.

DANIEL RUDD,
10 FEBRUARY 1888

CONTENTS

Preface ix

Acknowledgments xi

Introduction xiii

1 • Daniel Rudd and the Establishment of the
   American Catholic Tribune 1

2 • A New Civilization Based on the Fatherhood
   of God and the Brotherhood of Man 37

3 • Archbishop John Ireland's Masterly Plea
   for Justice 55

4 • Justice for African Americans 83

5 • Beyond Concerns of Race 109

6 • The Colored Catholic Congress Movement,
   1889–1894 141

7 • Daniel Rudd's Post-*ACT* Years in the South 167

Conclusion 189

Notes 191

Selected Bibliography 221

Index 229

PREFACE

In 1969 David Spalding, C. F. X., published a groundbreaking article on the Colored Catholic Congresses of the nineteenth century. In "The Negro Catholic Congresses, 1889–1894," Spalding identified Daniel Arthur Rudd (1854–1933) as the "chief architect" of this important lay initiative.[1] Prior to the article's publication, Rudd's contribution to the work of the Catholic Church in America had been largely forgotten. Spalding's study, however, inspired subsequent scholars, including Dom Cyprian Davis, O.S.B., who in 1990 published his seminal work, *The History of Black Catholics in the United States*.[2] One important historical character foregrounded in Davis's work is Daniel Rudd. Davis's study of this black Catholic leader has inspired scholars to devote attention not only to Rudd but also to his newspaper, the *American Catholic Tribune*, a black Catholic weekly published from 1886 to 1897. In particular, Joseph H. Lackner, S.M., has to date published three articles examining Rudd and the *American Catholic Tribune*: "Daniel Rudd, Editor of the *American Catholic Tribune*, from Bardstown to Cincinnati" (1994); "The American Catholic Tribune and the Puzzle of Its Finances" (1995); and "The *American Catholic Tribune*, No Other Like It" (2007).[3]

This book will build on the work of Davis and Lackner by exploring the nature of the "cry for justice" lifted by Rudd throughout the years of his newspaper's publication. My primary thesis is that from 1886 through the newspaper's collapse, circa 1897, Rudd promoted a church-centered vision of justice that presumed for the Catholic Church a vital role in the establishment of a racially equitable society in America. Appealing to the "Fatherhood of God and Brotherhood of Man," the editor of the *American Catholic Tribune* employed the theologically rich nomenclature of the day. These convictions regarding the fundamental unity of the human family found support both in the teachings of Jesus and the Christian Doctrine of Creation. Rudd argued the best hope for African Americans living in late nineteenth-century America was the Catholic Church. He believed that through its mission and ministry justice would indeed prevail in American society. Moreover, during this same period Rudd found sufficient evidence and encouragement from church leaders to believe that this divine institution would play a pivotal role in society's eventual recognition of the full equality of African Americans.

The primary source material for this book is the *American Catholic Tribune*. There are 285 extant copies of this publication at the Philadelphia Archdiocesan Historical Research Center, and the newspaper is also available on microfilm at several libraries. Though Rudd began publishing the *American Catholic Tribune* in August 1886, the earliest extant copy of the newspaper is dated 18 February 1887. The last extant copy, published in Detroit, is dated 8 September 1894.

ACKNOWLEDGMENTS

This book owes a debt of gratitude to many fine people. To my father and mother, James and Alene, whose faith and service to the most needy in our community make me want to be a better person. To my wife, Lori, the mother of our ten children, who has loved and served me devotedly since we met. As a result of her love, I experienced what can only be described as a renaissance. Looking back at my journals from the early years of our marriage, it is evident that she drew out of my inner being a set of abilities and gifts that had lain buried beneath a heap of self-doubt. For years she has encouraged me to write, and I have finally begun to listen. To my brother Tim, ever the generous one, and always nearby when I need him; it was he who paid for my first year of doctoral studies. I thank the members of the two congregations I have been fortunate to lead: the Hopewell Church of God and the Beechwood Church of God. They afforded me the time to research and write this book. Two individuals above all others deserve thanks at the University of Dayton. First, Cecilia Moore, who in spite of her busy schedule agreed to supervise the reading course that introduced me to Daniel Arthur Rudd. And, finally, William L. Portier, my dissertation adviser. His third-floor office door is always open to students and faculty alike. Many times I made use of this generous gift. His patience, expertise, and at times toughness helped me better understand the vocation of the scholar. The fruit of his years of study and his deep love for the church have improved not only this manuscript but also me as a person.

INTRODUCTION

On 6 January 1892, Daniel Arthur Rudd, a former slave and the proprietor and editor of the *American Catholic Tribune,* answered an invitation to speak before the Apostolate of the Press, an organization of Catholic editors and publishers, gathered in New York City. The youthful and energetic Rudd was at the zenith of his career. His many accomplishments up to this crowning moment demonstrate a man driven by deep resolve. Despite the bondage of his youth, Rudd, with the help of heretofore unknown benefactors, managed to get a well-rounded primary education, subsequently completing his high school training in Springfield, Ohio, following the Civil War. While residing in Springfield, Rudd became an accomplished printer and editor. In 1886 he and partner James Theodore Whitson, M.D., established a newspaper, the *American Catholic Tribune,* which subsequently became a national publication boasting 10,000 subscribers by 1892. This remarkably large subscription base made the *ACT* one of the most successful black newspapers of its era.

Daniel Rudd was among the most visible and influential lay Catholics of his generation. In demand as a lecturer, he traveled extensively. On these excursions Rudd met and won the confidence and cooperation of many distinguished church leaders, including James Cardinal Gibbons (1834–1914), archbishop of Baltimore; Henry Edward Cardinal Manning (1807–1892), of Westminster, United Kingdom; and Charles Cardinal Lavigerie (1825–1892), archbishop of Carthage and Algiers and primate of Africa. Rudd and several delegates to the first Colored Catholic Congress held in Washington, D.C., in 1889 were even hosted by President Grover Cleveland (1837–1908).[1]

At the same time Rudd was addressing the members of the Catholic press in New York, not far away in Philadelphia the delegates of the Colored Catholic Congress were meeting. Rudd was the visionary founder of this same organization established three years earlier. Moreover, Rudd appears to have been the initiator of the interracial lay Catholic congress movement. This important lay initiative was subsequently formed with the aid of influential German Catholic laymen William J. Onahan (1836–1919) and Henry J. Spaunhorst.

Despite Rudd's amazing accomplishments, his decision to answer the invitation to speak before the members of the Catholic press was accepted with "some temerity." Rudd's sense of the moment, however, trumped his reservations; the editor of the *American Catholic Tribune* confessed that this same platform afforded "one of the greatest opportunities" offered him to discuss issues of importance.[2]

Employing in his speech the jeremiad, a convention common to nineteenth- and twentieth-century African American social critics, Rudd reminded his audience that the "bas[ic] proposition of the American Government" was that "all men are born free and equal." "Its primal law declares that no one shall be molested, in life, in liberty or in the pursuit of happiness." The editor of the *American Catholic Tribune* argued that these same egalitarian principles were, in fact, "Catholic to the core," the church and state "fully agreeing in these premises." True to the jeremiadic construction, however, Rudd informed the members of the Catholic press that his race was "receiving more than their fair share of the ills that lay authwart [*sic*] the pathway of American life." Yet Rudd, ever the optimist, held out hope that African Americans would in the not too distant future be afforded the opportunity to thrive in the United States.[3]

In this same address, Rudd voiced his conviction that the Catholic Church would play a pivotal role in the establishment of justice and in the recognition of the full equality of blacks in the United States. Rudd also argued that equality for African Americans was set forth in America's founding documents, the Declaration of Independence as well as in the U.S. Constitution. He called on Catholic editors not only to take up this work on behalf of blacks, but also to make it the "very highest class of the current literature of the day." Further, Rudd reminded his audience that as a result of the church's "matchless charities," the "absolute equality before her altar," the "magnificent rites and ceremonials," and the "soundness of her philosophy," it had gained the "admiration" and "confidence" of a "developing race."[4]

In this same speech, Rudd urged his predominantly white Catholic audience to make a conscious effort to reach out to blacks. On behalf of African Americans, Rudd called on Catholics to "cast within their reach" the "anchor chain of Catholic Hope, Love and Charity." This could be done, he further explained, on several fronts, the "church, the schoolroom, in societies for young men and women, through the press, in business and commercial circles, and in every walk of life."[5]

Rudd urged Catholics to ignore the "accursed custom of American prejudice." The editor specifically called on fellow religionists involved in trade unions to "demand that every barrier be beaten down," allowing African Americans entrance. Similarly, he asked Catholic business owners to employ blacks on the same terms as other employees, "upon the ground of merit."[11]

Rudd's speech delivered to the Apostolate of the Press established the high-water mark of his influence in the Catholic Church. Only a month after his address, a group of black Catholics in Philadelphia, colleagues of Rudd's, began publishing the *Journal,* a rival black Catholic newspaper that appears to have adversely impacted the *American Catholic Tribune.*

This book traces Rudd's understanding of justice as it developed over time. Though he consistently maintained a vision of justice that included for blacks the recognition of their full equality, his understanding as to the best approach for achieving this objective passed through three identifiable stages. In his early years, during the Springfield period, Rudd was an integrationist. His approach for winning the rights of blacks may be characterized as a campaign of direct editorial advocacy, very much like the confrontational approach employed by Frederick Douglass (1818–1895) during the post-Reconstruction era. The Cincinnati/Detroit period of Rudd's life corresponds to his publication of the *American Catholic Tribune.* During this time, Rudd used his newspaper to promote a vision of justice that presumed for the Catholic Church an essential role in bringing about racial equality. After 1897, during the southern period, subsequent to Rudd's move from Detroit to Mississippi, it appears he may have dropped not only his campaign of direct editorial advocacy for the rights of blacks, but also his conviction that the Catholic Church would take a leading role in advocating for racial justice. Instead, in his biography of Scott W. Bond (1852–1933), Rudd promoted a vision of justice that shared much in common with Booker T. Washington's (1856–1915) accommodating, self-help approach for racial uplift.

Daniel Arthur Rudd (1854–1933). (Courtesy of the University of Notre Dame Archives.)

CHAPTER 1

Daniel Rudd and the Establishment of the *American Catholic Tribune*

We also had the great pleasure to meet our old instructor the Rev. Jno. S. Verdin S.J. . . . How well did we remember the musical sound of his kind voice. It seemed like childhood days again, when in Bardstown at old St. Josephs we received words of counsel and listened to his matchless oratory.

D. RUDD
13 OCTOBER 1888

Slavery in Bardstown

Bardstown, Kentucky, was the childhood home of Daniel Arthur Rudd. It was one of the few rural communities south of the Ohio River with a numerically significant Catholic population. The region surrounding this community became known as Kentucky's "Catholic Holy Land." Bardstown's first Catholic colony, made up of twenty-five pioneer families primarily from Maryland, was led by Basil Hayden. In 1785 this group of immigrants established the Pottinger Creek settlement about three miles from Bardstown. By 1792 six distinct Catholic settlements were located near the town. In 1808 Pope Pius VII (1742–1823) established America's first inland diocese at Bardstown. Bishop Benedict Joseph Flaget (1763–1850), the diocese's first bishop, subsequently purchased the Thomas Howard plantation near Bardstown. Here the prelate constructed St. Thomas Seminary. In 1816 Flaget laid the cornerstone for the first cathedral west of the Allegheny Mountains, the Basilica of St. Joseph Proto-Cathedral. Over the next couple of years the structure was completed.[1]

Elizabeth (Eliza) Frances Smith Rudd, Daniel's mother, was born 25 February 1807. She may have been the offspring of an interracial union. Both the 1870 and 1880 censuses list her racial classification as "mulatto." At an early age the young girl was accompanied by her grandmother to Bardstown. Sometime between 1840 and 1845, Eliza was acquired by Bullitt County, Kentucky, native, Charles Haydon, and his wife, Matilda Rose Smith Haydon. Given that Eliza's maiden name was "Smith," it is possible prior to being acquired by the Haydons that she may have served as a slave in the home of Matilda's family.[2]

About 1846 Charles Haydon constructed an elegant home to accommodate his growing family. This grand brick structure would, by a subsequent owner, be named "Anatok."[3] The home of Charles Haydon where young Daniel Rudd presumably served as a slave was located only a couple of hundred yards southeast of St. Joseph Proto-Cathedral. In the time of Daniel's youth, one could presumably stand on the front porch of Anatok, look out beyond the oak trees, and enjoy a commanding view of the majestic cathedral, its impressive columns, and towering steeple. This view of what one observer called the "most stately and capacious house of worship in the state" would have, no doubt, made an indelible impression on the young Daniel.[4]

Charles and Matilda were the parents of four children. Maria Haydon, the couple's third child, was born in 1840; the fourth, John Polin Haydon was born in 1843. Following their births there would have been plenty of additional work around the Haydon household. Eliza, Daniel's mother, may have been acquired to meet this need.[5]

Robert Rudd, the father of the subject of this book, was born 15 May 1801.[6] His first owner was Richard Rudd, a Catholic. By 1833 Richard's estate totaled more than 650 acres. Throughout his life the Bardstown native owned over thirty slaves. In 1833 Richard died, perhaps falling victim to the deadly cholera epidemic that struck the region in the spring of the same year.[7] Robert had been sold or transferred to a second owner prior

Anatok, where Rudd presumably served as a slave for Charles and Matilda Haydon, his Catholic owners in Bardstown. (Courtesy of the Nelson County Genealogical Roundtable, Nelson County Public Library, Bardstown, Kentucky.)

to Richard's death, but a review of the slaveholder's assets from this same year gives us a glimpse of the estate on which Robert previously had served. When Richard's estate was appraised in 1833, he counted among his earthly possessions over 110 hogs, eighty-nine sheep, a herd of cattle numbering about thirty, three oxen, and twelve horses. The farm had roughly 100 acres of corn under cultivation, and Richard was a partner in another 70 acres. At the time of his death, the estate records indicate Richard owned twelve slaves valued at $3,035. The oldest slave on the Richard Rudd estate in 1833 was a fifty-four-year-old male who carried the same name as the subject of this book, "Daniel Rudd." This same slave, born in 1779, was valued at $250. Considering that this elder Daniel worked on the same plantation as Robert, and was about twenty-two years his senior, it is plausible the

This portrait is believed to be of Charles Haydon. (Courtesy of the Nelson County Genealogical Roundtable, Nelson County Public Library, Bardstown, Kentucky.)

elder Daniel was Robert's father. This would have made the elder Daniel Rudd the grandfather of the subject of this book.[8]

Having been transferred from the farm of Richard Rudd sometime before 1833, it is unclear where Robert and a group of twenty-one other slaves previously owned by Richard Rudd labored. It may have been they were transferred or sold to one of Richard's three surviving brothers: James, William, or Christopher Rudd. In 1840, however, this lot of twenty-two slaves was willed to Richard's widow, Margaret, and to their two sons, James and John Alexander. At this time, Margaret, who appears to have been slighted in her late husband Richard's will, received eight of the twenty-two servants. Robert, aged forty by this time, was among them.[9]

Basilica of St. Joseph Proto-Cathedral, Bardstown, Kentucky. (Courtesy of the Nelson County Genealogical Roundtable, Nelson County Public Library, Bardstown, Kentucky.)

Robert Rudd and his wife, Elizabeth, worked as sextons at St. Joseph Proto-Cathedral. During this same period, church records show the Jesuits contracted with one referred to as "Black Man Bob" for services rendered to the pastor of the cathedral. Presumably, this individual was Robert. The baptismal records of the cathedral in Bardstown also reveal that between 1845 and 1854 Daniel's father served as a sponsor for the baptisms of three black Catholics. While in the employ of the cathedral, Robert appears to have continued to serve on the Rudd estate nearby.[10]

Robert and Eliza were permitted by their owners to marry in 1831, even though slave unions were not legally binding and could be nullified at the discretion of one's master. The covenant between Eliza and Robert, despite its legal tenuousness, produced twelve children; Daniel was the eleventh. He was born on 7 August 1854 on the Haydon plantation. Elizabeth was about forty-seven at the time of his birth. In 1858 Daniel had reached the tender age of four. At this time, records show his worth was accessed at $250.[11]

On 7 June 1865, only months after the conclusion of the Civil War, the Rudd home was visited by tragedy. Daniel's father, Robert, died. He was about fifty-three years of age at the time of his death; young Daniel was an impressionable ten. Subsequent to Robert's passing, the care of Eliza became a priority of Rudd's older siblings. William, one of Daniel's brothers who lived in Bardstown, took the family's matron into his home. Eliza apparently made her home with Daniel's older brother until the time of her death in 1893.[12]

Because Daniel Rudd was a slave, his dreams, ambitions, as well as his creative potential were subjected to the narrow economic interests of his master. In such a system, the growing boy's latent talent was of little concern except in how these same abilities might be harnessed for the good of the slaveholder. But Rudd's story is just one of millions. No doubt, one of the most disturbing legacies of the institution of American slavery was its incalculable opportunity cost, a cost measured in the loss of the collective human aptitude of tens of millions of enslaved persons. The question is begged: How many potential leaders, inventors, writers, doctors, and teachers of the caliber of Ida B. Wells-Barnett (1862–1931), T. Thomas Fortune (1856–1928), Frederick Douglass, Sojourner Truth (ca. 1797–1883), and Daniel Rudd were simply never afforded the opportunity to be educated or fully actualized. Moreover, how many of these same victims were ultimately denied the opportunity to contribute in a meaningful way to the good of society? The names of these enslaved victims, along with each one's undeveloped potential, lie buried beneath the diabolical and bloody institution of American slavery.

There are 285 extant copies of the *American Catholic Tribune* (hereafter *ACT*). In most of the issues Rudd contributed editorial columns. Only in a select few of these articles did the editor comment on his upbringing. In these editorials Rudd made no mention of his enslavement. Nor did he anywhere print the names of his former owners, Charles and Matilda. One can only speculate as to why. Perhaps he feared that drawing attention to the fact that he had been the property of a Catholic family would put off the African American audience he was trying to evangelize. Or maybe the shame of being born in such a condition made broaching the subject difficult.

As to the nature of Rudd's servitude, one can only speculate. Testimonies of former slaves reveal that individuals experienced the "peculiar institution" in the Blue Grass State differently. Though slaves worked to circumvent and otherwise minimize the most egregious aspects of the inherently cruel institution, the condition of slavery for Kentucky's blacks depended largely on the character and personality of individual slave owners.[13] Some former Kentucky bondsmen and bondswomen developed deep friendships with their masters and, following emancipation, were reluctant to leave them.[14] Others, on the other hand, related stories of the cruelty they had suffered at the hands of their overseers and masters.[15]

Nineteenth-century Catholic leaders held divergent opinions on the practice of slavery in the United States. Though some prominent Catholic liberals opposed slavery, many in the Ultramontane camp remained sympathetic to the southern cause.[16] A number of these same conservative Catholics supported the institution of slavery because they were opposed to liberal definitions of individual autonomy and liberty. Other Catholics possessed more pragmatic reasons for opposing immediate emancipation. Martin John Spalding (1810–1872), who at the time of his death served as Archbishop of Baltimore, feared for the temporal and spiritual well-being of slaves prematurely emancipated. For this reason, he favored a more gradual process of liberation. This approach he imagined would be more beneficial to the slave and would also ensure that no financial injury would be done to the slaveholder. As a rule, most Catholics seem to have followed the moral teaching set forth in 1841 by Francis Patrick Kenrick (1797–1863), who preceded Martin J. Spalding as archbishop of Baltimore. In a manual he authored to train Catholic priests, Kenrick argued domestic slavery as practiced in the United States was not inconsistent with natural law. In short, the prelate did not condemn slavery as an institution, but sought rather to make it more "humane." According to Kenrick, slaves were to be instructed to distinguish themselves by obedience to their masters; and masters were, in turn, responsible for employing bondsmen and bonds-women "moderately." To avoid sin, the slaveholder was also required to provide his charge with adequate food and clothing. In addition to the above directives, the master was forbidden to beat his slave "cruelly" or oppress him "with too much work."[17]

Statistics show many of Kentucky's Catholics owned slaves. For example, in the early nineteenth century, the Cartwright Creek region of Kentucky near Bardstown was the state's largest Catholic community. Of the residents living in this region in 1810, 70 percent would own slaves sometime during their lives. In antebellum Kentucky, between 1810 and 1860, Catholics in the area around Nelson and Washington counties, were more likely to own slaves than non-Catholics.[18]

Despite their faith, Catholic slaveholders in and around Bardstown treated their slaves no more humanely than their Protestant counterparts. Given the relatively small number of slaves on the typical Kentucky farm, husbands and wives were often not owned by the same individual. Routinely, slaves were sold to Catholic and non-Catholic buyers alike with little regard for family or religious ties. In some cases these charges were sold to southern concerns for profit; when this occurred, it appears little thought was given to the temporal or spiritual well-being of the persons being transacted.[19]

Bits of information from various censuses and court records indicate Daniel Rudd's family experienced not only the "affectionate bond" that sometimes formed between slaveholder and servant, but also the brutality of the "peculiar institution." Given the fact that Eliza and all her children are listed as "mulatto" in both the 1870 and 1880 censuses, it is possible that she or her mother were victims of sexual violence. The unique power dynamic in these master/slave relationships meant female slaves were often unable to stave off the sexual advances of their white masters and overseers.[20]

Catholic and Protestant slaveholders alike were culpable when it came to subjecting the family bonds of slaves to the owner's narrow economic interests. In 1833, for example, Richard Rudd's twelve slaves were partitioned into four lots, making it possible for his human capital to be equally divided among four heirs. How such a determination was made is instructive. To be fair, each heir would receive a slave lot worth $763.75. In one of the lots it appears a nursing mother and her seven-month-old daughter, Elizabeth, were grouped together, both going to the same heir. In two of the lots, however, children under ten were bequeathed to an heir without a woman in the group. In one of these lots, for example, Bill, a twelve-year-old, and Lucy, a seven-year-old girl, were grouped with a fifty-year-old man named Thomas.[21]

A review of the above data shows the dark side of the trafficking of human property was not restricted to humiliating public slave auctions. Moreover, the exodus of black Catholics from the church following the Civil War is a damning bit of evidence for those who would otherwise contend that Catholic slaveholders treated their slaves more humanely than did their Protestant counterparts.[22]

In 1860 there were approximately 225,000 slaves in the commonwealth of Kentucky. Thus, they comprised roughly 20 percent of the population. The majority of slaveholders held four or fewer slaves. A mere 1,555 of 22,000 slaveholders held more than 20 slaves. But this small percentage of slaveholders produced 50 percent of the corn and tobacco raised in the state. This same group produced about 66 percent of the state's wheat and 95 percent of the state's most important slave crop, hemp. According to some nineteenth-century observers, slavery as an institution found its most benevolent American manifestation in Kentucky. Foreign visitors to the South almost unanimously agreed that Kentucky's slaves fared better than those on cotton and sugar plantations farther south. Manumissions of slaves, however, were less commonplace in Kentucky than in other border regions of the United States, including Maryland and parts of Virginia.[23]

The typical bondsman or bondswoman residing in Kentucky, often referred to as a "servant," lived in a cabin or hut constructed of wood. If the master was zealous for the comfort of the slave, the cabin or slave quarters would have been well built. These dwellings, located some distance from the master's home, were frequently situated near one another and in close proximity to other out-buildings, including the corncrib, wood-shed, or smokehouse. Often, slave huts consisted of only one room, some-times containing a loft above. Servants typically slept on mattresses stuffed with corn shucks or straw. As a rule, clothes were issued to slaves twice a year, once in the spring and once in the fall. Winter clothing was made of linsey-woolsey, and summer clothes were sewn from inexpensive cotton goods. Sometimes the clothes worn by slaves were made of flax and hemp cultivated on the plantation and subsequently dyed with natural dyes made from herbs or berries. If clothes were purchased, they might have been previously advertised as "Negro goods" to distinguish them from better-quality clothing produced for whites. Will Oats, born in Wayne County, Kentucky, remembered that slaves on his plantation wore home-made cotton clothing, heavy shoes, and heavy underwear. If shoes wore out before the spring, he added, you had to do without till fall.[24]

For slaves, the allocation of food also depended in large measure on the goodwill of each individual master. Though some former servants from the Blue Grass State were reported to have subsisted on meager rations including cornbread, molasses, and scraps from the master's table, many others testified to having plenty to eat. The standard ration was between three to five pounds of pork and a peck (eight quarts) of cornmeal. Slaves drank sweet milk and buttermilk, kept vegetable gardens, and sometimes raised their own poultry. Bert Mayfield of Garrard County, Kentucky, recalled the use of an outside yard oven to cook bacon and to bake bread. Rabbits, raccoon, fish, and opossum augmented the pork and chicken allotted to slaves. During her captivity, Mayfield recalled baking opossum with sweet potatoes.[25]

The African American slave residing in antebellum Kentucky gen-erally worked either as a farm worker or a domestic around the "big house." The standard workweek was five and one-half days, Sunday being an off day. Because Rudd did not speak specifically of his childhood enslavement, it is difficult to determine the type of work for which the young boy would have been responsible. Will Oats, who was raised in Wayne County, Kentucky, was born the same year as Rudd. Though very young during the days of slavery, he was expected, nonetheless, to give his services to the master. Will's duties included cutting wood, milking, and tending the stock. George Henderson, who was born in 1860 near Versailles, recalled having to pull weeds, feed chickens, and tend the plantation's pigs.[26]

Though it is impossible to determine the exact nature of the work Rudd performed as a young slave, an 1887 editorial from the *ACT* may offer a clue. In this same article, Rudd stated that his family had labored at St. Joseph Proto-Cathedral in Bardstown long before the start of the Civil War.[27] This may mean instead of principally being employed on the Haydon estate as a farmhand, the youth may have helped with cleaning duties around the church. As a helper to the sexton, Daniel would have had the opportunity to become more intimately familiar with the nuances of Catholic faith and practice.

After slave chores were completed on Saturday afternoon, work typically ceased. On the weekend, Kentucky's servant population, among other activities, tended their own vegetable gardens, fished, quilted, and visited neighbors. For many bondsmen and bondswomen, attending Sunday worship services was a part of the weekly routine. On some larger plantations, as well as in select cities, including Lexington, churches were established for enslaved blacks. Slave owners at times, however, displayed cautiousness with regard to the religious activity of their servants, especially when these services included more formal instruction or were being led by black preachers. Beyond these concerns, slave owners either encouraged or were indifferent to the religious training of their servants. When blacks did attend the church of their master, they were forced to sit in a separate section of the building. Former Kentucky slave, Dan Bogie, remembered that he and the other slaves on the plantation on which he labored went to "white folks" church at the Freedom Meeting House and were seated in a separate gallery. He recalled seeing his mother baptized in Paint Lick Creek. Bert Mayfield remembered attending church services every Sunday with her master at the Old Fork Baptist Church about four miles from Lancaster. Aunt Belle Robinson, a former slave of Garrard County in central Kentucky, also recalled being taken regularly to church by her "Mistus."[28]

Some of Kentucky's slave masters were negligent with regard to the spiritual care of their charges. After interviewing a number of former servants of Boyd County, one interviewer wrote, "As negroes, in slavery days, were regarded as beasts of burden not much interest was taken in the welfare of their souls. Some kind hearted masters would allow them the privilege of meeting in religious service, where some one of their race in spite of the conditions of the times, could read and explain the Bible, would preach. Other masters would not allow this to be done."[29] At other times, blacks living in antebellum Kentucky established their own religious meetings. Some of these were sanctioned by their masters; others were clandestine.

Though a number of Kentucky's slaveholders may have neglected the spiritual care of their charges, in the main this does not appear to have occurred in central Kentucky's Catholic settlements. Pioneer priest Fr. Stephen T. Badin (1768–1853), the first Catholic priest ordained in the United States, insisted slaves be catechized. Fr. Charles Nerinckx (1761–1824), who served central Kentucky's Catholics, also possessed a special concern for slaves and attempted, albeit unsuccessfully, to establish a community of black sisters.[30] Similarly, Walker Gollar's study of St. Rose Church in Washington County demonstrates blacks not only were baptized but also regularly attended church.[31] Catechism classes were designed for black Catholics both at St. Joseph Church in Bardstown and at St. Pius in neighboring Scott County.

Rudd was baptized subsequent to his birth, and despite his status as a slave he was free to practice his faith. In an editorial dated 3 June 1887, Rudd wrote, "The editor was baptized [at St. Joseph] in August 1854 at the same font where all the rest, white and black were baptized without discrimination except as who got there first. At confession all knelt in whatever order they came and waited their turn to relieve their sin burden."[32] Rudd's sponsor for baptism was Maria Haydon, the fifteen-year-old daughter of his owner.[33]

During the Civil War, Bardstown was a hub of military activity. As the conflict escalated it became impossible for students at St. Joseph's College to focus on their studies. In September 1861, Union forces of Indiana's Tenth Infantry under the command of General Don Carlos Buell (1818–1898) encamped at Bardstown. In October of the same year, school officials were asked to use army provisions to bake bread for Federal soldiers. Subsequently, convalescing northern soldiers made use of about half of the available space in the college. By the spring of 1862 all the students, an overwhelming number of whom were Southerners, had fled the school; subsequently the campus became little more than a Jesuit residence.[34]

In September 1862 Confederate soldiers under the command of General Braxton Bragg (1817–1876) advanced toward Louisville. Upon their arrival at Bardstown they took over the college campus. Their stay was relatively short, however. Then, in January 1863, Union forces moved back into the area, seizing the church and using it for quarters. Federal soldiers did not remain in the community long, and by May 1863 the campus at Bardstown was free of combatants.[35]

With the departure of the students from St. Joseph College, most of the Jesuits at the school sought transfers to other Midwestern institutions. By the fall of 1862, there remained only four priests and five coadjutor brothers. In previous years as many as thirty-five were needed to maintain the operations at the college. For the four remaining Jesuits, the suspension of classes at St. Joseph College appears to have resulted in at least two new ministry foci. The first was certainly the care of wounded soldiers from both the Union and Confederate Armies. The second ministry focus, apparently led by acting rector Fr. John S. Verdin, S.J., directly, was an attempt to improve the participation of blacks in catechetical classes.[36]

In the fall of 1862 it had been determined that "catechetical instruction unsupported by other appeal, made but a feeble impression on the Negro mind." Only with difficulty could ten or twelve blacks be gotten together. In June 1863 it was decided the singing of Catholic songs and hymns would be instituted in catechetical classes. This inclusion seems to have yielded remarkable fruit among the recently emancipated blacks. African Americans began to attend these instructional meetings in ever increasing numbers, some classes containing as many as sixty to seventy indviduals.[37]

Among those positively impacted by this new ministry emphasis was the eight-year-old Rudd, who made his first communion along with other white communicates in June 1863. In the following quote he attempted to emphasize the equality he experienced as a youth at St. Joseph Proto-Cathedral:

> The editor of the TRIBUNE made his first communion there after the long course of study and instruction one must go through with prior to that event and during the time he and all the other Colored and white children sat together and when the late venerable Archbishop Spalding, then Bishop of Louisville, on the same bright June morning in 1863 administered the sacrament of confirmation.

The TRIBUNE man knelt beside as fair a damsel as ever bowed before that rail and thought nothing of it.[38]

Given the Jesuit's genuine efforts to accommodate the religious preferences of blacks in need of catechetical training, and Rudd's positive experiences among Catholics at St. Joseph in Bardstown, he from an early age developed a positive view of Catholicism. Following Rudd's subsequent move to Cincinnati, this conviction would mature and the editor would become an outspoken proponent of a church-centered platform of justice.

Rudd, in his adult years, became an accomplished entrepreneur, lecturer, author, and editor. He also established and managed a printing school. Rudd was bilingual, and he wrote and spoke German. The editor of the *ACT* also appears to have acquired some level of competence in timber management, agriculture, and mechanics. Given Rudd's career achievements, it seems likely his education would have begun at an early age, sometime prior to the official emancipation of Kentucky's slaves.[39]

In Kentucky there was never a law against educating enslaved blacks. Many whites, however, disapproved of the practice. For this reason a large percentage of African Americans residing in antebellum Kentucky did not receive formal academic instruction. Kentuckian Dan Boogie recalled, "White folks did not teach us to read and write. I learned that after I left the white folks." George Henderson, a former slave also from Kentucky, stated that the slaves on the estate on which he lived were not permitted by their master to attend school. Despite these examples, some slave owners disregarded public sentiment, seeing to it that their servants could read and write. Though private instruction of one's slave would have aroused less notice, there were schools in both Lexington and Louisville that educated servants.[40]

Rudd's early education was begun in Bardstown and subsequently completed when the youth moved to Springfield, Ohio.[41] As to the specifics of his early academic training, however, not much is known. In all likelihood, Rudd benefited from the instruction of a private tutor, either Verdin himself, one of the other Jesuits, or perhaps a teacher provided by the Haydon family.[42]

Emphatically Rudd declared there was no color line in the Catholic parish of his youth. Though members of his family were considered the human property of the Haydon's, the Rudd's managed to earn a measure of respect among black and white Catholics in the Bardstown community. For example, upon the death of Daniel's mother, Eliza, Fr. C. J. O'Connell postponed the funeral so he himself could officiate. At the memorial service, O'Connell explained how Elizabeth had "merited and received the love and respect of her own race and the ventration [*sic*] of the people of all other races who knew her." He further declared that "if the colored people followed her saintly example there would be no race problem to vex and fret them." Given their experience of Catholicism in Bardstown, it appears Daniel's family maintained strong and healthy ties to the church. This may help explain why Rudd remained a Catholic after emancipation when so many former slaves exited the church.[43]

Coming of Age in Springfield

The Union victory over the Confederacy came in April 1865. On 18 December of that same year, the Thirteenth Amendment officially freed Kentucky's slaves. In search of gainful employment, many blacks from Kentucky traveled north. Some former bondsmen made their way to southern Ohio, where the demand for farm laborers remained high through the late 1860s.[44] In 1865 Daniel Rudd's older brother, Charles Henry, and sister-in-law, Jemimah, migrated to Springfield, Ohio, a regional center of manufacturing in the nineteenth century.[45] The city's location on the National Road and its infrastructure, including excellent rail service, facilitated the growth of its manufacturing base. As a result Springfield's population grew rapidly in the decades following the Civil War. During this period of growth mills in the city produced agricultural implements, mill machinery, woolen goods, carriages, and flour. The companies founded in Springfield from 1860 to 1880 include E. W. Ross Company; James Leffel and Company; Springfield Agricultural Works; Springfield Coffin and Casket Company; J. Redman and Son Company; McGregor Brothers Company; Springfield Brass Company; Thomas Manufacturing Company; Mast, Foos and Company; Crowell and Kirkpatrick Company; Springfield Malleable Iron Company; and the Champion Chemical Company.[46]

A number of African Americans who made their way to Springfield in the years after the Civil War went to work for William Whitely, the entrepreneurial force behind a variety of business enterprises in the city, including the Champion Machine Company, a manufacturer of agricultural implements.[47] In the *ACT,* Rudd praised Whitley, referring to him as the "Reaper King." The editor of the *ACT* noted that this same entrepreneur was the "first great manufacturer in the United States to give the colored mechanic a full and fair showing."[48]

Sometime before 1876, perhaps as much as a decade earlier, Daniel Rudd moved from Bardstown, Kentucky, to Springfield, Ohio, in order to complete his secondary education. Springfield's primary school remained segregated throughout Rudd's early years in the city. One history of Springfield contends the city's schools were integrated in 1885; a second Champion City history gives 1887 as the date.[49]

In Springfield, Rudd went to work for the G. S. Foos Company.[50] Gustavus S. Foos supported the Whig Party in his younger years, and he became a zealous Republican later in life. One historian described him as "exceedingly liberal-minded" on many subjects. Gustavus and his brother William partnered in various mercantile, real estate, and banking ventures in the city of Springfield, only to see their respective fortunes vanish during the economic panic of 1873.[51] At the time Rudd went to work for the G. S. Foos Company, the firm was manufacturing "hardware and specialties."[52] Rudd apparently boarded at the company located at 81 Mechanic Street. The following year, he worked and boarded at Springfield's European Hotel, located at 36–38 East Main Street. The name of the *ACT*'s editor does not appear in the 1879–1880 issue of the Springfield city directory. However, Rudd was reported to have lived for some time in Columbus, Ohio. It is possible that he moved to Columbus after 1880, subsequently returning to Springfield by 1883. Rudd's name reappears in the 1883–1884 edition of the city directory. After his return to the Champion City, he boarded at 47 Madison, in the city's second ward, with his brothers Charles, Robert, and William. Rudd apparently resided at this address until his move to Cincinnati in 1886.[53]

While residing in Springfield, Rudd attended St. Raphael Church. There were two Catholic parishes in the city at the time of the editor's arrival, St. Raphael and St. Bernard. St. Bernard Parish was predominantly a German parish. St. Raphael, founded in 1849, was the older of the two churches. It also held the distinction of being the first Catholic Church founded in Green County, Ohio. During Rudd's years as a member of St. Raphael, the parish was led by Fr. William H. Sidley, the congregation's fifth pastor.[54]

Sidley was born in Geauga County, in northeastern Ohio. This region was decidedly more progressive with regard to issues of race than was the southern portion of the state.[55] Sidley studied at the University of Notre Dame; subsequently, he attended seminary in the cities of Cleveland and Cincinnati. The priest was ordained in Springfield in 1870 and became St. Raphael's pastor in 1873. Sidley served the congregation for twenty-nine years.[56]

Relations between the editor of the *ACT* and Sidley appear to have been cordial. In the fall of 1889, Lincoln Valle, one of Rudd's traveling agents and an active member of the Colored Catholic Congress movement, visited the city of Springfield in order to promote the *ACT*. While in Springfield, Valle stayed in the home of the editor's brother, Henry Rudd. On this visit, Valle, accompanied by the Rudd family, attended Mass at St. Raphael Church. He "cordially welcomed" the work of the *ACT* in the city. Further, Sidley gave Valle a "beautiful notice before his congregation" encouraging members to support the newspaper and the propagation of the Catholic faith among blacks. Evidence from the *ACT* shows relations between Rudd and his former pastor remained strong even after the editor's move to Cincinnati. For example, in November 1891 Sidley invited Rudd back to Springfield to give a lecture.[57]

While residing in Springfield Rudd became a strong advocate for the rights of African Americans. Though he retained his campaign for full equality for blacks throughout his life, one can discern, over time, signs of development in his thinking as to which would be the most promising and practicable method for achieving justice for African Americans. This development in strategy is identifiable in the work of many black leaders of the nineteenth century, including Frederick Douglass.[58] Rudd throughout his lifetime espoused at least three different strategies for attaining equal citizenship and full equality for blacks. These three approaches correspond to three distinct periods in the editor's life. As a young man during the Springfield period, 1881–1886, Rudd pursued a "Douglass-like" direct editorial advocacy in the hopes of protecting the civil rights of African Americans. Throughout the Cincinnati/Detroit period, 1887–1897, the *ACT*'s editor championed a church-centered approach pursuant to the full equality of blacks. Sometime subsequent to the collapse of the *ACT,* and during the southern period from 1900 forward, Rudd promulgated a "Washington-like" economic, self-help approach as the most promising method by which African Americans might hope to achieve full equality. Given Rudd's affiliation with the NAACP in 1919, however, it is plausible he joined the ranks of other blacks in moving back toward a more direct approach for attaining political and civil rights for blacks, especially as violence in the South continued and the limitations of Booker T. Washington's program of self-help became more evident.

Throughout the nineteenth century blacks utilized both the written and spoken word as their major vehicle for protest. This was especially true of Rudd, who while in Springfield began working to establish himself in the newspaper business. During Rudd's early years, 1881–1886, the nature of his activism was similar to the approach employed by Frederick Douglass, the most prominent African American of his era. In the final decades of the nineteenth century, Douglass lifted his voice in strong support for the immediate recognition of full citizenship rights for blacks, even as many race leaders were moving in the direction of a more circumscribed, self-help, economic advancement platform. During the Springfield period, Rudd, like Douglass, demonstrated a commitment to a direct editorial campaign for full equality, a more confrontational approach that included a commitment to political and judicial activism.[59]

Daniel Rudd's first job as a journalist appears to have been with the *Sunday News,* where early in the 1880s he worked as a printer, reporter, and editor. Sometime around 1883 Rudd founded a new publication, the *Review.* After the *Review*'s board of directors relieved Rudd of his responsibilities as editor, he founded a newspaper in 1884 called the *Tribune.* Following a brief return to the *Review,* he began publishing the *Ohio State Tribune* (hereafter *"OST"*) in 1885. Boasting a new editorial purpose, in August 1886 the *OST* was rechristened the *American Catholic Tribune.*[60]

As a youth residing in Springfield Rudd became involved in Republican politics. Though by 1879 a number of the state's black leaders, including notable legislator and historian George Washington Williams (1849–1891), were already expressing dismay at the duplicity of some members of the Republican Party, Rudd, on the other hand, appears to have retained his confidence in the GOP. The reason for this position may have been related to the party's support of black rights, including the 1875 Civil Rights Act.

In September 1881 Rudd carried his direct activism a step further when he joined other African American leaders to protest the local school board's discriminatory policies. On this occasion, Rudd objected to the refusal on the part of Shaffer Street Elementary School officials to admit the children of two black residents, George Reynolds and J. W. Gazaway. When a split in the African American community occurred over whether to push for equal school facilities for blacks or to attempt to integrate Springfield's schools, Rudd sided with the latter group. In the hopes of raising the funds needed to present their grievances in the U.S. Circuit Court of Appeals, the editor was chosen to petition Clifton Nichols, a potential donor. Rudd declared:

> It is pleasant and profitable for us to be here as we are to-night to take steps right and proper for our advancement. Last fall, at the opening of the schools, quite a commotion was created in our midst by a little lady, Miss Eva Gazaway (who I have the pleasure of presenting you), going to the public school in her district and being refused. Her father, doing as none of our citizens have done heretofore, demanded to know why she might not be admitted as well as her next door neighbor, and he was informed that she was black. Hence the reason of the suit and of our presence here to-night. The citizens met and appointed a committee to carry the case, if necessary, even to the Supreme Court of the United States.
>
> Of individuals, families, and communities our Nation is composed; when all work in harmony and good feeling the general good of the Nation will be secured. This suit is not for Miss Gazaway alone nor for the rights of the children in this community or State, but for all the children.[61]

Despite Rudd's efforts, the court ruled against their petition.[62]

Raising a "Cry for Justice" from Cincinnati

Sometime in 1886 Daniel Rudd and his business partner, James T. Whitson, M.D., moved to Cincinnati to publish the *ACT.* The Pennsylvanian-born

Whitson was an accomplished man in his own right. As a youth in Pennsylvania he attended a Catholic elementary school. Completing his secondary education in Pittsburgh, Whitson was one of Central High School's first black graduates. For a time he served as the principal of an elementary school for blacks in Ripley, Ohio. Subsequently, he enrolled at the Western Reserve Medical College graduating in the spring of 1885. In Springfield he and Rudd met.[63] Rudd was successful in persuading the physician to join forces with him in the establishment of the *ACT.* Whitson assumed the role of business manager for the newly established paper traveling the country in order to promote the publication. The Rudd/Whitson partnership ended with some acrimony in the summer of 1888. At this same time, Whitson allowed Rudd to purchase his stake in the *ACT.*[64]

Why Rudd and Whitson chose Cincinnati as the operational base for the *ACT* is unclear. Their business model seems to suggest the company intended to offer not only a uniquely focused newspaper but also a whole menu of printing services. In 1886, however, there were some 130 printing establishments already operating in Cincinnati. Close to 10 percent of these were located on Fourth Street, the same thoroughfare on which the *ACT* would locate. The decision to headquarter the newspaper in the Queen City may have had more to do with Archbishop William Henry Elder's (1819–1904) strong endorsement of the newspaper than other business or marketing considerations.[65]

At the time of the *ACT*'s establishment, many of the city's blacks resided in three neighborhoods. The most notorious of these was pejoratively labeled "Bucktown." Situated south of the courthouse and just west of Mt. Adams in the city's sixth ward, this ghetto community located between Sixth and Seventh streets was bounded on the west by Broadway and on the east by Culvert Street. A second neighborhood, "Little Africa," was located in the city's eighth ward, along the levee near the Ohio River. It was bounded on the south by the river, on the north by Third Street, on the west by Central Avenue, and on the east by Vine Street. Though many of the city's blacks lived in the two above-mentioned neighborhoods, a fair number of African Americans also resided in a third neighborhood known as "Little Buck," located at Sixth Street and Freeman Avenue, in the western part of the city. [66]

Upon their arrival in Cincinnati, Rudd and Whitson set up shop at

A WORD OF APPROVAL.

Cincinnati, May 28, 1889.

EDITORS:

AMERICAN CATHOLIC TRIBUNE:—
I am very much pleased with the great labor you are applying to make THE AMERICAN CATHOLIC TRIBUNE a useful and interesting factor in advancing the best interests not only of your own immediate people, but of the whole country. And I am glad to see your very satisfactory success, and to learn of your steady progress.

You are obtaining for yourselves both the esteem of your readers, and the blessing of God.

I give you my blessing. Your faithful servant in Christ,

† WILLIAM HENRY ELDER,
Archbishop of Cincinnati.

In the *American Catholic Tribune,* Rudd proudly published the endorsements of members of the Catholic Hierarchy, including this one from Archbishop Henry Elder of Cincinnati. (Courtesy of the Philadelphia Archdiocesan Historical Research Center.)

233 W. Fourth Street, close to the business district downtown, in the city's eighteenth ward. They then began assembling a staff to support their newspaper and attached printing operation. By 1887 they had hired a Harrison Avenue resident and dressmaker, Cora Turner, to keep the company's books. In October 1887, Rudd informed his readers the *ACT* had outgrown its Fourth Street facilities. Anticipating an increase in the size

of the office staff, as well as the installation of a new cylinder press, Rudd announced the newspaper would be relocating to 355 Central Avenue in the city's sixteenth ward. Further, Rudd stated the Central Avenue location would also house a school for students interested in learning the art of printing.[67]

After arriving in Cincinnati, Rudd took up residence at 150 Central Avenue. The editor later made his home at 286 George Street in the city's seventeenth ward, just west of the central business district. Rudd's George Street home appears to have been located in an integrated neighborhood outside the boundaries of the three previously described black neighborhoods. Not more than 300 yards to the east and south of his George Street residence was the Holy Trinity Parish. Approximately 400 yards south of his home was St. Patrick Catholic Church.[68]

Despite their proximity, the editor of the *ACT* attended neither the Holy Trinity Parish nor St. Patrick Church, but rather a predominantly black congregation, St. Ann's Parish. Rudd went to this congregation even though it was located about one mile from his George Street home. St. Ann's had been founded in July 1866 at the request of a number of its African American members. Francis Xavier Wenniger, S.J., a missionary priest assigned to Cincinnati, was a driving force behind the parish's establishment. The Jesuit clergyman raised $4,000 to found the mission church. The first pastor of the congregation was Fr. Adrian Hoecken, S.J.; he was born in Holland and came to the United States in order to work among Native Americans.[69] In 1887 St. Ann's Parish was located on New Street, at Broadway and Culvert near Bucktown. At the time Rudd arrived in Cincinnati, Fr. John Driessen, S.J., was the pastor. Driessen was also born and educated in Holland and was subsequently ordained there in 1867. While serving in Holland he answered the call for volunteers to come to America. Assigned to the Jesuit rectory at St. Xavier's College in Cincinnati, Driessen not only served as the pastor of St. Ann's but also ministered as a chaplain in a number of the city's hospitals.[70]

Post-Reconstruction America

Following the Civil War, African Americans were granted the rights of full citizenship. The era of Radical Reconstruction, from about 1865 to

1877, was a period in which blacks not only won the right to vote but also held political offices in every state of the former Confederacy. At the local level, they served as coroners, surveyors, treasurers, tax assessors and collectors, jailors, solicitors, registers of deeds, clerks of court, police officers, marshals, firemen, and mayors. At the state level blacks held posts including, among others, state land commissioner, superintendent of education, secretary of state, and supreme court justice. Pickney Benton Stewart Pinchback (1837–1921) of Louisiana even served for a brief period in 1872–1873 as the first nonwhite governor of a southern state.[71] During Radical Reconstruction blacks were also elected to federal office. For example, Hiram R. Revels (1827–1901) in 1870 became the first black citizen to be elected to the U.S. Senate, taking over the seat formerly held by Confederate President Jefferson Davis (1808–1889).[72]

The America of the post-Reconstruction period, however, was a nation in retreat from its declared egalitarian principles. After the Hayes-Tilden compromise of 1877, blacks in the South found their newly won citizenship rights were in jeopardy. The federal government, beset by accusations of corruption, left the southern states to govern their own affairs with little interference from Washington, D.C. The victory in the disputed presidential election of 1876 was granted to Republican Rutherford B. Hayes (1822–1893). In exchange, federal troops were withdrawn from the last two states where they remained, Florida and Louisiana.[73]

President Rutherford B. Hayes ignored the issue of African American civil rights, as would his successors, including James Garfield (1831–1881), Chester A. Arthur (1829–1886), Grover Cleveland (1837–1908), Benjamin Harrison (1833–1901), and William McKinley (1843–1901). Rayford Logan identifies Hayes as the chief architect of white supremacy in the post-Reconstruction South. He further explains that because of the president's concerns over sectional strife, and the possible eruption of a new civil war, he left southern leaders to pursue their own strategy with regard to the place of blacks in American society. Logan further argues that by the turn of the century McKinley would complete the ignoble work of his presidential forerunner, Hayes.[74]

Evidence of McKinley's failure to uphold the civil and political rights of southern blacks was demonstrated by the president's decision not to intervene when the right of enfranchisement for African Americans was threatened by Louisiana's notorious, constitutional "grandfather clause."

Further proof of the president's failure to uphold the rights of African Americans was exposed by his refusal to protect the suffrage of blacks disenfranchised by North Carolina's constitution, which was ratified in 1900.[75]

Southern politicians showed little interest in encouraging African American suffrage, not only because of their sentiments with regard to black inferiority, but also because most blacks were loyal to the Republican Party well into the twentieth century. Southerners, therefore, used intimidation and violence as tactics to keep blacks from participating in the electoral process. Buttressed by the fear of social equality and race "amalgamation," southern politicians now freed from federal interference cheered the Supreme Court's repeal of the 1875 Civil Rights Bill. The ruling was a de facto acceptance of the state's right to do as it pleased with African Americans. Moreover, the repeal of this important law in 1883 opened a flood gate of legislation aimed at eliminating the newly won rights of blacks. Following this decision Justice John Marshall Harlan (1833–1911), the only member of the court to oppose the ruling, was disappointed. He further feared the amendments representing the ideals of freedom and equality articulated by Lincoln in the Gettysburg Address, as well as the moral justification for the bloody Civil War, were being renounced.[76]

Evidenced by the meager support offered to black schools in the South, and by the campaign of terror and intimidation waged by white supremacist terror groups, it became clear the window of opportunity for African Americans in the post-Reconstruction South was rapidly closing. During this same period, southern state governments circumvented the intent of the Fourteenth and Fifteenth Amendments and began rewriting their constitutions with the intention of disenfranchising blacks. For example, Florida ratified a new constitution in 1885, Mississippi in 1890, South Carolina in 1895, Louisiana in 1898, North Carolina in 1900, and Virginia in 1902.[77]

Even before the end of Radical Reconstruction, states began enacting laws establishing segregation. For example, in 1870 Tennessee enacted the nation's first law against interracial marriage. Five years later, this same state established the first in a series of Jim Crow laws. Other states followed Tennessee's example. Encouraged on with the repeal of the Civil Rights Bill of 1875, states barred blacks from hotels, barbershops, restaurants, and theaters. By 1885 most southern states had established laws requiring separate schools for blacks. By 1900 both major political parties had for all intents and purposes given up on protecting the rights of blacks.[78]

In the Catholic Church, attitudes toward racial issues generally followed societal trends. However, a unique door of opportunity and promise remained open for blacks in the Catholic Church throughout the 1880s and 1890s. This fact is demonstrated by the church's position on two important bellwether issues. First, during this period influential church leaders worked for the ordination of black priests. Second, Catholic officials in the latter decades of the nineteenth century demonstrated a willingness to allow parishes to remain racially integrated.

In the church, progressive views on race relations eventually gave way as southern states moved to institutionalize racial segregation. For example, by the 1890s recalcitrant attitudes held by prejudiced church officials were dampening the work of advocates of black vocations. Even John R. Slattery (1851–1926), who had consistently been the Catholic Church's strongest advocate for the ordination of African Americans, seemed to acquiesce to pressure from southern bishops who refused to receive black priests into their respective dioceses. The few African American priests who were ordained during this period lived lonely lives marked by isolation and harassment.[79]

Offering a window into worsening racial relations, Dolores Egger Labbe has identified three phases in Catholic Church leaders' attitudes toward racially integrated parishes in Louisiana. In phase one, 1888–1897, Francis Janssens (1843–1897), the pragmatic archbishop of New Orleans, established segregated churches for the benefit of African Americans whom he hoped to keep actively involved in parish life. During this period, it was understood that blacks would be free to attend the parish of their choosing. A second transitional phase existed from 1897 to 1909. By 1909, however, the move to force blacks into segregated black parishes was well under way. The forced racial segregation of parishes in New Orleans was due in large part to the Americanization of the city, a city which traditionally had been the home of a large population of Catholic free people of color. The changing sentiments of church leaders toward blacks in this important southern diocese appear to mirror a similar trend in the larger church community.[80]

John R. Slattery as the first superior general of the St. Joseph's Society of the Sacred Heart (Josephites) was a strong advocate for the cause of black priests. (Courtesy of the Josephite Archives.)

The Black Press and Daniel Rudd

One of the important ways African Americans worked for the promotion of equality and racial justice was through the black press. The nation's first black newspaper, *Freedom's Journal,* was published in 1827 in the city of New York by Samuel Eli Cornish (1795–1858) and John Brown Russwurm (1799–1851). Given the fact that racial prejudice was prevalent in American society in the antebellum period, it is no surprise Cornish and Russwurm sought to speak out on behalf of the nation's blacks. The decision to do so was an exercise in black agency. As a result of this action, Cornish and Russwurm blazed the trail for subsequent African American newspaper publishers, including Daniel Rudd.[81]

The publishers of *Freedom's Journal* set out to accomplish five goals related to Rudd's editorial agenda. First, Cornish and Russwurm sought to offset misrepresentations of African Americans in the white press. These caricatures were unflattering and offensive to blacks. Second, this New York publication endeavored to help African Americans become "useful members of society." Third, the paper sought to promote character development among blacks. Fourth, the paper aspired to encourage its African American readers to protect black civil rights and to vote in the interest of the race. Finally, the newspaper attempted to provide reading material that would encourage blacks to "enlarge their stock of useful knowledge."[82]

Daniel Rudd, founder and proprietor of the *ACT,* worked for racial uplift and to overthrow the widely held conviction that darker-skinned races were inherently inferior to white Europeans. He believed race justice would be realized only when African Americans were free to enjoy the same rights and opportunities as their white brothers and sisters. Though similar in its aspirations to conceptions of justice promulgated by other black leaders of his generation, Rudd's vision of justice promoted in the *ACT* cannot be explicated apart from the essential role he believed the Catholic Church would play in its coming to fruition.[83]

For Rudd, the press, secular and sacred, was to play a critical role in the attainment of justice for blacks in post-Reconstruction America. Early in his journalistic career Rudd declared, "The press is the mirror of our daily actions. . . . The editors shape the very destinies of nations—yes, civilization. Take away our printing presses and in two centuries we would be as far backward as we have advanced in 200 years."[84] In 1887 he wrote, "If the press would unite in teaching man his moral duty, how much less trouble there would be in the affairs of life."[85] During the years of the *ACT*'s publication, 1886–1897, Rudd was an active member of the Colored Press Association. In January 1891 he led a delegation of Cincinnati's African American leaders in a successful effort to get the association to select the Queen City as its next meeting site.[86]

While serving as a member of the Colored Press Association, the editor of the *ACT* proposed a number of suggestions as to how the national black press might be more effective. First, he believed the association should combine and purchase material as a cooperative. Second, he believed it would be advantageous to maintain a single engraving department for all association members. Finally, he believed the association needed to be linked more closely via the telegraph.[87]

The March meeting of the Colored Press Association, held in Cincinnati in 1891, seems to have been unusually productive. In 1893 the editor of the *Cleveland Gazette,* influential state legislator Harry C. Smith (1863–1941), wrote, "There is no denying the fact that the life infused into the Afro-American Press association at its Cincinnati, meeting in 1891 has been gradually ebbing ever since, until now the organization has about reached the low plane it occupied prior to the '91 meeting."[88] Following the Cincinnati gathering, Rudd's talents were acknowledged when he was asked to take on various leadership roles in this same national organization. For example, the editor of *ACT* was serving as chairperson of the press organization's executive committee in August 1893.[89]

Not only was Rudd involved in the Colored Press Association, but he was also an active member of the Catholic Press Association. He believed that by introducing blacks to the only religion that knew no color line, he was, indeed, striking a blow for justice. Beginning in June 1889, on page 2, the editorial page of the *ACT,* Rudd began printing a quotation from Daniel 12:3. This same quotation appears to be a loose translation from the *Vulgate.* It read, "They who instruct others unto justice, shall shine as stars in the Kingdom of Heaven." Rudd further claimed, "Such is the reward of the supporters of this journal."[90]

Daniel Rudd began his publishing career in post-Reconstruction America. During this era, blacks sought to retain the rights won during Reconstruction. Charles A. Simmons has identified nine periods in

African American Press history. As might be imagined, the most prolific period in terms of the creation of black newspapers was the "era of reaction and adjustment" occurring from 1877 to 1915. The number of newspapers established by blacks in this era seems to have swelled even as public sentiment toward African Americans hardened and violence against blacks increased. Of the roughly 4,000 African American owned newspapers established in the United States since 1827, 2,099 were started in this particular period. From 1880 to 1890, 504 black papers were established in the United States. One of these newspapers, published in Cincinnati, was the *ACT*.[91]

The Birth of the *American Catholic Tribune*

Though she likely missed some publications, Felecia Jones Ross identified fourteen black newspapers established in Ohio from 1877 to 1900. The immigration of blacks into the community and the hostility of whites toward their presence in the Queen City made Cincinnati a likely staging point for the emerging black press. During the latter part of the nineteenth century, the southern Ohio community was home to several black newspapers. For example, Cincinnati's *Colored Citizen* was one of the few black papers published in the United States during the Civil War. Charles W. Bell published the *Declaration,* Cincinnati's only black newspaper printed during the decade of the 1870s. In 1883 the *Colored Patriot* boasted that it was Cincinnati's only black Republican paper.[92]

Sometime before January 1885, prior to his move to Cincinnati, Rudd established a newspaper he titled the *Ohio State Tribune (OST)*. The young, enterprising Rudd faced a number of challenges in the early months of the *OST*'s publication. It was during this period that Rudd was criticized by the editor of the *Cleveland Gazette* for his failure to get a particular edition of the newspaper to print. By 1886 the *OST* appears to have been destined for failure. Evidence for the near collapse of the *OST* can be found in an article published in the *Observer*.[93]

In this same imaginative article, the narrator travels through a cemetery containing the city of Columbus's failed African American newspapers, where he happens upon a grave dug for Daniel Rudd's *Ohio State Tribune*. The caretaker of this cemetery speaks to the narrator, informing him the grave for the *OST* had, indeed, been dug, but "just before the funeral, its parent the energetic Dan Rudd, resurrected it back to life." The narrator further explains how Rudd "in the small, still hours of the night" had "placed the blanket of hope around it and carried it to Cincinnati, re-christened, the *American Catholic Tribune.*" The *ACT* is also identified as the "most successful journal in America" by this same individual.[94]

The first edition of the newly rechristened *ACT* was published on 22 August 1886. In the *ACT,* Rudd determined to create a national weekly publication that would "continue to fight for the eternal principles of liberty, justice and equality before the law." He also promised to "publish the news without tediousness of detail" and to "endeavor to encourage a high standard of moral manhood." The above listed objectives, originally associated with Rudd's *OST,* appear to have been carried forward to the *ACT.*[95]

A combination of motivations may have led Rudd to establish the *ACT.* Following the second gathering of the Colored Catholic Congress movement in July 1890, Rudd told a reporter of the *Cincinnati Times-Star,* "I have always been a Catholic and, feeling that I knew the teachings of the Catholic church, I thought there could be no greater factor in solving the race problem than that matchless institution whose history for 1900 years is but a continual triumph over all assailants." In this same interview, Rudd claimed, "we began a Catholic newspaper in this city with the view of removing, as far as possible, the misinformation which had emanated from the non Catholic press of the race as based upon the teachings of non Catholic white denominations."[96] Subsequently, Rudd claimed he started the newspaper in the hopes that it would do what no other black newspaper had done: "give the great Catholic Church a hearing and show that it is worthy of at least a fair consideration at the hands of our race, being as it is the only place on this Continent, where rich and poor, white and black, must drop prejudice at the threshold and go hand in hand to the altar."[97] Rudd's reasons for establishing the *ACT* likely stretched beyond his high-minded idealism. He was, after all, a shrewd entrepreneur. It is reasonable to assume, therefore, the opportunity to reach a niche readership with a uniquely focused newspaper also motivated the enterprising businessman.

The timing of Rudd's decision to establish the *ACT* could not have been better, coming as it did on the heels of the Third Plenary Council

(Baltimore III) held in Baltimore in 1884. In the meeting, Vatican officials seeking to build on what little progress had been made in the black apostolate since the Second Plenary Council (Baltimore II), held almost two decades earlier, urged American bishops to address the needs of African Americans. Seminary officials and religious orders were also encouraged to recruit adherents to work among blacks. Additionally, it was determined a special yearly collection would be taken up in all the dioceses across the United States in order to fund "Indian" and "Negro" missions. As Rudd was working to establish his newly founded publication, other advocates inside the church were working to improve the lives of African Americans. For example, St. Katharine Drexel's (1858–1955) fortune, donated to minister to blacks and Native Americans, was beginning to be distributed.[98] Also, during this same period, the American Josephites, led by the visionary John R. Slattery, was laboring to evangelize southern blacks in the hopes of elevating among their ranks a native clergy.[99]

Like other major black newspapers of the period, including the *Cleveland Gazette* and the *Washington Bee,* the *ACT* was four pages in length and offered either six or seven columns of print per page. The newspaper contained not only editorials promoting the Catholic Church but also stories copied from other major newspapers. Among the items printed in the *ACT* was news from the U.S. Congress and the Ohio legislature. The newspaper also featured anecdotes, humor, short stories, poetry, recipes, as well as articles on fashion, agriculture, and science.[100]

Most black newspapers were relatively short-lived. One reason for the failure of many publications was the lack of financial capital. In December 1887 Rudd bemoaned the difficulties currently being faced by African American newspaper men. One of the major obstacles, according to Rudd, was the fact that the proprietors were forced to "spend most of their time hunting the money to make the wheels go around."[101] In the hopes of raising the money needed to place the *ACT* on solid footing, Rudd early on petitioned white Catholics in Cincinnati. At times his solicitations were unsuccessful. For example, Mrs. M. Torrensdale, affiliated with a publication called the *Advocate,* discussed her refusal to support Rudd's fledgling newspaper in a letter to Fr. Daniel E. Hudson, C.S.C., the editor of *Ave Maria.* She had refused Rudd, in part because she knew the "state of their finances."[102]

Revealing a developed acumen for business, Rudd was able to raise the funds necessary to get the newspaper on its feet. The *ACT*'s printing business, which produced custom made cards, letterheads, envelopes, bill heads, statements, pamphlets, books, briefs, and "all kinds of legal and commercial work," provided an additional source of revenue. The sale of advertisements and money raised from his printing school also may have generated some income for the newspaper. Though the above mentioned streams of revenue may have contributed some dollars toward the cost of the *ACT*'s publication, they were not the main fonts of support.[103]

Two primary sources of revenue appear to have kept the *ACT* in the black. The first was the sale of newspaper subscriptions. By May 1888 Rudd employed five traveling agents who canvassed the country seeking subscription sales. For example, in 1889 Rudd's agents canvassed the northern part of the United States, from St. Paul, Minnesota, to Boston, Massachusetts. Other agents covered the central United States, from St. Louis, Missouri, to Washington, D.C. Though on one occasion Rudd claimed that if he had proper support he would spend half his time showing members of the race in southern cities the "fairness, the justice and the truth of Catholicity," evidence from the *ACT* reveals Rudd's newspaper was almost exclusively a northern concern. Rudd and his agents made precious few forays into the states formerly allied with the Confederacy.[104]

A second important source of revenue for the newspaper was direct contributions from white Catholics willing to spend home mission dollars in support of the evangelization of blacks.[105] Rudd solicited missional funds from Catholic clergy and lay members alike. These gifts and offerings appear to have been a vital source of revenue, especially in the *ACT*'s first year of publication. Speaking of the establishment of the newspaper in September 1887, Rudd wrote, "Grandly have the Catholics of America, from one end of the continent to the other, come to our assistance, and helped us to prove by their generosity that the Catholic Church is the 'only one where rich and poor, white and black, must drop prejudice at the threshold and go hand in hand to the altar.'"[106]

The collection of mission dollars from Catholics continued to be a source of revenue beyond the first year of the *ACT*'s publication. In 1889 Rudd wrote, "The American Catholic Tribune is a perpetual mission, and every dollar given or expended for it is a help in the mission."[107] The newspaper's largest cash supporter may have been Cardinal Lavigerie.

Rudd met the cardinal in Lucerne, Switzerland, in August 1889. Lavigerie was so impressed with Rudd and his work among blacks in America he committed to giving one thousand francs per year to Rudd's publishing enterprise. This amount was to be given for the remainder of the cardinal's life. The second largest contributor to the *ACT* in terms of dollars seems to have been Fr. Patrick Corrigan of Hoboken, New Jersey, who sent Rudd $100 yearly in order to purchase copies of the *ACT* to be distributed to prospective converts.[108]

Other Catholic donors seemed eager to donate home mission dollars to aid Rudd's evangelization efforts among blacks. For example, Monsignor John E. Burke, at the time serving as pastor of St. Benedict the Moor Parish in New York City, invited Rudd to speak on two occasions, only weeks apart. Following Rudd's speech to members of the parish in February 1889, Burke gave Rudd the following endorsement,

> Mr. Rudd is publishing a newspaper. It has been of incalculable benefit to the race. Without it we would not have had the Congress. It costs a great deal to publish a newspaper. I want to see him succeed . . . I will act as an agent for the American Catholic Tribune and propose to help him otherwise. I will not ask you to give me a collection for him, but I do want to take his paper and pay him for it. I have been taking it for two years and gladly recommend it. I now give Mr. Rudd as a donation to the cause fifty dollars. I do not give it for him, but for his paper. It is no charity for him, but it is an aid to his noble efforts.[109]

Among members of the American Catholic hierarchy, Rudd received financial aid and moral support from the Archbishop of Philadelphia, Patrick John Ryan (1831–1911), as well as from the Archbishop of Cincinnati, William Henry Elder.[110] The *ACT* was also supported by laymen who purchased their subscriptions in advance, sometimes commenting on the quality of the newspaper. For example, John Boyle forwarded Rudd six dollars to cover the subscription for three years commending the newspaper's "Educating qualities."[111]

Rudd also enjoyed help from Protestant supporters. When he or one of his traveling agents visited a city, they depended on locals to introduce them to prospective subscribers. On one occasion, Rudd commended William Ecton, a prominent, black Protestant leader in Washington

Court House, Ohio, who had played host to Rudd when the latter visited the central Ohio town.[112]

The *ACT*'s readership may have included more whites than blacks. Advertisements for skin bleaches, hair straighteners, and African American funeral establishments, which often appeared in black newspapers of the period, are largely absent from its pages.[113] Moreover, a major thrust of Rudd's marketing strategy was to sell subscriptions to mission-minded Catholics in predominantly white parishes throughout the country. In his lectures, the editor asked wealthy whites to contribute funds to the *ACT* so that free copies could be distributed to non-Catholic blacks. It is possible, therefore, to maintain the argument that though the majority of Rudd's paid subscribers were white, his target audience was black. As is evident from the pages of the *ACT,* Rudd used his newspaper both to instruct and encourage African American Catholics, as well as to proclaim Catholicism's merits to prospective black converts. In this manner he served his black readers even as he attempted to shape his white readership's perception of blacks.

An "Energetic Republican"

Early in Rudd's journalistic career, the editor placed faith in the political system as a means by which manifestations of racial injustice could be redressed. Rudd's brand of direct activism, which called for the immediate acknowledgment of black rights, was possible in the relative safety of Ohio, a northern state formally allied with the Union cause. In adopting this more direct and aggressive strategy, Rudd mirrored other black leaders in Ohio during the time period, including the fiery Harry Smith of the *Cleveland Gazette.* Smith also viewed politics as an effective means by which race justice and equality could be attained in society.[114]

Following the Civil War, the overwhelming majority of blacks remained loyal to the Republican Party. Rudd too was active in Republican politics before the establishment of his newspaper. In June 1887 he published an exchange from the *Commercial Gazette* that referred to him as a "level-headed Republican." On another occasion, the *Springfield Globe-Republic* labeled Rudd an "energetic young colored Republican." This designation fit the zealous Rudd. The year before he began publishing the

ACT, the editor conducted a vocal campaign to defeat Joseph B. Foraker's (1846–1917) bid to win the Republican nomination for governor of the state of Ohio. In the spring of 1885, the *Globe-Republic* observed that Rudd was "bustling around at the state Republican convention" doing all he could to defeat Foraker. Similarly, the *Commercial Gazette* of Cincinnati documented Rudd's political activities, including the editor's endorsement of D. K. Watson, a Republican candidate for the office of state attorney general.[115]

Though Rudd's involvement with Republican politics predated his arrival in the Queen City, he continued to remain active after 1886. There were a number of black political clubs in Cincinnati in the late nineteenth century. The Ruffin Club, the Elliot Club, the Grant Club, and the Blaine Club were all committed to the Republican Party. The Maceo Club was an independent political club. The Douglass League and the Duckworth Club were Democratic organizations.[116]

Rudd was a member of the Cincinnati-based Ruffin Club. This organization was named in honor of George L. Ruffin of Boston. Ruffin was the first African American ever to hold a "distinguished judicial position" in a northern state. The club was established for blacks who were apparently discouraged by some from joining the city's white Republican organizations. The Ruffin Club began with seven members in 1887. In May of this same year, the *ACT* said of the newly established organization, "Every earnest Colored Republican in the city is welcome to membership." A year later the organization had grown to 300 members, gaining along the way something of a national reputation. Wendell P. Dabney, a local black historian, claimed the Ruffin Club was the "rendezvous of the high livers" of the day. The club exerted "great influence" on local politics. This same author noted further that the organization was "strictly orthodox Republican."[117]

Rudd's church-centered vision of justice was probably still in development when he began the *ACT* in the late summer of 1886. He initially founded the newspaper to achieve the modest goal of giving the Catholic Church a "fair hearing" among blacks. But as Rudd became disillusioned with the political process generally and the Republican Party particularly, it appears over time he became more and more convinced full equality for African Americans could only be attained through the ministry of the Catholic Church.[118]

By the spring of 1889 Rudd was employing his newspaper to communicate a developed and coherent message concerning the essential role the Catholic Church would necessarily play in the establishment of an egalitarian society free from the tyranny of the color line. In April 1889 Rudd revealed the link between the Catholic Church and the "glorious future" awaiting African Americans when he wrote, "There is a glorious future before our race in this land; but it rests on one condition, viz—Christianity. No race can develop its manhood without God. We must become Christians and then shall we be men in every sense of the word. Not Christians of a lame divided Christianity, but of a whole, harmonious church."[119]Again Rudd gave voice to both his disillusionment with politics as well as his convictions about the important role the Catholic Church would play in bringing racial justice to society:

> This is a good time for the Negro. Just when the impulse of American politicians thought it a good time to throw the stalwart youth overboard and proceed with alacrity to carry out the idea, there steps in a force that is more potent than impulsive political parties and as steady as gravitation, and calls a halt. That force is the Holy Catholic Church whose foundation is the Savior and whose plea and law is the "Fatherhood of God and Brotherhood of Man." She will not be disturbed in her work of equalization until it is consummated.[120]

Rudd's bondage at the hands of his coreligionists, Charles and Matilda Haydon, did little to diminish his faith in the Catholic Church. Yet Rudd's church-centered vision of justice appears to have developed over time. As American Catholic Church leaders began taking positive steps to reach out to blacks, Rudd no doubt took notice. In the end, he became convinced for African Americans the most promising path forward was to link their collective destiny with that of the glorious and certain to be victorious Holy Catholic Church.

CHAPTER 2

A New Civilization Based on the Fatherhood of God and the Brotherhood of Man

The Whole Christian Religion is based on the unity of the Human race. Destroy this and fundamental laws are swept from existence. The Catholic Church has always taught this truth and by that teaching has made present civilization possible.

D. RUDD
31 MAY 1890

Justice as Full Social Equality

Beginning in 1827 with the establishment of this country's first African American newspaper, *Freedom's Journal,* black journalists and editors have been on the front lines of the campaign for racial justice. Prior to emancipation, these pioneers opposed the institution of slavery. Following the Civil War, African American contributors to newspapers and journals courageously labored to protect the civil rights won during Reconstruction. This they did by challenging perceived injustices and combating commonly held racial stereotypes.

The *ACT* was but one of hundreds of black newspapers promoting racial equality in the United States from 1886 to 1897. Taking up many of the concerns of his journalistic peers, Rudd waged a campaign to defend African Americans against negative stereotypes and to bolster race pride within the black community. He also declaimed the evils of race segregation both in the nation's schools as well as in public accommodations. In the pages of the *ACT* Rudd called on businesses to hire African Americans routinely denied jobs because of their skin color. Black newspaper men and women also found both the southern prison system and the crop mortgage system of agriculture to be unjust.[1]

Rudd's campaign for racial justice led him to speak out on the question of African American emigration. He further demonstrated a concern for the plight of people of color living beyond the borders of the United States. But the single most critical justice concern addressed by African American journalists during this period seems to have been the escalation of mob violence perpetrated against blacks. This particular category of racial crime often took the form of lynching. In the *ACT* Rudd vociferously condemned the lynching of blacks. Despite his concern over the violence being suffered by African Americans, however, he paid little attention in his newspaper to the injustices being faced by other ethnic groups, including, Native Americans, Mexican Americans, and Chinese Americans.

The campaign for justice and racial equality led by African Americans in the nineteenth century elicited a number of different responses. More radical white supremacists opposed any liberalization of race relations out of fear these provisions would prepare the way for social equality. Some members of America's dominant racial group, however, supported a limited equality for African Americans. These more progressive whites were, for example, willing to recognize the political equality of blacks and to allow them the same privileges enjoyed by whites in America's court system.[2]

Fr. John M. Mackey, a white priest who served for a time as the *ACT*'s coeditor, advocated a limited social equality for blacks. Though this Cincinnatian adamantly opposed "amalgamation," he nonetheless promoted a circumscribed social equality agenda. For example, he sanctioned the right of blacks to "practice all the trades. . . . side by side with white people." He also believed "well conducted" blacks should be permitted to "sit at table in the public hostelries." Further, Mackey supported African American Catholics' efforts to join parish schools, benevolent societies, and charitable confraternities.[3]

The Reverend Dr. John M. Mackey served as associate editor of the *ACT*. As rector of the Cathedral of St. Peter in Chains, he hosted the second Colored Catholic Congress in Cincinnati. (Courtesy of the Athenaeum of Ohio.)

In contrast to more restricted versions of racial equality, full social equality of the type Rudd promoted was an unqualified recognition of the unity of the human family and a comprehensive disavowal of any system of racial hierarchy. This sought-after social arrangement called for an acknowledgment of the fundamental equality of the races across all fronts, legal, political, civil, and social. A commitment to this principle meant the elimination of all vestiges of the color line, that tyrannous racial barrier that had effectively served to keep blacks from more intimate forms of social contact with whites. In short, full social equality meant the elimination of race prejudice in a completely integrated and free society.

Many whites residing both in the North and in the South refused to acknowledge social equality between blacks and whites. There is little question for some that the major objection was an impassioned opposition to interracial marriage and conjugal unions. This opposition was fueled by the widespread conviction that blacks were an inferior race of people. The belief in the inferiority of blacks was held even by some of the most progressive European Americans of the period. Further, some whites believed the offspring of these "illicit" interracial unions were morally and mentally inferior to children of the "parent races." Elaborate racial classifications based on skin color were constructed in the nineteenth century. The darker skinned "mulattos" were often viewed as "vain," "stupid," and "lazy," while it was widely believed the more light-skinned children had the chance of becoming "decent" sort of people.[4]

Whites were not the only group in American society opposed to interracial unions. Many blacks also objected to the practice on the grounds of race pride and solidarity. One such notable individual was John H. Smythe (1844–1908), a Washington, D.C., diplomat and lawyer who served as minister to Liberia from 1878–1881 and 1882–1885.[5]

Rudd's "cry for justice" was a campaign to win for African Americans the most extensive recognition of civil rights possible. This drive would have placed the editor in the company of African Americans who believed the prohibitions against interracial marriage were an insult to the dignity of the race. Yet evidence from the *ACT* demonstrates Rudd cared little to protect the right to the "ultimate amalgamation" of the races. On one occasion the editor stated he neither promoted nor condemned the practice. Rather, Rudd's view on the controversial question appears to have been similar to that of Archbishop John Ireland (1838–1918) of St. Paul, Minnesota, who stated, "As to social intercourse or intermarriage between the races, it is not a question of right or wrong. It is purely a question of taste."[6]

From Rudd's point of view, neither a limited equality before the law nor a measured social equality would meet his standard for racial justice. Despite Rudd's apparent ambivalence on the question of interracial marriage, evidence from the editorials and exchanges of the *ACT* demonstrates he considered full equality the only genuine expression of racial justice for American society. Like John Ireland, Rudd promoted a racially integrated model of society. Justice would only be achieved when all Americans, regardless of race or class, were viewed as children of the same Heavenly Father. When this occurred, African Americans would then be recognized as the equal of their white counterparts; they would, moreover, be able to enjoy the rights and opportunities guaranteed to all citizens by the nation's founding documents.

The vision of justice Rudd articulated would have likely been heard by whites as a call for social equality. In the pages of *ACT*'s editorials, however, the phrase "social equality" was very rarely employed. It is possible the term was so emotionally charged that the editor chose not to use it in conjunction with his own specific calls for racial justice. Evidence from the *ACT* proves, nonetheless, that Rudd promoted full equality between the races across all fronts.

Rudd's support of the full citizenship rights of blacks led him to condemn his peers who were promoting a less robust justice agenda. On one occasion, for example, Rudd printed an article from a black newspaper, the *Chattanooga Justice*. This same writer claimed the color line in society was so deep that "we expect it to continue in the church, in the family, in marriage and all the rest." The writer of this exchange merely requested that African Americans be granted equality before the law. Rudd was put off by this modest proposal. He wrote in response, "This is driveling nonsense, and the man who writes such stuff would be of more service to the race and to civilization if he go off and hide himself forever. Shame! Shame!"[7]

Similarly, Rudd contended with bigoted whites, many of whom detected a social equality agenda in every assertion of black rights. On one occasion, for example, Rudd reminded his readers, "It is not social equality for a man to be accommodated according to his means, in hotels, common carriers, and in places of public amusement." Rudd went on to say, "The Negroes neither North or South care anything about race mixing socialbly [*sic*] with the whites, they have had too much of that . . . against their will." In the above citation, Rudd affirmed his belief that blacks were not interested in "domestic intimacy."[8]

Given the exigencies of race relations in post-Reconstruction America, Rudd at times seemed willing to concede the fact that social equality and the full justice such a state of race relations implied was a condition realistically achievable only in the future. Yet, he seems to have communicated his own position on the subject when he printed an exchange from the *Cincinnati Post* that referred to social equality as a "beautiful blossom of the living, growing tree of Christian Civilization."[9]

Rudd actively promoted an agenda of racial equality prior to 1890. But in the spring of this same year, his campaign for full social equality received a significant boost from Archbishop John Ireland, who began to publicly support a similar platform. Three months after Archbishop Ireland, in a sermon delivered 4 May in Washington, D.C., articulated his support for the recognition of the social equality of blacks, Rudd confidently stated, "The basic proposition of all Christianity" is the "'Fatherhood of God and the Brotherhood of Man.'" Because God created all the nations of the earth, Rudd concluded, "there can be no possible inequality, except the inequality of accident," which, according to the editor "did not change the relations of men." He articulated in this same editorial his conviction that the Catholic Church would "solve the Negro problem on the right lines." According to Rudd, this would be done by making blacks the "absolute social and political equal of every other race."[10]

Rudd was an active Catholic prior to the birth of the *ACT*. It was, however, after the establishment of the newspaper when he began actively promoting the church as a transformational force able to bring justice to race relations. Over time, Rudd became more and more convinced of the central role the Catholic Church would necessarily play in ushering in a "new civilization," a more humane society characterized by full equality for all races. Moreover, Rudd came to believe the Catholic Church would be the "force" which would not only elevate black Americans but also teach members of white society more generally the truth concerning the fundamental unity of the human family—in short, the "Fatherhood of God and Brotherhood of Man." Throughout the years of the *ACT's* publication, Rudd continued to trumpet the essential role the Catholic Church would play in Christianizing society.

By late summer 1886, Rudd began making use of theological language common among Christian groups in the nineteenth century. Like his Protestant counterparts, he began promoting the recognition of the "Fatherhood of God and Brotherhood of Man" as the most complete expression of social equality. In the pages of the *ACT,* the editor claimed it was the Catholic Church that taught the fundamental unity of the human family. He further declared the "plea and law" of this divine institution was, in fact, the "Fatherhood of God and Brotherhood of Man."[11]

Rudd's use of the term "plea and law" to describe the commitment of the Catholic Church to the ideal of the "Fatherhood of God and Brotherhood of Man" is interesting. There are a couple of ways to interpret Rudd's language. He may have been trying to express in the strongest possible terms his views regarding the church's uncompromising commitment to the unity of the human family. Or perhaps Rudd was simply trying to communicate his belief that the relatedness of all people to God and to one another was not merely a peripheral Catholic doctrine, but rather a foundational one. Finally, Rudd may have used this phrase to make his polemical case for Catholicism, which he believed to be committed not only to living this "law" but also to prophetically proclaiming it for the benefit of society.

Though Rudd was not a professional theologian, he nonetheless couched his convictions about justice in theological terms. His use of the phrase "Fatherhood of God and Brotherhood of Man" no doubt made Rudd's message more palatable to fellow Christians, Protestant and Catholic alike. By employing this theologically laden language, the editor of the *ACT* was appealing to Jesus' New Testament teachings on the interrelatedness of all humanity under one Divine Father. Similarly, this popular theological formulation found support in the Christian Doctrine of Creation.

White skeptics, however, denied the fundamental unity of the human family and the equality of all races. They sought to exaggerate and even manufacture racial distinctions. These same critics claimed blacks were a lesser form of humans, if human at all. Belief in the inferiority of African

Americans and persons of color was a sentiment with deep roots in the United States. One extreme example of this conviction was articulated by Charles Carroll, who in 1900 argued that the white man with his "exalted physical and mental characters" and the Negro with his "ape-like physical and mental characters" could not be the "progeny of one primitive pair." Instead, Carroll reasoned, only whites were made in the "image of God." "Negros," he argued, were indeed not a part of the human family at all. They were part of the ape family. Carroll wrote, "All scientific investigation of the subject proves the Negro to be an ape; and that he simply stands at the head of the ape family, as the lion stands at the head of the cat family." Carroll blamed evolutionary theorists for perpetuating the idea of the essential unity of the human family.[12] Appealing to the "Fatherhood of God and Brotherhood of Man," Rudd challenged individuals like Carroll, who denied the humanity of blacks.

Those white supporters who defended a pluralistic theory of human origins were opposed by many members of the clergy who believed the flawed theory contradicted orthodox Christian teachings on both the genesis of humanity and the universal saviorhood of Christ. Various pluralistic theories of human origins, however, did appeal to some southern political, medical, and literary thinkers. The belief in multiple racial origins also gained scientific credibility when prominent scholars of the American School of Ethnology, including Samuel G. Morton (1799–1851) of Philadelphia and Louis Agassiz (1807–1873) of Harvard, supported it.[13]

For Rudd and his contemporaries, the Christian anthropology presupposed in their appeal to the "Fatherhood of God and Brotherhood of Man" was revolutionary. This ideal arrangement necessitated a model of egalitarian, societal relations free of race prejudice. For Rudd, as for Archbishop Ireland, the anthropological conviction implied in the use of this theological formulation was not accidental to the Catholic faith, but rather its most basic proposition. The editor's egalitarian claims, established as they were on his belief in the fundamental unity of the human family, reveal the very essence of Rudd's vision of justice. Moreover, in the pages of the *ACT* Rudd promoted a vision of justice and full equality inextricably linked to the mission and ministry of the Catholic Church.[14]

A Church-Centered Vision of Justice

Rudd's vision of justice communicated in the *ACT* can be described as church-centered for at least two reasons that will hereafter be explored. Firstly, Rudd believed blacks entering the Catholic Church would find a refuge from the inequities of the color line. Secondly, Rudd's vision of justice might be labeled church-centered because of the editor's convictions as to what has been termed the "Romantic apologetic for Catholicism."[15] Those espousing this hermeneutic for reading history looked with confidence to the civilizing effect of the Catholic Church; they believed it had been, and would continue to be, the principal ameliorating force in society. Rudd, like other Catholics of the period, believed the inequities of racial injustice would eventually be overcome thanks to the tutelage of the one divinely ordained church.

In Rudd's mind, the Catholic Church was a transnational institution with a universal and diverse membership of people drawn from all races.[16] Because of its transnational character, he believed the church was positioned to challenge the parochial race views of America's white population. Therefore, the editor spoke out against what he labeled "Americanism," or race prejudice. He believed this same Americanism, "unknown outside the United States," was what kept blacks from enjoying "full fraternal fellowship in the church organization." Rudd also confidently declared that Americanism had never been permitted to be a part of the Catholic Church's practice. He further declared that within the pale of the church "all are equal."[17]

This is not to say Rudd had given up on America or on its institutions. For example, Rudd made a distinction between an illegitimate "American Spirit" and what he termed a "true American spirit." Rudd believed a manifestation of the illegitimate and misguided American spirit was at work in the country doing all in its power to "crush out Negro Ambition." On the other hand, true American spirit was the "Fatherhood of God and Brotherhood of Man."[18]

In the *ACT* Rudd attempted to strike a delicate balance between his robust claims regarding the church's commitment to equality for blacks and the editor's pleas for individual Catholics to live up to the church's egalitarian teaching. Speaking of the Catholic Church, Rudd wrote, "Among the members discrimination is unknown. Recognizing the fact that all mankind are children of a common Father, all are welcome around the family circle, the Altar of the Sanctuary. The Church seeks to propagate the Faith and bring all the children of God unto Christianity. She teaches the Fatherhood of God and the brotherhood of man, and follows up her precepts with her practices." Challenging individual American Catholics who refused to acknowledge the church's teaching concerning the fraternity of the races, Rudd concluded, "Her followers can do no less than practice the same principles."[19]

Beyond Catholicism, Rudd could see no organization offering the country's African American population "such possibilities of assistance." Again speaking of the Catholic Church, the editor of the *ACT* wrote, "Broad and liberal as she is, we can make headway within her pale that greatly advance us toward that social equality which we must reach in order to stand as full citizens, above the reach of prejudice, which so restrains our civil equality, notwithstanding the great number of special statutes intended to obviate that effect."[20]

Rudd believed the Catholic Church to be the only institution in the United States really committed to recognizing the full equality of blacks before the altar. In January 1887, Rudd claimed blacks entering the church would be received as equals. On another occasion, Rudd printed an exchange from the *Negro American* that declared the Catholic Church was the only church "offering the Negro communion on terms of equality."[21]

In support of his claims, Rudd, on many occasions, wrote about the hospitality he himself had received at the hands of white Catholics. For example, in September 1887, after his return from a meeting of the German Verein held in Chicago, Rudd wrote, "The editor of this paper will always remember with deepest gratitude the courtesy shown him by the many Catholics he met in Chicago this week. Truly the Catholic Church is the place for the Negro if he wants to meet unadulterated Christian kindness."[22]

Because of Rudd's faith in the "equalizing force" of the Catholic Church, he invited members of the race into this divine institution. He believed the Catholic Church would provide African Americans a sanctuary free of racial bigotry, a place where blacks would be viewed not merely as the equal of whites, but also as members of the same family. Rudd wrote, "If the American Negroes want to smash the overflowing bowl of prejudice in church circles in America they should step as a single man, into the folds of 'The only church on this continent where rich and poor, white and black must drop prejudice at the threshold and go hand in hand to the altar.'"[23]

In January 1891 Rudd published the following editorial describing the fraternal relations between the races in the Catholic Church: "The close and intimate personal relations existing among members of the Catholic faith is well known and recognized. A brother in the church is indeed a brother in all that term implies, no difference what his race or complexion may be." Emphasizing the egalitarian spirit widely embraced by Catholics, the editorial claimed this sentiment was not merely the result of the "dictation of the priesthood."[24]

Rudd believed the Catholic Church to be an essential agent of uplift for African Americans. True to the Romantic impulses inherent in nineteenth-century American Catholicism, Rudd believed God had been at work in each historical epoch lifting the downtrodden. Those in the church embracing this Romantic theology identified the Incarnation as a watershed event in the uplift of humanity. In the Incarnation, the divine nature elevated all of human nature by being united in a single person, Christ. As a result of the Incarnation, a new principle promising to bring progress to society had been released in history.[25] Blacks entering the church would, therefore, experience the full benefit of this lifting force.

By means of conversion, Rudd hoped to initiate blacks into the Catholic Church. He imagined the church to be a universal institution, a true fellowship undivided by sectional, racial, or class divisions. The editor believed the Catholic Church in the United States to be a visible community committed to living out the "Fatherhood of God and Brotherhood of Man." Rudd encouraged his white Catholic readers in their attempts to welcome blacks into the church. On one occasion, for example, Rudd said he had been often asked how to "bring the Negro into the Church." In response he offered the following: "First Pray. Then, build up all the Catholic institutions that he has begun or that have been started for him. Build up to respectable proportions the convents of the Oblate Sisters at Baltimore, St. Louis and Leavenworth. Rebuild the Convent of the Sisters of the Holy Family at New Orleans. Wherever there is a Negro school where secular teachers are employed let the teachers be of the race. Help the Negro Catholic press, encourage the Negro to do for himself; and the question will answer itself."[26]

Rudd's use of the ideal of the "Fatherhood of God and Brotherhood of Man" was not unique to Catholic writers; for a number of years, for example, the masthead of the *Christian Recorder* of the A.M.E. Church bore the words "God Our Father, Man Our Brother." Rudd recognized that the unity of the human family was a theological conviction espoused by other Christian denominations. He believed such a communal spirit of equality, however, could only come to realization in society through the mission and ministry of the Catholic Church. This conviction at times introduced a polemical tone to some of Rudd's editorials.[27]

Rudd believed other Christian denominations had failed to welcome African Americans as equals into their churches. For example, the editor of the *ACT* wrote of the Episcopalians, "while the Episcopalians have done something for the colored people they have neither the depth of Christian charity nor the discipline to place the Negro on the same footing as themselves under any and all circumstances in the church."[28] In December 1887 Rudd declared the Presbyterians "have not the right sort of Christianity." Rudd further speculated as to how these same "so called Christians" would answer at the bar of eternal justice for "wrapping the gospel in elegant furs and resting it within hearts of prejudice?"[29] On another occasion, Rudd attacked the Presbyterian Church for its handling of the one question "upon which all Christianity itself is based. All mankind are of one origin." In this same article, Rudd argued that the "true animus of Protestants" was revealed in this action, "they would use the poor Negro" but not "allow an equal show in their churches."[30]

As a nineteenth-century Catholic, Rudd would have no doubt been familiar with the type of polemical arguments developed by Catholic defenders of the faith, including Spanish priest and Catholic apologist Fr. Jaime Balmes (1810–1848). On one occasion, Balmes wrote that "Protestantism, when viewed in a mass, appears only a shapeless collection of innumerable sects, all opposed to each other, and agreeing only in one point, viz. in protesting against the authority of the Church."[31] Rudd's critique of other Christian denominations is predictable. He viewed Protestant Churches as impotent products of human creation, expressions of what he termed "lame, divided Christianity."[32] He would have presumably viewed Protestantism's tendency toward division as an intrinsic feature of the misguided movement. The editor also believed Protestants were operating outside the authority of God's true church.

Rudd, for example, spoke out against a proposal by Presbyterians to organize blacks into "separate existence." He argued that this plan to segregate African Americans was ill-conceived and did not have the backing of legitimate church authority. Instead, he believed it was the result of "private judgment."[33] In the end, Rudd simply could not imagine that such a divided form of Christianity, operating as it did outside the divinely sanctioned authority of the Catholic Church, would be able to address the virulent race prejudice held by so many white Americans

Rudd and the Romantic Apologetic for Catholicism

One might describe Rudd's vision of justice as church-centered for a second reason. Rudd held a Catholic perspective as to the vital role the church had played in the emergence of Western civilization. In short, Rudd espoused what has been termed the "Romantic apologetic for Catholicism." Those who embraced this worldview believed that the credit for the development of Western civilization largely belonged to the Catholic Church. Through the church's patient tutelage over a period of centuries, society's barbarism had been ameliorated. These same proponents believed that as the Catholic Church had been an active force in the civilization and uplift of Europe's pagan populations, so it would continue to lead modern society toward a more flourishing existence. Further, many Catholics of this period held this position in contradistinction to Protestants who viewed the Reformation and the birth of Protestantism as the watershed event in the progress of human civilization and freedom. Moreover, proponents of Romantic theology believed the lifting power of the church extended beyond the ranks of the faithful to members of society more generally. For those who embraced this view of history, the Catholic Church was the divinely commissioned teaching agent for society. In the minds of the faithful, the church had been responsible for improving the lives of America' s downtrodden inhabitants, including, among others, blacks, women, and Native Americans.

Rudd was committed to idea that the work of Christ was ordained to be continued through the teaching mission of the Catholic Church. He further believed the church had received this divine commission for this work from the "Almighty Emperor [sic] of time and eternity."[34] For

Rudd, this educational mission was centered in the papacy. Commenting on an article in the *Connecticut Catholic,* which listed the names of each pope, Rudd wrote, "It is through this unbroken line stretching across nineteen centuries that the Catholic Church received from the Master the mission to preach and to teach."[35] The teaching ministry of the church, and its civilizing effect on society was sometimes highlighted in articles Rudd printed in the *ACT.* One article, for example, spoke of the benefit Native Americans were receiving as a result of being brought into contact with the civilizing power of the Catholic Church.[36]

Key figures in the propagation of the Romantic apologetic for Catholicism were European Catholic apologists such as Jaime Balmes and Count Charles de Montalembert (1810–1870), a French journalist, politician, and historian. In Balmes's seminal work, *Protestantism and Catholicity, Compared in Their Effects on the Civilization of Europe,* the author examined the effects of Protestantism and Catholicism on European civilization. One of Balmes's primary antagonists was François Pierre Guillaume Guizot (1787–1874), who challenged the Catholic hermeneutic for reading European history. For example, in one of Guizot's best-known works, *History of Civilization in Europe,* the author argued that in the period from the fifth century to the twelfth century, church leaders had almost always "been led to range themselves on the side of power and despotism against human liberty, regarding [liberty] only as an adversary . . . taking more pains to subdue than to secure it."[37] Guizot linked the spread of civilization with the emergence of Protestantism. He viewed the Reformation as a "great movement of the liberty of the human mind . . . an insurrection of the mind against absolute power in the spiritual order."[38]

Guizot believed the reactionary forces dispatched by Rome to battle against Protestantism, specifically the Jesuits, did so unsuccessfully and to the detriment of civilization. He further argued the Jesuit campaign against "modern civilization" and the liberty of the "human mind" resulted in no "splendor" nor "grandeur" and no "great events"; nor did this reactionary campaign put in motion "powerful masses of men." Conversely, Guizot claimed the force being attacked by the Jesuits had conquered with splendor: it did "great things" by "great means"; "it aroused the people, it gave to Europe great men, and changed, in the face of day, the fashion and form of states."[39]

Balmes challenged the idea that Protestant reformers of the sixteenth century contributed much to the development of science, art, human liberty, and various other elements comprising what may be termed "civilization." Balmes, for example, argued European civilization owed to the Catholic Church "its finest ornament," the "abolition of slavery." He further argued, "Before Protestantism European civilization had reached all the development possible for it." In fact, Balmes concluded, "Protestantism perverted the course of civilization, and produced immense evils in modern society."[40]

The Romantic apologetic for Catholicism was an interpretation of the development of Western civilization that would subsequently be embodied in the work of a number of American Catholic apologists, including, among others, Isaac Hecker (1819–1888), founder of the Paulists, and Archbishop John Ireland. These defenders of the Catholic faith believed democracy (rightly conceived), the emergence of individual civil rights, as well as improvements in the plight of the poor and women, were all the result of Catholicism's civilizing influence on society.[41]

Rudd too developed a Catholic hermeneutic for reading Western history. He was convinced the Catholic Church had performed, and would continue to perform, an essential pedagogical role in the gradual improvement of society. For example, on one occasion Rudd wrote, "That the Catholic Church, like a beacon light, points out the only sure way to a higher and perfect civilization is attested by the nineteen centuries that have rolled back into the past since She received Her commission from Her Divine Founder."[42] In the editor's mind, the Catholic Church's efforts to improve American society were going to benefit blacks as well as whites.

That some nineteenth-century Catholic apologists applied their polemical hermeneutic of reading history to America's race question is no surprise. Those who did created an interpretation of history similar to the one developed by A. J. Faust, a black photographer from Washington, D.C. In an address delivered at the first gathering of the Colored Catholic Congress in 1889, Faust argued the Catholic Church, in its early days of existence, attempted to ameliorate the condition of the Roman slave. He further declared that the church had worked on behalf of the slave and the oppressed "before the African was stolen from his home by English slavers." In this same speech, Faust also emphasized the civilizing and uplifting effect of Christianity on those in bondage.[43]

Faust defended the Catholic Church against critics of its record on the human institution of slavery. He argued, for example, that the church in the early years of its existence remained "passive" on the "great moral blight" because "immediate emancipation" would have been "extremely hazardous," even if it could have been accomplished. "Time was required to prepare society and the slave population for a change of such vital consequence," he declared. Faust also argued when the "counsels" of the church were followed, "nations advanced in law and liberty." It was Pope Gregory the Great (540–604) who had freed his slaves, he reminded his readers. Faust further explained that during the time of the Crusades, manumissions were granted to soldiers who volunteered to free the Holy City from the yoke of the infidel. Similarly, Faust pointed out that the first writer to condemn the African slave trade was Dominic Soto (1494–1560), the Dominican friar and confessor of Holy Roman Emperor Charles V (1500–1558).[44]

In his encyclical "On the Nature of Human Liberty," Pope Leo XIII (1810–1903) also applied the Romantic apologetic for Catholicism to the "Negro problem." In this nineteenth-century encyclical the pope claimed the "powerful influence of the Church" had "ever been manifested in the custody and protection of the civil and political liberty of the people." He further claimed, "The impartiality of law and the true brotherhood of man was first asserted by Jesus Christ," stating that Jesus' "apostles re-echoed His voice, when they declared that there was neither Jew or Gentile, nor barbarian, nor Scythian, but all were brothers in Jesus Christ." This Catholic hermeneutic for reading history made it possible for the pope to conclude "slavery, that old reproach of the heathen nations was mainly abolished by the beneficial efforts of the Church."[45]

Like other nineteenth-century Catholics concerned with the rights of blacks, Rudd applied the Romantic apologetic for Catholicism to America's racial dilemma. In a telling address given at the first Colored Catholic Congress gathering, Rudd declared the "great Church of Christ is destined to lift humanity to its highest planes of perfection; and in the moral and mental elevation of mankind, she must of necessity lift the Colored race."[46] On another occasion, the editor of the *ACT* wrote, "the great church of our Lord and Savior is quietly pursuing her divine mission, to 'teach all nations,' placing the seal of her approval at all times upon Justice and equity and condemning in all seasons the injustice heaped upon the poor and despised Negro."[47] Similarly, Rudd wrote, "More than one-sixth of a vast population, each in law the equal of another, yet, in fact, debarred from common justice, stretch forth their hands to the Church asking that She teach mankind a decent respect for itself and God."[48]

During the years Rudd published the *ACT,* he was in demand as a lecturer. On his speaking tours around the country one of the editor's major themes appears to have been the important role the Catholic Church would necessarily play in the establishment of racial justice in the United States. On one occasion, for example, Rudd printed an exchange from the *Commercial Gazette* of Cincinnati, which said the following of the *ACT's* editor: "Mr. Rudd has prepared a new lecture he being gifted with oraorical [*sic*] powers as well as literary capacity. Its title is 'The New Civilization.' As a devout Catholic Mr. Rudd naturally and very justly ascribes to his religion vast potentialities in the way of elevating his people."[49]

In June 1887 the *Louisville Courier Journal* reported Rudd had given "The New Civilization" speech to a large crowd gathered at Jackson Hall in Lexington, Kentucky. Rudd said, "the new civilization has for its basis Christianity, and this embraces all that is charitable in social intercourse, fair in diplomatic relations and commercial exchange, and beautiful and pure in art and music, elegant and Christianly in literature and pleasing to God." Rudd continued, the "spark of civilization, the recording of past events and prophesy of that which was to come, was kept aglow . . . by the monks and Catholic Priests during the dark ages." Rudd stated enough was known of these "forces" and "resources" to "place the whole human family in speaking distance." He further stated if the black man was to keep pace with his "fair hued brother" he must be "grounded in truth and fairness, girdle about him the robe of energy, and enter every field where the genius of man avails to conquer."[50]

According to Rudd, with this speech he hoped to "dispel some of the misinformation that exists among a portion of my race concerning the Roman Catholic Church: second, to show that the Colored man has been the equal of every other man before the altars of the Catholic Church, beginning with the wise men of the East, who followed the star of Bethlehem and bowed in adoration of our Lord in the manger until this living hour." Rudd further explained, "I want to show [blacks] that

to-day, greater than ever before, Holy Mother Church is striving to educate and build up the unfortunate of every race and tribe, of every tongue
and clime. . . . Her members are members the world over, her priests are
priests in all the earth."[51]

The Triumph of the Catholic Church

At times, Rudd confidently communicated his belief that Catholicism
would eventually unite all African Americans under one religious banner.
Responding to T. Thomas Fortune's article on Catholic efforts to evangelize blacks, Rudd wrote, "Mr. Fortune is right, as eventually, every tribe
and tongue and nation will be found under one religious banner, no matter if they do differ now."[52] On another occasion, Rudd wrote, "It is use-
less for people to try longer to hide the fact that the Colored people of
America are coming in large numbers to the one true Church. Because
they find there that great spirit of real Christianity, which makes all men
equal before the altar of the Lord."[53]

Rudd went on to declare Protestant groups were wrong for denying
that the black man had the "same right" as other people "to go into any
and all of their meeting places under similar circumstances." They were
further wrong in leaving the "great highway defined and established by
the Incarnate Son of God." "When Christ commissioned the Church to
teach, He thereby left His law in the keeping of men especially chosen
for this purpose," Rudd reasoned. The editor concluded blacks were
coming to see the deficiencies in Protestantism and would in a "few years
be found largely in the Catholic Church."[54]

CHAPTER 3

Archbishop John Ireland's Masterly Plea for Justice

Bishop Ireland, of Minnesota, and those who are like him covered by the protecting aegis of God's Holy Word, shall shine in triumph like the stars of heaven. One can feel in this man's splendid courage something of the assurance of the Rock of Ages.

ALBERT WHITMAN
QUOTED IN THE *ACT*
21 JUNE 1890

Allies in the Campaign

Rudd found in the Catholic Church an organization that facilitated his development academically, spiritually, and professionally. This same institution also supported him in the refinement and promotion of his church-centered platform of racial justice. During the decade of the 1880s, the editor of the *ACT* became part of a Catholic chorus dedicated to promulgating racial equality in the United States. Further, Rudd's personal encounters with members of the American Catholic hierarchy, individual priests and lay persons alike, convinced him the church was sincere in its efforts to deliver full equality to African Americans.

Archbishop Elder of Cincinnati and Archbishop John Ryan of Philadelphia were two of the members of the Catholic hierarchy particularly concerned with the plight of America's black population. Elder came to the aid of Rudd when the editor was working to establish the *ACT.* In a letter penned to the archbishop in 1888, Rudd wrote, "Dear Archbishop, I have every reason to thank you for your kindness to us and to the American Catholic Tribune for it was by your approval that the paper was able to stem the tide for that most dangerous period of the life of any newspaper, the first year. It was your approval also that gave us standing among the prelates and clergy of this country."[1] Elder also demonstrated his concern for the cause of blacks by participating in Rudd's Colored Catholic Congress movement. He spoke to the congress at its first gathering in January 1889, and the next summer he hosted the meeting in Cincinnati.

Similarly, Rudd found in Archbishop John Ryan of Philadelphia an ally in his quest for racial equality. Rudd wrote, "Archbishop Ryan was one of the first to send us a check for $25 when the American Catholic Tribune was battling for a foothold."[2] In January 1892, this same church official hosted the third gathering of the Colored Catholic Congress in Philadelphia.

Rudd's positive assessment of the church's efforts on behalf of the race was further encouraged by supportive members of the Catholic clergy. On their marketing trips throughout the United States, Rudd and his staff met many supportive priests. Fr. John E. Burke of New York City Patrick Corrigan of New Jersey were particularly helpful to Rudd in that they heartily supported the editor's journalistic campaign to evangelize blacks.[3] Rudd's agents also regularly reported on the aid given to them by clerics serving in cities around the country. For example, in November 1890 Lincoln Valle spoke of the warm hospitality given him by the family of Fr. Thomas Burke. Following this meeting, the *ACT* reported that Valle and Fr. Augustus Tolton (1854–1897), who had been traveling with Rudd's agent, were received "as all Catholics receive their friends."[4]

Rudd's faith in the Catholic Church's advocacy for the rights of blacks was bolstered by the church's ongoing campaign to end the international slave trade. On one occasion, Rudd printed Pope Leo XIII's appeal for donations to stop the trafficking of slaves.[5] Commenting on the pope's appeal and the subsequent circulars issued by American bishops, Rudd wrote the following:

> While Negroes in the United States may be abused by enemies and pretended friends, his case is still not a hopeless one; for while the Catholic Church exists, She will labor to elevate mankind the world over, with out regard to race or complexion. She has, in all ages, faced the prejudices of all the people of all the nations with God's eternal truth, the equality of all the sons of men.[6]

Rudd's faith in the church was further encouraged by Cardinal Lavigerie's antislavery efforts in Africa. In the *ACT,* Rudd published an exchange detailing the pope's commissioning of Lavigerie for this noble endeavor. The exchange further reported that a donation of 300,000 lire from the pope had been forwarded to finance the cardinal's work.[7]

Rudd found more proof of the church's commitment to racial equality in the ordination and subsequent ministry of the nation's first openly recognized African American priest, Father Augustus Tolton. For example, Rudd described the High Mass conducted by Tolton at Cincinnati's Cathedral of St. Peter in Chains as the "same awful ceremony performed precisely like the same solemn services are performed from the 'Rising of the sun to the going down thereof the earth around.'" Though Rudd acknowledged Tolton was only one of seven million blacks in America qualified to "offer the Divine Oblation," he nonetheless argued that "if there were thousands of others all of them would be accepted as priests of God in any and every Catholic [Church] on the face of the earth." For the editor of the *ACT,* Tolton's presence in the church was evidence this divine organization was at work "'curbing the great ynd [*sic*] raising the low.'"[8]

Rudd's faith in the advocacy of the Catholic Church was also encouraged by his experiences at the meeting of the first lay Catholic congress convened at Baltimore in 1889. At this same gathering, Rudd himself was honored for the important role he had played in organizing the assembly.[9] The spirit of equality that pervaded this meeting was observed not only by the editor of the *ACT,* but also by other journalists who attended. For example, following this gathering *Ave Maria*'s correspondent wrote, "The Negro, the Caucasian and the Indian, were all received alike, socially and otherwise. It was a deep feeling of Christian love and respect that caused great and wealthy Irishmen, Germans, and

Though his racial heritage was not widely known Bishop James A. Healy was the first African American bishop ordained in the United States. (Courtesy of the College of the Holy Cross)

Fr. Augustus Tolton, the nation's first openly recognized African American priest. (Courtesy of the Archdiocese of Chicago's Joseph Cardinal Bernardin Archives and Records Center.)

others—all true American citizens to kneel at the feet of the negro priest to ask him to invoke the blessings of Almighty God upon them."[10]

Moved by the spirit of this same gathering, Rudd published the comments of another participant at the lay congress who noted the extent to which the color line had been removed. The contributor wrote, "It was indeed a scene never to be forgotten by those who had the happiness of witnessing it. There were no distinctions, there were no side issues, there were no 'ifs' and 'wherefores' but there was one grand and cordial enthusiastic and practical demonstration and acknowledgement of the great brotherhood of man." Commenting on the article, Rudd added, "We hope the above is plain enough for our able and distinguished contemporaries."[11]

During the years of the *ACT*'s publication, Rudd had occasion to witness firsthand the Catholic laity's commitment to the cause of racial equality and justice. For example, in November 1890 Rudd and a Jewish guest, Mr. Geza Berger, were invited to attend the fifth annual council gathering of Kentucky's branch of the Catholic Knights of America. However, Dr. Henry DeGruyter, Kentucky's representative for the Cincinnati newspaper the *Volksfreund,* declared he considered it beneath him to sit at the same table "with a negro and a Jew."[12] Acting to defend the dignity of their invited guests, the entertainment committee moved to inform DeGruyter that he himself would not be permitted to attend. Moreover, it was determined this same committee could "recognize no distinction of race or color."[13]

A banquet was held on the last evening of this same gathering. During this banquet, Rudd was asked to respond to a toast. The *ACT* reported, "This was the signal of the grandest ovation of the evening and when Mr. Rudd arose the scene that followed could not well be described. The great audience almost went wild in its ovation to Mr. Rudd, the cheering lasting several minutes." The editor addressed the gathering of approximately three hundred delegates after his toast. The *ACT* commented, "Mr. Rudd's address was scholarly and dignified, and his allusion that he was privileged to address those about him as brother Catholics brought forth renewed applause."[14]

Archbishop John Ireland's Promotion of Full Equality for Blacks

Perhaps for Rudd the most convincing evidence of the church's good will toward the cause of racial equality was found in the sermons and speeches of St. Paul's Archbishop, John Ireland. This same visionary and courageous church leader campaigned for the immediate recognition of the full social equality of blacks. No doubt Rudd would have concurred with one journalist who declared the "principle of the brotherhood of man was better embodied in the Archbishop than in any other prelate of this country."[15] Ireland's campaign for racial equality made an impression not only on the black Catholic community, but also on many black Protestants as well.[16]

John Ireland, archbishop of St. Paul, Minnesota, was an advocate for the recognition of the full equality of blacks. (Courtesy of the Archdiocese of Saint Paul and Minneapolis Archives.)

Ireland, affectionately referred to as the "consecrated blizzard of the West," was a member of the liberal wing of the American Catholic hierarchy sometimes referred to as the Americanist party. Other prominent members of this movement were Isaac Hecker; John Slattery; Bishop John J. Keane (1839–1918), the first rector of Catholic University of America; and Bishop Denis J. O'Connell (1849–1927), bishop of Richmond, Virginia. Ireland had served in the Civil War as a chaplain for the Union army. His political sympathies were with the Republican Party, though it is difficult to determine to what extent Ireland's political views impacted his position on racial justice. Regardless of his politics, however, Ireland would have understood the church's responsibility to advocate on behalf of one of the nation's most vulnerable populations.[17]

Ireland's linkage of Romantic theology to the "Negro problem" would not itself have distinguished his work from other American church leaders of the late nineteenth century. Among Catholic leaders of this period almost all would have acknowledged the "Fatherhood of God" and the essential unity of the human family. What distinguished Ireland from most other white church leaders of his era was that he dared promote the immediate recognition of the full social equality of blacks.

"Amalgamation," a term used to describe the intimate interaction between the races, was opposed by many Catholics, even in the liberal camp. This list included Cincinnati church officials Archbishop John Baptist Purcell (1800–1883), his brother Fr. Edward Purcell, as well as one-time *ACT* associate editor John Mackey. "Race mixing" would have been odious not merely because of an aversion to racial integration, but also because such unions would have violated nineteenth-century American class norms. Other nineteenth-century opponents of amalgamation believed that only in the distant future would the social equality of blacks be recognized. This recognition would come after the race had advanced enough to achieve parity with whites.

There were a relatively small number of blacks living in the archdiocese of St. Paul in the last two decades of the nineteenth century. Those who did would have directly benefited from Ireland's relatively progressive position on social equality. Though Ireland held no institutional authority to implement his ideals on racial integration beyond his diocese, the prelate became an inspirational ally of African Americans generally, and of black Catholics specifically. Evidence from the *Northwestern Chronicle* and the

ACT reveals some in Ireland's diocese may have begun promoting the controversial call for the recognition of the full social equality of blacks as early as April 1890. This was the same year a Louisiana law, Act III, was passed, forcing blacks to ride in Jim Crow cars. An issue of the *Northwestern Chronicle* dated 11 April set forth a number of Ireland's specific pronouncements concerning the race question. The prelate believed for America's "race problem" there was "but one solution . . . to obliterate the color line." Ireland supported the political rights of blacks. The archbishop further argued African Americans should be treated as whites in all "public gatherings" and in "all public resorts," including hotels. Many of Ireland's progressive contemporaries would have supported him up to this point. Ireland, however, refused to draw a color line even in the sacrosanct institution of marriage. Instead, the prelate voiced his approval of interracial unions, a controversial position that presumed absolute equality between the races.[18]

In April 1890 Rudd's *ACT* produced a series of speeches delivered at a benefit to raise funds for the establishment of St. Paul's first black congregation, St. Peter Claver Church. Speeches were given by Fr. John Gmeiner, Fr. John T. Harrison, and Archbishop Ireland himself. The "justice" expressed in these same addresses was heartily endorsed by Rudd. Commenting on these speeches, the editor declared them to be "remarkable in their clearness and justice." Gmeiner addressed the tendency on the part of national groups to "exalt their own nationality or race above all mankind." This, Gmeiner argued, whites had done at the expense of "Africans." In this same speech, he further argued no "essential difference" could be identified between "Africans and whites." Gmeiner insisted, "The greatest apparent difference between Negroes and whites, consisted in the color of skin. Yet also this difference is only accidental."[19]

Though Gmeiner stated he did not believe "Africans" had "yet reached the full height of modern civilization," he reasoned this unfortunate fact was to be explained by the "discouraging circumstances in which they had been placed for generations." Further, Gmeiner spoke of the "remarkable progress" made by African Americans since they had been given "a fair chance." He stated he believed the majority of blacks would remain in the United States. He further held out the hope that African American missionaries would someday evangelize Africa.[20]

When Archbishop Ireland addressed this same assembly, he blamed the "race problem" on "simple prejudice." Ireland declared he believed the race question could be solved "if we put ourselves squarely on the broad platforms of American citizenship and the Christian religion." Ireland pointed out that though "liberty," "fraternity," and "equality," were "mere vibrations of the air" in Europe, they were, in fact, realized in this country, but only for the "white man." Ireland asked, "Why for him only? Why draw a line before the simple accident of color?" He further asked, "Are not the black man and the white man children of the same ancestry? Does not the same human blood course through their veins?" Ireland argued it was a "stain upon the pages of our country's history that there were ever men beneath our flag whom we refused to treat as our equals." He urged amends be made by treating "our black brother as a man, our equal in matters political, civil or social."[21] Speaking of the injustice of slavery forced on African Americans, Ireland declared, "We take slavery as an excuse for denying equality to day to the Negro. We loaded him with chains, we strove to keep him in ignorance, to degrade him and the effect of our own cruel treatment is cited as a justification of his social inequality. Why, in very shame we should hurry to take away from him all possible signs of our past conduct towards him; in very justice we should press upon him all rights to which a man is entitled from his fellow man."[22]

Ireland also spoke of the incompatibility of Christianity and race prejudice. He argued, "We are not merely Americans, we are Christians, and the cardinal principle of religion is one brotherhood for all men. Christ died for all; we are all laved in the same Baptismal waters; and the same hope of heaven is extended to all. How one Christian can repel from his side another, simply because he is of a different color, passes my understanding." The solution to the "race problem," according to Ireland, was to "obliterate absolutely all color line." He explained to the African Americans in his audience "soon you will be recognized equals of your fellow citizens: and soon it will be as impossible to exhibit towards you political or social ostracism, as it would be impossible to-day to bring back upon your limbs the chains of servitude."[23]

Ireland urged blacks to "take refuge in the Catholic Church." On behalf of the Catholic Church, he promised African Americans "justice." In the end, Ireland said he refused even to acknowledge that a "Negro problem" existed, declaring instead, "there is no problem to be solved. I know no color line, I acknowledge none." The archbishop was well aware of how his words would be received, even by those whose opinions he held in "high value." Yet he also confidently affirmed, "I believe I am right." He continued, "Aye, untimely to-day my words will be to-morrow timely. My fault, if there were a fault, would be that I am ahead of my day. The time is not too distant when Americans and Christians will wonder that there was a race prejudice."[24]

At the conclusion of this meeting, Father Harrison, rector of the cathedral in St. Paul, invited his African American listeners to join St. Peter Claver Church. He referred to prejudice as a "monster," which, thanks to the leveling influence of the "old Church," was becoming a thing of the past.[25] Though one might expect that such an extraordinary set of speeches would have been better covered in the African American press, an examination of the *Christian Recorder,* a prominent black newspaper of the day, yielded no comment through May 1890.

Equality Carried "Too Far"

The lack of commentary in the black press following the St. Paul speeches may have been because a record of the lectures of Gmeiner, Ireland, and Harrison do not appear to have been widely circulated. In May 1890 Ireland sought to remedy this lack of publicity. On 4 May of this same year, Ireland's controversial sermon on the color line was delivered in dramatic fashion before a packed house at St. Augustine Church in Washington, D.C. It appears Ireland had agreed to preach in Fr. Michael J. Walsh's black parish on the condition Walsh would have Ireland's sermon published in the *Catholic Mirror.* The prelate was fifty-one and at the zenith of his career in 1890, almost a full decade before the archbishop's reputation would be tarnished by Pope Leo XIII's 1899 condemnation of a constellation of ideas termed "Americanism."[26]

The atmosphere in the historic black church was electric with expectation as Ireland stood to deliver his sermon. The import of this address was enhanced by the attendance of a number of notable politicians, including Minnesota's delegation to the U.S. Congress: Secretary of the Treasury William Windon; Senator William D. Washburn (1831–1912) of Minnesota; Senator Powers; and Auditor of the Treasury John R. Lynch. In this sermon, Ireland courageously addressed the "race problem." He placed much of the blame for the dilemma on whites. He further stated whites were in need of "lessons in charity, benevolence, justice and religion."[27]

Ireland urged America to make amends for slavery by "recognizing [blacks] in the enjoyment of all their rights." He referred to the teaching of the Catholic Church, drawing attention to the "corner-stone" of its tenets, the "equality of all men." "The solution of the question," according to the archbishop, was that individuals should "look one another in the face as members of the same family, children of the same God." Further, he pointed out, "No church is a fit temple of God where a man because of his color is excluded or made to occupy a corner." "The color line," he said, "must go and soon, too." "The line will be drawn at personal merit," he concluded.[28]

In this historic sermon, Ireland spoke directly to white Catholics. He reminded the crowd whenever Catholics "gave way and yielded" to race prejudice "they contradicted the teachings of their hearts as given by God as to equality and fraternity." He further asked Catholics to "extend the right hand of fellowship to their Colored brethren and say that there was not and could not be a color question between Catholics." This, according to Ireland, would be the "true and only solution" to the race question. [29]

In a manner that did not seem to cool the audience's appreciation for Ireland, the prelate reminded his black listeners that they needed to exercise patience. He assured them their "recognition" would be in "accordance with their merits." He encouraged his audience to show themselves worthy of "religious and social equality." Ireland further urged the crowd to educate themselves and their children, to save money to purchase a home, to be loyal subjects of the state, law-abiding citizens seeking redress for injustices "where it should be given and in a proper spirit." Finally, the archbishop encouraged his African American listeners to "judiciously and sternly" "stand for their rights," specifically the right to vote.[30]

Complying with Ireland's request, the *Catholic Mirror* did print the archbishop's sermon prefaced by the following words of introduction:

> We have long wished for an ending to the discussion on the Negro question, but we cannot reach the end until the matter is settled and settled right. The venerable Archbishop of St. Paul preached a sermon in Washington recently that has awakened the deepest interest in every thing that pertains to the conversion of the Negro as well as to show conclusively that the race prejudice is a crime

that we must as Catholics, lift ourselves above it or go down under Just retribution.[31]

If publicizing his revolutionary position on the race question was what Ireland sought, the prelate's sermon delivered at St. Augustine accomplished his purpose. The words and ideals found in Ireland's sermon caused a stir around the country and received reviews in a number of newspapers, Catholic and Protestant alike. Rudd commented on the archbishop's speech in an *ACT* editorial. Rudd's enthusiasm for the ideals set forth in Ireland's sermon is evident. Moreover, the editor of the *ACT* urged black newspapers to publish the prelate's message. Rudd editorialized, "If the Colored press of the United States mean to be fair to the race and the cause of equality the sermon of Archbishop Ireland will be reproduced in every Negro paper in the United States. . . . Justice must and will prevail." He further called the speech a "revelation" and urged his readers to "Read it."[32]

Newspapers throughout the country responded immediately to Ireland's controversial sermon. Many praised the archbishop's remarks. One black writer, presumably Protestant, called him "the man of God— the Elijah of this age."[33] The *People's Advocate* declared the ideals in Ireland's message to be "aggressive and radical, the legitimate results of conviction and moral courage." A contributor to this same publication recognized the significance of Ireland's sermon, in part because of the archbishop's "official position" in the church.[34] The *Catholic Mirror* printed Ireland's speech, allied to the claim that "the equality of all men, in the eyes of the Common Father of mankind, can not for one moment be questioned by a follower of Jesus Christ. . . . This is the corner-stone, the groundwork for the Christian system."[35] The *Catholic Columbian* of Columbus, Ohio, stated the Catholic Church "does not draw the color line." "She teaches, God is our Father and that we are brothers in Christ."[36]

For many blacks, Ireland's St. Augustine sermon provided evidence that the Catholic Church was sincere in its campaign for racial equality. Predictably, the archbishop's address was praised in a number of African American newspapers. The *New Orleans Pelican,* a secular black paper, affirmed Ireland's position concerning the color line. This publication echoed the archbishop's claim that the color line existed only "in the minds of those whose intellects were clouded by unjust reasoning."[37] A contributor to the *Chicago Conservator* agreed that the color line was substantiated only in a prejudicial mind. He further argued that, though the Catholic Church may have had its "superstition" and "error," it did, however, "recognize in every human being a child of God."[38] T. Thomas Fortune's newspaper, the *New York Age*, also commented on the sermon. Presumably, Fortune himself noted the "startling truths" communicated in Ireland's "remarkable" sermon on "Social Equality." Particularly noteworthy to the editor was Ireland's claim that African Americans would be assured "absolute social and religious equality" in the Catholic Church.[39]

Among the other important black newspapers of the day commenting on Ireland's sermon was the *Washington Bee*. Ireland's address, said one contributor "created a great deal of commotion among protestant denominations and the colored people generally." This writer claimed through Ireland, the Catholic Church had essentially declared "the first truth of the gospel . . . [t]hat all men are human and being so have souls." This, according to the columnist, was the "element which determines equality." The *Bee* recognized the Catholic Church as the first to "extend the hand of fellowship and declare in favor of a universal brotherhood and equality." This same publication further claimed that the archbishop should be congratulated for "both his just expressions as well as for his diplomacy."[40]

Rudd declared he could have included in the *ACT* many positive reviews of Ireland's message from Catholic papers as well as from other black papers; but enough had been referenced to show Archbishop Ireland had "an army of honest, open-hearted men behind him and with him in his magnificent demand for simple Justice." Rudd prodded his readers to drop their "foolish conceits and labor to lift to a higher level, all the children of men." "This is Christianity," he concluded.[41]

Opposition to Ireland's Justice

As might be expected, not every journalistic response to Ireland's sermon was positive. In June 1890, for example, Rudd printed an exchange from the *New York Tribune* acknowledging the fact that Ireland had been "roundly abused" in southern journals.[42] Similarly, the *New Orleans Times Democrat* took issue with Ireland's controversial proposals. The editor of this newspaper decried what he termed the "social equality" sentiments espoused by the archbishop. This same publication claimed the color line had been "fixed by nature herself." Those preaching Ireland's brand of "equality theory" were opening the way to "race demoralization," the publication declared.[43] Another of the archbishop's detractors argued that had the archbishop delved "a little farther into . . . physiology," he would have discovered blacks and whites had "distinct, clear characteristics, which prove that they are essentially of different kinds." He further claimed Ireland had misrepresented his religion.[44]

Ireland's call for the obliteration of the color line also evoked expressions of reservation from high-ranking Catholic Church leaders, including Archbishop Ryan of Philadelphia and Archbishop Michael Augustine Corrigan (1839–1902) of New York. On 20 May 1890, Ryan penned a letter to Corrigan expressing his reservations over Ireland's 4 May sermon. Ryan wrote, "Archbishop Ireland has created a sensation in Washington and through the country, by declaring that Catholics should admit negroes to social as well as political and religious equality. His enthusiasm sometimes leads him too far, but his purity of intention is unquestionable. Social equality is always the last attained, and only time and merit on the part of the Negroes can affect it."[45]

John M. Mackey's Response to Ireland

There is little question Rudd and other black Catholic leaders were encouraged in their campaign for racial equality by Ireland's historic St. Augustine sermon. The archbishop, however, did not speak for all American Catholic Church leaders. Perhaps the most surprising opposition to the prelate's position on social equality and racial justice came from an unlikely source, none other than John M. Mackey, who at the time was serving as the associate editor of the *ACT*. As pastor of the Cathedral of St. Peter in Chains in Cincinnati, Mackey would that same summer host the second Colored Catholic Congress. He must have, therefore, been viewed as an advocate for blacks. The cathedral boasted more African American members than any other parish in the city. Further, Mackey took special interest in the cathedral's black membership; he himself conducted a class on the sacraments for them. In a July 1890 sermon, Mackey outlined his own more circumscribed view of social equality.[46]

Mackey's opening homily, delivered at the second Catholic congress, has for some time puzzled scholars, in part because his remarks concerning "amalgamation" seem oddly out of place. Both Spalding and Lackner have expressed some level of puzzlement over Mackey's comments. For example, Spalding noted that the optimism of the members of the second Colored Catholic Congress seemed to have been "unshaken" by the opening sermon delivered by Mackey.[47] Subsequently, Lackner labeled this same opening sermon an "improbable" one.[48]

Evidence from the *ACT,* however, illumines the context for Mackey's otherwise puzzling comments. The pastor's address before the delegates of the second Colored Catholic Congress was given only about two months after Archbishop Ireland's controversial sermon was delivered in Washington, D.C. In Ireland's watershed sermon, the archbishop had declared the color line existed only "in the minds of those whose intellects were clouded by unjust reasoning." Ireland said the color line was a product of imagination in individuals infected with racial prejudice, and it therefore must be eliminated, he concluded.[49]

Knowing the merits of Ireland's proposal were being discussed around the country, especially among African American Catholics, Mackey sought to declare his disapproval of Ireland's radical position. Given this context, Mackey's comments before the second Colored Catholic Congress in Cincinnati in July 1890 make sense, even if they express the sentiments of many in the church who felt Ireland's campaign for social equality had gone too far. Mackey declared, "The white race does not desire amalgamation with the Negro race. The individual of either race who disregards this line of demarcation drawn apparently by nature herself, is no credit to either race. The races will go down the stream of time to the end on parallel lines as they have reached us, equal in the fatherhood of God and brotherhood of man."[50]

In attributing the color line to nature, Mackey echoed the same sentiments as Ireland's critics, including the contributor to the *New Orleans Times Democrat* mentioned above. In the opening lines of Mackey's sermon, the associate editor of the *ACT* directly challenged Ireland's claim that the color line was a product of race prejudice. Instead, Mackey attempted to legitimize the color line by declaring it had been established by "nature herself." Similarly, Mackey's opening comments concerning his disapproval of "amalgamation" illumine the fact that the cathedral's pastor did not support Archbishop Ireland's position on interracial marriage. Given the context for Mackey's sermon, his comments regarding those who might "disregard the color line" can only be viewed as a repudiation of Ireland's call for the immediate recognition of the social equality of blacks.[51]

Mackey's comments on social equality delivered to the congress were calculated. He simply wanted to distinguish his position from the more radical stand taken by Archbishop Ireland. At the same time, Mackey was cognizant of the appeal Ireland's ideals concerning race justice and social equality held for African Americans. Ironically, on the last day of the second congress, Mackey spoke "in forcible language the attitude of the Church toward the races," all the while claiming to occupy a position "squarely on the same platform with Archbishop Ireland."[52]

Justice from Ireland's Church

Following Ireland's St. Augustine sermon, Rudd appears to have more closely monitored the archbishop's comments on race and the color line. Further, the editor appropriated Ireland's statements to agitate for his own similar claims on racial justice and equality. In January 1891, for example, Rudd again printed Ireland's prescription for race justice and social equality in the pages of the *ACT*. In an address to a crowd celebrating the twenty-eighth anniversary of emancipation, Ireland had attacked the evils of the "nefarious" slave system, which he claimed "could not long endure" in a society "imbued with Christian principles." "Christianity," Ireland continued, "emphasized the brotherhood of man." In this same speech, the archbishop of St. Paul also called into question the alleged inferiority of African Americans.[53]

Though Ireland acknowledged many blacks were uneducated and undeserving of certain "political privileges" or "social favors," he did insist these less fortunate blacks should be treated the same as "ignorant" and "boorish" whites. Ireland further pointed out that pride kept whites from treating African Americans as brothers. The archbishop argued blacks should be the equal of whites before the law. In this same speech, he again voiced his approval of interracial marriage. Though many liberal-minded individuals would have agreed that the civil and political equality of blacks ought to be recognized, few would have supported the absolute and immediate removal of the color line. For doing so would have been tantamount to endorsing interracial marriages.[54]

The archbishop further proposed that blacks ought to enjoy the same political rights as whites. He believed any previous inadequacy in education, which had resulted in the black man being "unfit" to hold office or vote, should hurriedly be remediated "for his sake and our own." Ireland also favored the opening of all "professional avenues" for black employment. He further argued gentlemen of whatever hue should have equal access to public accommodations. For Ireland, social equality and personal interaction between the races was largely a "matter of taste," but as to the archbishop's stand on the issue, the prelate confidently claimed, "my door is open to men of all colors, and no one should blame me."[55]

Ireland's position on justice for African Americans resonated with Rudd. The editor of the *ACT,* commenting on the above speech, called it a "masterly plea for justice to the negro."[56] Many aspects of the address appealed to Rudd: Ireland's refutation of the alleged inherent inferiority of blacks, his call to open all avenues of employment for African Americans, as well as the archbishop's demand for strict equality based on merit rather than on the accident of skin color.

About one year after Ireland's controversial sermon, Rudd again referenced this important message. The editor of the *ACT* had recently begun a tour of the "far South." While traveling Rudd discovered Archbishop Ireland's words were "on the lips of almost every Colored man we met there." Based on the editor of the *ACT*'s communications with both blacks and whites in this region, and the popularity of the archbishop's solution for settling the race question, Rudd estimated it would not take long to convert that section of the country. Rudd wrote, "The gospel of humanity, of love and forgiveness, the gospel of equality before the altar, as preached by the archbishop has taken deep root and means more than any passing commentary from us could explain."[57]

In May 1891 the editor of the *ACT* again referenced Ireland's efforts on behalf of African Americans. Commenting on the prelate's participation in the confirmation of a large group of children from the diocese of St. Paul, the correspondent described the "delightfully Christian spectacle of a white child walking up the nave of the old cathedral by the side of a black one to receive the sacrament of confirmation from the hand of one who never misses an opportunity to raise his voice in favor of the colored man." The writer further stated the "color line" had been "broken down in St. Paul."[58]

Again, in late November 1891 the *ACT* reported on a speech given by Archbishop Ireland. This address was delivered to an audience gathered to voice their opposition to separate car legislation that had been recently passed in Tennessee. Ireland, in this address, declared he was "proud to call all men" his "brothers." Similarly, he stated, "Before the Omnipotent we are equals, We are all his children."[59]

In December 1891 Rudd traveled to Washington, D.C., to meet with Catholic congress leader W. S. Lofton. Rudd did not realize Archbishop Ireland had been scheduled to preach the following Sunday at St. Augustine Church. In his Sunday sermon, the prelate urged his African American hearers to proclaim their rights. He also spoke the following Tuesday for the Knights of St. Augustine Commandery No. 2. After Ireland had been introduced, the crowd gave him an ovation lasting five minutes. The archbishop then urged the Colored Catholic Congressional delegates to go to Philadelphia to "tell the Catholic world what you want, and demand it."[60]

Proof that Ireland was viewed as something of a patron for African American Catholics is also found in Philadelphia's black Catholic publication, the *Journal*. This publication routinely led its editorial column with the following words from Ireland's 4 May 1890 sermon: "They who exercise prejudice against their colored brethren contradict the principles of justice and charity of the Father of Mercy, who lives on the altar. No institution that closes its doors on the colored orphan is worthy of the name of charitable or religious." Demonstrating the importance of the archbishop's remarks to black Catholics, it should be noted a second quotation from Ireland was included on the *Journal*'s editorial page. This quotation read, "The white people now stand in need of lessons in charity, benevolence, justice and religion, for they have permitted unreasonable causes and prejudices to sway them."[61]

One of the dilemmas Rudd was forced to address in the pages of the *ACT* was the existence of bigoted Catholics who refused to recognize the full equality of African Americans. For Rudd's part, he simply did not allow the prejudicial behavior of individual Catholics to impugn the work of the entire church. In other words, the editor of the *ACT* made a distinction between the sinful behavior of individual Catholics and the official teachings of the church.[62]

In September 1888 Rudd wrote, "We believe there are some bad Catholics, who bring about a misunderstanding by their willful disobedience of Catholic teachings, but the Church does not approve their work."[63] Speaking of bigoted Catholics, Rudd wrote, "If here and there one finds some person or persons who profess to bolong [sic] to the Catholic Church, who are blinded by race prejudice, they learned it elsewhere than in the teachings of Mother Church."[64] Rudd also had in mind sinful Catholics when on another occasion he wrote, "The Father should not be held accountable for the bad doing of his son unless it is evident that he is the cause of his son's bad conduct."[65]

At times Rudd was placed in the uncomfortable position of having to defend African Americans from prejudicial attacks leveled by white Catholic newspapers. In the fall of 1889, for example, the editor of Cleveland's *Catholic Universe* claimed whites were destined to rule America's inferior black race. Sympathy should be given to white Southerners forced to employ "natural law" in their efforts to preserve "Caucassian [sic] domination" the journalist continued.[66] Rudd took this same Catholic editor to task when the former responded with the following:

> Are we to understand that the hundreds of thousands of Negroes who have been murdered for doing what the law, in its plainest terms, says they have the right to do were murdered according to "natural law"? Is the unmerciful beating of innocent and helpless women and children in the still midnight hours, by masked and bloodthirsty scoundrels a part of that "natural law"? Is the burning of the hard earned homes and chasing of trembling and unarmed men with rifles and shot guns, a part of that "natural law?"

In response to the above insult, Rudd reminded his readers that in the South whites had a higher illiteracy rate than blacks. He also claimed blacks had learned crime from their "Caucasian brother."[67]

Adam, The Catholic Journal of the New South, published in Memphis, also expressed sentiments at odds with Rudd's vision of racial justice. On one occasion, this Memphis publication declared that the benevolence of Katharine Drexel was wasted on African Americans. The paper further proposed that she should have bequeathed her fortune to benefit members of her own race.[68] On another occasion, this same publication expressed disgust at the fact that interracial marriage was permitted in twenty-three North American states and territories. Rudd responded by referring the editor to the writings of Archbishop Janssens of New Orleans, who had defended the practice.[69]

Rudd was certainly aware of the race discrimination blacks suffered at the hands of their white Catholic brothers and sisters. For example, he published the comments of William S. Lofton and Charles H. Butler, both of whom were influential members of St. Augustine Parish in Washington, D.C. These two laymen strongly criticized church leaders for failing to open Catholic schools to blacks residing in the nation's capital.[70] Similarly, in July 1887 Rudd printed a *Western Appeal* exchange highlighting the refusal on the part of the Sisters of Mercy to serve Vintrolia Vanbansher, a black sixteen-year-old who had come to their hospital for treatment.[71] But despite these incidences, the optimistic Rudd maintained his conviction that the best hope for blacks seeking full equality and justice in America was to be found in Catholicity. The editor believed the truths of Christianity could not help but ameliorate over time the prejudiced attitudes of wayward members within the Catholic Church.

Tellingly, leading magazines and newspapers of the period were willing to concede the fact that caste prejudice was "minimized in the Catholic Church."[72] On one occasion, for example, Rudd wrote, "Such papers as the A.M.E. *Recorder,* the *Detroit Plaindealer,* the New York *Freeman,* (later the *Age*) and A.M.E. *Church Review* . . . improve each opportunity to show that whatever else may not be in accordance wsth [*sic*] their views, Catholic Unity and the absolute equality of all people, of every race, before Catholic Altars are deserving of the highest commendation and meet their unanimous approval."[73]

On another occasion, the *Detroit Plaindealer* claimed that the Catholic Church was stirring up Protestants to do their duty. Though this publication was critical of the church's past dealings with African Americans, it still declared that with the emergence of Catholic leaders, including "Boyle," "Ireland" and "Lavigerie," times had changed.[74]

Bishop Benjamin Tucker Tanner (1835–1923) of the highly regarded black magazine the A.M.E. *Church Review,* on another occasion wrote, "The Catholic Church is in dead earnest in the work undertaken among the colored people of the country." He further stated, "Rome draws no 'color line' in Christianity as in the hierarchy . . . it is well understood by the most ignorant or the most prejudiced Catholic, that when he appears as a worshipper before the altar he must leave his prejudice behind."[75]

While conceding that race prejudice was not as prevalent in the Catholic Church, other Protestant newspapers attempted to raise the conspiratorial specter of a mass conversion of blacks to Catholicism in order to urge Protestants to take a more just stand toward African Americans. For example, the *Star of Zion,* an organ of the A.M.E. Zion Church claimed:

> In Catholic churches, as a rule, there is but little race prejudice, and all races worship together with the slightest friction; but when the Negro goes into a white Protestant church, as a rule, he is ordered to the gallery and if he refuses to go, is generally ejected—and yet this is called advanced Christianity. . . . There are thousands, who, like us, are yielding, and will yield, to the cajolery and inducements offered by the ever active and ingenious Catholic priests and sympathizers, who promise them equal rights and privileges with them in Church and State, until at no distant date they will possibly divide and decimate our ranks to such a startling extent, that [we] will be almost powerless to stem the tide of their insidious encroachments.[76]

Despite Rudd's claims regarding equality, justice, and the Catholic Church, some black newspapers questioned the editor's pronouncements. The Catholic Church was vulnerable to this challenge, in part because there were so few black priests serving in the American church. In 1890 August Tolton was the only openly recognized black priest serving in the United States. On one occasion, a Protestant newspaper, the *Philadelphia Sentinel,* reported, "The Negro finds himself never advancing beyond the altar railings in the Roman Church. If he is capable and has the ability and this cursed race prejudice do [*sic*] not show itself, then make them priests or let them advance to the highest position in the Roman Church." In answer to this criticism, Rudd drew attention to the beatification of St. Peter Claver (1580–1654), "a Negro, who went beyond the railing in the Roman Church."[77] Defending the Catholic Church's record on the ordination of black priests, Rudd subsequently commented, "Every Negro in the United States knows, if he has read his exchanges, that in this country there are Colored boys studying for the priesthood in Catholic Colleges."[78]

Though only one openly recognized black priest served the church in America in 1890, there was reason at the beginning of the last decade of the nineteenth century for Rudd to be optimistic. For during this period the American Josephites, under the able leadership of John Slattery, worked diligently for the ordination of African Americans. Moreover, at this historic juncture Slattery found allies for the cause of black vocations in the Holy See, as well as among influential Americanist church leaders, including Archbishop John Ireland and Bishop John J. Keane.[79]

Despite Rudd's effort to defend the Catholic Church's record on African American vocations, many church officials, especially in the South, opposed the ordination of black priests. Embracing the same prejudicial attitudes widely held in American society, the historical record shows many in the church believed blacks incapable of remaining celibate. They also believed African Americans were unable to meet the academic requirements of seminary training. The American Josephites worked against such sentiments. They recruited individuals they believed could serve as catechists and as priests. Those competent to meet the rigorous training and deemed fit to represent the race gained entrance into seminary; a few blacks were even ordained. But because an overwhelming number of African Americans resided in the South during this period, the efforts of Slattery and other advocates of a native priesthood for blacks required the cooperation of both southern bishops and the white clergy, who were to work alongside their black peers in ministry. This cooperation was not in any meaningful way forthcoming. In the end, the American Josephites, who led the campaign to ordain black priests in America, were able to promote only three candidates to the priesthood before the end of the first decade of the twentieth century, at which time the door to black vocations in the United States was all but closed. The three black priests ordained by the Josephites were Charles Randolf Uncles (1859–1933) in 1891, John H. Dorsey in 1902, and John J. Plantevigne (1871–1913) in 1907. The cause of black vocations suffered in the years following Plantevigne's ordination; not until 1941 was another black priest ordained by the order.[80]

In the United States, the Catholic Church's commitment to full equality for blacks was also questioned because of the existence of racially segregated parishes. The Catholic Church in the South remained integrated during the period of the Civil War. In the Archdiocese of New Orleans, where most black Catholics resided, several factors kept parishes integrated through the late 1880s. For example, free people of color who dominated black leadership in the city were proud of their contribution to the church, even if they resented being forced to sit in the same pew formerly reserved for slaves. Wishing to remain in their existing churches, these same leaders preferred to push for "better conditions" in regular parishes. Furthermore, most black Catholics resided in the French sections of New Orleans as Canon Peter L. Benoit of the Mill Hill Fathers discovered on his visit to the city in 1875. It is likely the priests of these integrated parishes also opposed segregation because they wished to retain the financial support of their black Catholic members. Finally, the shortage of priests in the diocese impeded even normal growth in the number of parishes, let alone the development of segregated black churches.[81]

Dolores Egger Labbe has argued the establishment of the American Josephites and Katharine Drexel's order, the Sisters of the Blessed Sacrament for Indians and Colored People, actually encouraged the creation of racially segregated institutions. The irony is neither of these groups openly advocated segregation. The move toward segregation occurred, however, because bishops seeking to work among blacks in their diocese could take advantage of missional support from these well-meaning organizations only if they were grouped in segregated parishes.[82]

The decision to establish segregated parishes in New Orleans was led by Archbishop Janssens, widely viewed as a progressive on race issues. Janssens, who served during the height of the Americanist influence on the church, attempted to adapt Catholicism to the American context. For the archbishop, this meant acquiescing to the city's changing racial norms. The prelate's move to create segregated parishes was motivated in part by his fear that African Americans were leaving the Catholic Church in large numbers because they were not afforded the opportunity to participate fully in parish life. The archbishop believed blacks in racially segregated churches would have more occasions to join parish sodalities and societies, sing in choral groups, and serve as altar boys and acolytes. For this reason, Janssens looked to the national church paradigm as a way of creating voluntarily segregated parishes.[83] In actuality, the archbishop did more to move the city's churches toward forced segregation than did his predecessors, who largely ignored the concerns of blacks. Moreover, Janssens's efforts were opposed by many of the city's leading "Afro-creoles."[84]

Rudd was sometimes forced to defend the existence of segregated parishes. On one occasion, the editor of the *ACT* wrote, "It is a well-known fact that every so-called Colored Catholic Church in this country was built at the earnest request of its Colored members, and, against the wishes and solicitation of the white members of the parishes from which they separated."[85] Rudd's position on the existence of black parishes reveals his ambivalence toward their creation. Rudd was an integrationist. Though the editor abhorred the indignity of the color line in the church, he didn't detail exactly what he hoped to see accomplished by its elimination. It is unlikely he would have been satisfied with African Americans merely being afforded the right to attend integrated churches or schools. What he wanted was the complete elimination of any racial hierarchy in both church and society.

Rudd's defense of the existence of segregated parishes is puzzling. He had, after all, vigorously opposed segregation in Ohio's schools because he believed segregated schools fostered racial prejudice. It will be recalled that Rudd fought against racial segregation in the state's schools even when other black leaders warned that the establishment of integrated schools would endanger the jobs of Ohio's black teachers.[86]

Despite Rudd's opposition to segregation in Ohio's schools, he reluctantly endorsed the establishment of black parishes. Rudd wrote, "WE have not been outspoken in favor of the organization of what is termed 'Colored Catholic' churches. Nor in fact any other sort of class churches, except on the basis of language; because the Catholic Church is big enough and broad enough to hold all the races and all the classes on planes of absolute equality."[87] Rudd went on to explain that non-Catholic blacks "demand" and "have organizations and work through them. The creation of these segregated parishes was an attempt to "counteract this vast influence." Rudd further claimed this arrangement was voluntary. He wrote, "Not that we can not, but we do not avail ourselves of the opportunities and invitations given us by the Church to enter any and all of the Catholic Churches where we please."[88]

Other Catholics more vociferously opposed the creation of racially segregated parishes. For example, a Canadian Catholic from Kamloops, British Columbia, John F. Smith, questioned Rudd on the practice:

> I do not endorse [the practice] not being able to see clearly the good that would arise from it, but the evil that may be the outcome—the erection of Colored Churches for our people, schools for Colored children, ordaining Colored priests for Colored people, and Colored teachers for Colored children etc., for it will, in my opinion, result in a still wider breach than that which now exists, and may culminate in a complete separation of the two races in the Church.[89]

Having seen no segregated church in his travels, Smith further surmised the practice of building race churches was an American innovation.[90]

In the subsequent issue of the *ACT,* Rudd responded to Smith: "Out of one flesh and one blood, God created all the nations of the earth. The Catholic Church teaches within her domain the absolute religious equality of all mankind before her altars. . . . This thing of color distinction is not in her teachings, never has been there and never will be. Any one claiming to be a Catholic and who varies from this rule will have to answer for direliction [*sic*] of duty at the bar of eternal justice."[91] The editor of the *ACT* recalled his family's positive experiences in St. Joseph Church at Bardstown. He further recounted how the white members of St. Joseph had urged their African American brothers and sisters to remain in the parish after the latter group purchased property with the intention of establishing a black church.[92]

In the winter of 1888, Smith again wrote the *ACT* expressing his concern over the establishment of separate churches for blacks. In his letter, published in the 3 February issue of the newspaper, he wrote the following:

> Are the majority of Colored Catholics in the States of so degrading a type as to necessitate the erection of separate buildings for their worship? Not having been brought face to face with the affairs and conditions of these people, I refrain commentation, but, will say the same as was said on a previous occasion, that separate church is purely an American rule and not that of the church. It is to be hoped that the authorities of the church having at heart the interest of church and people, will adopt the best means available to reconcile the two races, especially in the church.

He went on to argue, "There certainly can be no better means instituted in fostering the existing breach, than the establishing of separate church[es] and schools."[93]

It appears that John Slattery was recruited by Rudd to offer an answer to Smith's query. In the 17 February issue of the *ACT,* Rudd published Slattery's defense of the existence of black parishes. Slattery argued the primary reason for the establishment of separate black churches was white "prejudice." He bluntly stated, "Many Catholics dislike the Negroes." Slattery further acknowledged the existence of "many bad Catholics." He claimed even some "good Catholics" were prejudiced against African Americans. Slattery saw no need to "run counter to these prejudices" by forcing blacks and whites into the same parishes. He further expressed his conviction that segregated churches did more to break down racial prejudice than "any other influence in the land." Segregated parishes served as mission stations for African Americans, Slattery contended. He also argued that because blacks desired separate parishes, this alone was "reason enough why they should have them."[94]

Slattery's defense of the existence of racially segregated parishes was subsequently challenged by Charles Butler. The black Catholic leader called into question Slattery's suggestion that race prejudice must be allowed to gradually die out. Butler further argued the church had "conquered worse enemies than prejudice." He also contrasted Slattery's misguided defense of segregated churches with a less tolerant view of prejudice articulated by John Boyle O'Reilly. In a previous letter O'Reilly had declared, "It is as it ought to be in the Catholic Church, that a man's skin is forgotten by both white, black, red and yellow. All men's souls are alike, and all men's hearts answer to the same keys. Prejudice of Color or Country is the chief narrowness and ignorance. Those who receive communion together are wretched christians if they refuse to sit together at their common tables."[95]

Slattery's defense of racially segregated parishes also evoked a substantive response from Smith, who believed Slattery was speaking from an "American point of view," since such sentiments could not be traced to the "teachings of the Catholic Church." Smith could find no justification for accommodating prejudiced Catholics. Further, the Canadian Catholic objected to members of the church dictating to Catholic leaders on questions of principle. Speaking of the church, Smith declared, "Except in the present case we can find no instance where she has catered to the whims of the greater or smaller portion of her congregation when the principles of the Church are envolved [*sic*]." Nor could Smith reconcile Slattery's use of the term "good" in relation to prejudiced Catholics. He argued, "A community could not be declared good if hatred is cherished in their midst." Smith reasoned rather pointedly, "From the argument used in justification of separate churches and the source from which it emanated [Slattery], we do not wonder at the Colored Catholics preferring their own churches and pastors."[96]

Rudd's position on the existence of separate black parishes seems to have paralleled that of Archbishop Ireland. For example, when Ireland dedicated a new black parish in the city of St. Paul in 1892, the prelate expressed some ambivalence over the matter. He stated the establishment of a separate church for African American Catholics was only a temporary measure designed to benefit blacks. Further, Ireland desired all races to worship together. He also emphasized the fact that blacks were free to attend any of the city's parishes.[97] Rudd, echoing something of the same sentiment, wrote the following:

> There is no desire on the part of the Church to set apart separate churches for Colored people, and where there are Colored churches as in this city, Washington, Baltimore, New York, Louisville and elsewhere, they are largely attended by whites and the Colored people go into any other Catholic church that may be convenient to them, and they are welcome. . . . If every so-called Colored Catholic church in the world was done away with instantly the Colored Catholics would be at home in any other Catholic church beneath the Sun.[98]

For Rudd, racial justice was inextricably bound up in the recognition of the full equality of blacks. It was supported by the editor's conviction that people of all races were indeed brothers, the offspring of one divine father. Rudd's vision of justice may be appropriately termed "church-centered" because he believed that, once in the Catholic Church, blacks would experience true fellowship untainted by the color line. Moreover, the editor's embrace of the Romantic apologetic for Catholicism and its hermeneutic for reading history allowed him to cling to the hope that the Catholic Church would in time be the agent to deliver racial justice for African Americans.

CHAPTER 4

Justice for
African Americans

*The Colored race wants simple justice at the hands of its
fellow-citizens. We love America because we have a right
to love her. We have earned the right to live here, and pro-
pose to enjoy that well-earned privilege.*

D. RUDD
5 JULY 1890

A Prophetic Voice

Throughout his journalistic career Rudd consistently raised "a cry for justice." In the *Ohio State Tribune,* the forerunner to the *ACT,* Rudd campaigned for "the eternal principles of liberty, justice and equality before
the law."[1] Subsequent to the establishment of the *ACT,* Rudd continued
to promote racial equality. He believed race prejudice kept African
Americans from experiencing justice and the full equality such an interpretation of justice presumed. Misguided public sentiment also kept blacks
from enjoying all the benefits of American citizenship inspired in the
Declaration of Independence and guaranteed by the U.S. Constitution.
Despite Rudd's promotion of racial equality in the editorials and exchanges
of the *ACT,* it appears he did not, in any meaningful way, consider the

plight of other marginalized groups in the United States, including Native Americans, Mexican Americans, and Chinese Americans.

Rudd's campaign for recognition of the full equality of African Americans was but one manifestation of a larger, black, racial uplift movement. Vincent Harding has traced the genesis of American black protest and justice seeking back to Africa and the beginnings of the European slave trade. For Harding there is a connection between those early justice seekers and the twentieth century civil rights leaders who protested racial segregation in post–World War II America. All these courageous individuals, in their quest for freedom and justice, have throughout American history launched many "creative black initiatives," he contends. Harding's work makes it possible to link Daniel Rudd's activism with the contributions of other black leaders concerned with racial uplift and justice, including Paul Cuffee (1759–1817), Nat Turner (1800–1831), Frederick Douglass, Ida B. Wells-Barnett, T. Thomas Fortune, Booker T. Washington, Martin Luther King Jr. (1929–1968), and Malcolm X (1925–1965).[2]

Because of Rudd's commitment to a church-centered vision of justice, the editor could not let claims regarding the inherent inferiority of blacks go unanswered. To this end, he promoted a race pride agenda in the *ACT.* Rudd's church-centered vision of justice assumed the essential equality of all members of society regardless of race. The editor imagined for America a racially integrated society. He opposed race leaders who promulgated the emigration of blacks from the United States, and he fought against the discrimination of African Americans seeking employment. As an integrationist, he also opposed racially segregated schools and separate coach legislation.

Rudd's sense of justice was offended by the mistreatment of African Americans, including those unfortunate individuals trapped in unfair crop mortgage agreements. He was also disturbed over the fate of those languishing in less than humane conditions in southern prisons. But after the infamous vigilante murders of Thomas Moss, Calvin McDowell, and Will Stewart in Memphis in March 1892, the issue that most offended Rudd's sense of justice was the crime of lynching, a crime that had in the last decade of the nineteenth century increasingly targeted the nation's black population.

Defending the Dignity of Blacks
by Promoting Racial Pride

As early as August 1886, the same month Rudd's *OST* was rechristened the *ACT,* the editor spoke out against the "invidious discrimination" and "caste prejudice" he claimed was "ever bobbing up to thwart the American Negro in his manly efforts to make himself an honest and upright citizen." Rudd further claimed the chief cause for the unjust state of race relations in the United States was the fact that "one class is and has always been taught that they are better than the other, and people who [have] known otherwise had rather submit to the injustice than worry themselves enough to correct this evil."[3]

Rudd believed the widespread acceptance of the theory of white superiority was at the root of the unjust state of race relations in nineteenth-century America. Therefore, the most fundamental component of Rudd's race justice agenda involved correcting this myth. By using his newspaper to highlight the accomplishments of African Americans, Rudd fostered racial pride in his black readers. This editorial approach also served to educate his white audience as to the accomplishments of blacks.[4]

In his weekly editorial column on page 2 of the *ACT,* Rudd sometimes published the comments of critics of the race. He did this in order to rebut them. For example, on one occasion Rudd published the criticisms of Rabbi Edward N. Calisch, of Richmond, Virginia:

> The Negro today in America betrays only too clearly his close kinship to his savage and present brothers in African wilds. In spite of all learning, contact and association with the whites, he is dominated by a superstition, as gross, as powerful as ever held sway over the weaken[ed] minds of primitive man. . . . Marital ties are spiders' webs. . . . Thus far education has been powerless to affect the emotional nature.[5]

Rudd defended the race and the cause of justice and equality by arguing that the "rabbi's knowledge of the Afro American is about on par with the knowledge [of] nine-tenths of all the other white men who take up their little pens to solve the Negro Problem. He has met some barbers, some Pullman car porters and some hotel waiters. Then he has probably stood outside or perhaps inside of some church where some ignorant Afro

American preacher has 'explained the Bible,' the words of which he could neither pronounce or define."[6] Rudd went on to declare if the rabbi were to enter one of the "refined homes of Afro-Americans in Richmond or any other considerable town he would, we think, form a new opinion."[7]

At times, the dignity of African Americans was attacked by bigoted Catholics. For example, in February 1891 *Adam, The Catholic Journal of the New South* published an article that raised questions as to the effectiveness of converting southern blacks. The contributor wrote:

> It is a waste of time and money to endeavor to inculcate the doctrines of Catholicity into the cranium of a full grown Southern darkey. . . . You know but little of the negro people until you live among them, then you will be forced to the conclusion that it takes a mighty sight of religion to keep the negro from robbing a hen roost if a favorable opportunity is presented.[8]

In response, Rudd argued that he had experience in the South with members of his race. He defended Katharine Drexel's expenditure of funds for African American missions. He further declared that the black convert made "as good a Christian as a white man."[9]

In order to foster racial pride, Rudd routinely introduced his readers to successful African American Catholics. For example, in March 1887 Rudd published a biographical feature accompanied by a sketch of Fr. Augustus Tolton, referring to the priest as the "most conspicuous man in America." Rudd seems to have taken particular pride in the nation's first openly recognized African American priest. As early as 1888 Rudd marketed portraits of Tolton.[10]

Rudd attempted to inspire racial pride in his readers by featuring other distinguished African American Catholics, including W. S. Lofton from Washington, D.C. Lofton had graduated from the dentistry program at Howard University and subsequently became an influential leader in the Colored Catholic Congress movement. Rudd also featured lesser-known, albeit successful, African American Catholics. For example, the editor of the *ACT* printed an exchange from Philadelphia eulogizing Mary Frances Augustin. This accomplished woman had been one of the city's most distinguished caterers. Similarly, Rudd introduced his readers to James Armstrong, a respected black lay Catholic leader from Chicago who was an important and influential ally of Fr. Tolton.[11]

Rudd's campaign to foster racial pride featured non-Catholic black leaders as well. For example, in April 1891 Rudd printed a large sketch of the acting president of the Colored Press Association, John Mitchell Jr. (1863–1929). In September 1887 the editor referred to the achievements of a former slave who had moved to China and subsequently gained ownership of a syndicate bank. Also, Rudd highlighted the accomplishments of W. McGwinn, a black student at Yale who had taken second highest honors at the law school. On another occasion, the editor drew attention to the work of J. A. Carpenter, an African American inventor.[12]

Rudd's effort to bolster racial pride by highlighting the accomplishments of African Americans was not limited to male examples. For instance, in the newspaper he made mention of a Cincinnati native, Miss Ida Gray Nelson (1867–1953), who had been elected vice president of her dental class in Ann Arbor, Michigan.[13] Similarly, Rudd praised the work of Consuela Clark, who had graduated from medical school and was serving as a physician in St. Louis.[14] Moreover, Rudd took particular pride in the existence of African American religious orders and the work these same women of color had undertaken. Consequently, the editor promoted the ministry of the Oblate Sisters of Providence, as well as the Sisters of the Holy Family of New Orleans. Rudd's decision to feature women of color in nontraditional roles may also yield clues as to his leanings on gender justice issues.

Rudd also served his vision of justice and equality by educating both blacks and whites as to the important historical contributions made to the nation by African Americans. This function was all the more important because these same contributions were often overlooked or ignored altogether by American historians of the period. In the spring of 1889 Rudd suggested blacks honor their own race with monuments. For example, when a group of African Americans from Illinois proposed a monument to honor Abraham Lincoln (1809–1865), William H. Seward (1801–1872), Charles Sumner (1811–1874), Wendell Phillips (1811–1884), and John Brown (1800–1859), Rudd wrote that "one of the greatest crimes is [the Negro's] shortsightedness." He continued, "Are there no Colored men among the living or the dead who were contemporaries and co-workers with these great men in the struggle for liberty? Are we to forever extol the praises of the white man and find nothing in Negro courage, virtue, character and devotion worthy of monument?"[15] Similarly, Rudd ran several exchanges informing his readers of the progress being made on a monument to honor African American patriot Crispus Attucks (1723–1770), who was believed to have been the first to die in America's war for independence.[16]

Through the early 1890s, as the South became more racially segregated, public criticism of blacks escalated. At the Colored Press Association meeting held in Cincinnati in March 1891, the condition of African Americans living in the South was a topic of discussion. This forum was precipitated by a felt need on the part of the delegates to defend the record of the race. Internal evidence from the *ACT* during this period reveals that a number of detractors from around the country were claiming blacks were becoming less rather than more civilized over time.[17] Subsequent to the press meeting, Rudd announced the *ACT* would join the *Detroit Plaindealer* and Ida B. Wells-Barnett's *Memphis Free Speech* in dispatching a correspondent to "report on the condition of the Southland." Rudd wrote, "The letters of these correspondents will certainly prove highly interesting, to those, who are interested in the development of the race. It is sheer nonsense to talk about the Colored people going backward; they are doing no such thing."[18]

In the summer of this same year, Rudd published a report from Sarah Cole, a Cincinnati schoolteacher who had spent a month in the South. In this report, Rudd discussed Cole's observations. She had observed that blacks in the South owned property, were involved in business, and were pursuing education.[19] Rudd's own correspondent, Edward Reed, who had traveled to the South in the summer of 1891, also argued against the charge that blacks were regressing. As evidence for his claim, Reed highlighted the success of an enterprising black grocery store owner from Jackson, Mississippi.[20]

Rudd's Opposition to Racial Segregation

A second race justice issue addressed by Rudd throughout the life of the *ACT* was racial segregation in American society. Despite the fact that Rudd attended a racially homogeneous parish in Cincinnati, Rudd promoted an integrationist platform. He believed the color line as it was then being drawn in various sectors of society was a gross injustice forced on African Americans by prejudiced whites. The editor believed segre-

Ida B. Wells-Barnett, an African American journalist and civil rights activist who vociferously opposed lynching. (Courtesy of Library of Congress.)

gating the races exacerbated race prejudice. He further believed equality could not be achieved in a society that sought to maintain a color line between the races. On one occasion, Rudd took issue with an article printed in the *New Orleans Crusader*. The contributor seems to have given voice to Rudd's own opposition to separate exhibits, bar associations, and the like.[21] Following this same logic, the *ACT* detailed Rudd's opposition to a plan to create a separate state for African Americans. In fact, he labeled the effort "some queer nonsense." Rudd believed the flag of the United States should rightly float over all "one country, one people with equal and unabridged privileges."[22]

Early in the *ACT*'s publication there was considerable coverage given to Rudd's opposition to racial segregation. For example, in the late winter and early spring of 1887, Rudd repeatedly made reference to the passage of the Ely-Arnett Bill, legislation which not only dismantled Ohio's Black Laws but also made provision to desegregate the state's public schools. In the first extant issue of the *ACT*, Rudd wrote, "The cry of justice is heard."[23] Rudd enthusiastically penned these words in response to the passage of this historic legislation.[24]

Rudd, a strong advocate of racially integrated schools, believed the separate school system made the state "an aider and abettor" in the crime of "prejudicial-fostering." He stated his opposition to segregated schools the summer before the passage of the Ely-Arnett Bill:

> We called attention to the system of public schools which educating the races apart made the state an aider and abettor in the crime of prejudicial-fostering between different races of her citizens. No one seemed to see the crime. We have not ceased however, nor will we while God permits us to wield pen and tongue to write and declaim against an out rage, blacker than even human slavery itself, until the foul blot is removed.[25]

Rudd believed those who opposed desegregating Ohio's schools—for example, Cincinnati educator William H. Parham—did so out of economic self-interest. Though Rudd acknowledged the fear of black leaders, he took exception with claims that the *ACT's* position on racially integrated schools would result in the elimination of the black teaching profession in Cincinnati. As a result of his position on this controversial issue, the editor received criticism from some within the black community.[26]

The *Christian Recorder's* position on the question of integrated schools put it at odds with the *ACT's* editorial stand. During this time A.M.E. Church educational philosophy was committed to the preparation of African American schoolteachers. Consequently, church leaders were quite concerned over the anticipated closure of Ohio's black schools. It was in black schools, after all, that the overwhelming majority of Cincinnati's African American teachers served.[27]

Some African American leaders opposed integrated schools not merely to protect the jobs of black teachers, but also for cultural reasons. Many believed white teachers were prejudiced toward their black students and therefore could not serve as positive role models for them. Some contributors to The *A.M.E. Church Review,* including F. L. Cardozo, voiced their support for racially segregated schools. Cardozo believed integrated schools would be the ideal but feared that the "odious race distinction" would be wiped out only over several centuries.[28]

Rudd believed the eradication of the color line in Ohio's schools was a major step toward a more just society. He informed his readers that

Cincinnati's superintendent, E. E. White, had a "reputation of fairness." The editor, therefore, was confident White would appoint black teachers to the newly integrated schools. Rudd believed that if black teachers were in fact fired from the city's schools the community would be capable of challenging the dismissals. He told his readers no "cry" would be made until there was a need. Rudd warned, however, that "we will guard with jealous care the interests of the race and dispute at every point the march of un-American prejudice."[29]

In the years after the passage of the Ely-Arnett Bill, Rudd took Cincinnati's school board to task for its failure to comply with the state's ruling against school segregation. He also decried the failure of the city's school board to appoint black teachers to integrated schools. In June 1889 Rudd discussed the proposed closing of the city's Gaines High School, attended primarily by blacks. The editor wrote, "If Gaines High School is to be allowed to stop where it is, then invidious discrimination against well qualified teachers must end." Rudd threatened that if the discrimination did not end, they would find themselves "in the hottest fight on the School Question that has yet occurred in this State." He further added, "We want justice or nothing."[30]

In September 1890 Rudd again articulated his opposition to the city's segregated schools. Further, he criticized Cincinnati's school board for its refusal to appoint qualified black teachers. Rudd asked, "What right has the state to draw taxes from all people for school general purposes and then to discriminate against any class of citizens?" The editor called for the resignation of White's successor, Mr. W. H. Morgan, because he believed Morgan was not broad enough "to do justice to all classes." In September 1891 Rudd proposed a bitter fight with the city's school board because of its decision to send a delegation to St. Louis to seek advice on segregating Cincinnati's schools. The next month, Rudd advised his readers to seek an injunction to stop payment for the "illegal schools" rather than to assemble yet another public meeting concerning the matter.[31]

Discrimination in Public Accommodations

The practice of denying African Americans equal access to public accommodations and public transportation could not be reconciled with Daniel

Rudd's vision of a just, egalitarian society. On a regular basis, therefore, the editor drew attention to instances in which blacks were discriminated against in the public sphere.

Like other southern Ohio communities, Cincinnati had continued to be influenced by southern racial norms throughout the post-Reconstruction period. But by the 1890s the move toward racial segregation in public accommodations in Ohio had gained broad-based support.[32] Blacks who had received some protection under the federal Civil Rights Bill of 1875 seemed even more vulnerable after this same legislation was ruled unconstitutional in 1883. Subsequently, state legislatures in the northern part of the United States passed laws banning discrimination against blacks. Ohio's provisions, however, were widely underenforced. Moreover, the financial penalties for violation of these same laws were often insignificant.[33]

Even after state codes criminalizing racial discrimination in public accommodations were passed in 1884, blacks in Cincinnati were routinely denied equal accommodations. For example, in 1890 state representative John Green of Cleveland was refused lodging in several of the city's hotels. Though the following year Green was able to secure accommodations in the city's prestigious Gibson House, he was expected to take his meals in the hotel kitchen.[34]

As a part of his campaign to protect civil rights, Rudd employed the editorial page of the *ACT*. On one occasion he declared Cincinnati was being "outraged" because businesses were refusing to serve blacks. Rudd also targeted African Americans for refusing to take whites to task for practicing racial discrimination. He wrote, "When the best known and ablest Colored men can be insulted by any one who sees fit to do so and no one speaks in resentment then it is time to ask, what is the Negro good for?" Rudd further threatened, "We have rested under this thing long enough and shall no longer be silent. . . . We know this will strike hard. But we are prepared to give and receive hard blows."[35] The above quotation seems to illustrate Rudd's willingness to move beyond editorial advocacy to direct advocacy on behalf of blacks.

The editor of the *ACT* sometimes published the names of local businesses guilty of practicing discrimination against African Americans. For example, Rudd drew attention to a sign in John Heider's West Fifth Street eatery informing blacks they would be permitted to eat only in the rear of

JUSTICE FOR AFRICAN AMERICANS

the restaurant. Given the insult, Rudd questioned his readers as to whether they would continue to patronize the establishment.[36] On another occasion, Rudd published an anonymous letter detailing how Coney Island, a local amusement park, had refused entrance to African Americans. The same letter bemoaned the fact that discrimination in some localities in Ohio was getting worse rather than better. The letter also detailed the legal liability of any person choosing to discriminate against the state's black citizenry. Further, the letter urged action on the part of Cincinnati's African American population, declaring "there is but one way to stop these infernal outrages, and that is by making an attack all along the line, upon every hotel, every restrurant [*sic*] and every place of public amusement, that violates the Statutes of this State in these matters."[37]

Rudd demonstrated his own willingness to directly confront businesses who refused to serve blacks. In the spring of 1890, for example, he took legal action against the P. C. Butler Delicatessen after being denied service. Rudd had visited the establishment with the Strauss Brothers, white tailors who advertised with the *ACT*. Stung by the insult, the editor subsequently secured the legal services of attorney J. R. Foraker. The courts ruled in favor of Rudd, awarding him a judgment of $100 in the case. Commenting on this same ruling, Rudd wrote, "The putrescent sore of United States prejudice, is a cancerous growth and should be speedily removed."[38]

Throughout the years of the *ACT*'s publication, Rudd fought against laws that segregated public carriers. The first state to pass comprehensive legislation to separate the races traveling in railroad cars was Tennessee in 1881. This same state legislature, apparently unaware of this 1881 bill, passed another Jim Crow law in 1891. Other states joined in adopting similar Jim Crow legislation, including Florida in 1887, Mississippi in 1888, Texas in 1889, Louisiana in 1890, and Alabama, Georgia, and Arkansas in 1891.[39]

As early as October 1887, Rudd had identified the practice of racial segregation in seating on public transit as an "injustice" that demanded redress.[40] He believed separate coach legislation to be an "outrage." These laws, according to the editor, were the result of "accursed prejudice" and therefore worked against the spirit of nineteenth-century progress. When Kentucky, his commonwealth of birth, considered enacting its own separate coach law, Rudd remained confident that the legislation would not pass. After the state legislature subsequently approved the bill, Rudd was deeply disappointed and adamantly voiced his disapproval. He wrote, "Men of Kentucky, this is criminal. Who can tell how many of these latter day saints sucked their infantile nourishment from black paps? The white men of Kentucky have robbed the Negro race of its identity, and now that they have done so wish to hide the crime drawing an artificial line. The separate coach law is an outrage. How long O Lord, how long?"[41]

Employment Opportunities

In the editorials and exchanges of the *ACT* Rudd promoted hiring African Americans to skilled jobs. Early in the life of his newspaper he commented on the efforts of those blacks seeking to win jobs in racially integrated schools. That blacks were being routinely denied the opportunity to join labor unions and to work in various industries remained a consistent topic of editorial for Rudd throughout the life of the *ACT.*

In 1890 African American representation in less desirable and less lucrative divisions of labor was roughly double the percentage in the total U.S. population. For example, blacks made up 21.7 percent of agriculture, fishing, and mining workers and approximately 22.6 percent of the nation's service workers. Conversely, in this same year African Americans made up only 3.6 percent of the nation's manufacturing workers, 4.3 percent of trade and transportation workers, and 3.6 percent of the country's professional workforce. As the above data illustrates, in the more skilled fields of employment, blacks numbered less than one-third of their percentage in the total U.S. population.[42]

In the editorials and exchanges of the *ACT,* Rudd repeatedly condemned discriminatory hiring practices. In September 1887 he pointed out that fire departments around the country were routinely refusing to employ blacks. When the city of Cincinnati continued its practice of employing only white firefighters, the editor responded:

> Do the Firemen forget that many of them are paid with money collected from Negro citizens? . . . From this day on, we demand of the authorities of this city a recognition of the 20,000 Colored people, citizens here; recognition in the fire department and we propose to keep up the cry until it is done. If the authorities want it, meetings will be held to enforce the demand.[43]

Three years later, Rudd again condemned the fire department of Cincinnati for its refusal to hire African Americans.[44]

Though Rudd complained that whites often refused to hire qualified blacks, he did not believe African Americans should sit idly by, passively waiting for white sentiment to change. Rudd was a strong advocate of black agency. He believed if African Americans established their own businesses, there would be a steady supply of jobs for blacks. On one occasion, Rudd remarked, "One business firm is worth more to a community, than a thousand politicians."[45] On another occasion, the editor of the *ACT* stated, "There is not any reason why there should not be a large number of business houses run by Colored men in this city." Further, he believed the local market around the Queen City would support such enterprises.[46] In April 1888 Rudd urged African Americans to enter the mercantile business. In this same editorial, he challenged the notion that whites would not patronize a well-run African American owned clothier.

> If Colored men wish their sons and daughters to occupy important positions in life, those of us who have money must launch into business. We must commence if necessary on a small scale and aim to increase our stock and trade as our means and opportunities afford. We must learn to do business with all classes of people. As the demands of our businesses require more help let us employ Colored men and women or employ some Colored and some white and in this way set the example for our white brethren.[47]

Black Emigration from the South

Rudd's vision of justice compelled him to take a stand on a much-debated topic during the post-Reconstruction era, whether or not blacks should emigrate from the South. The American Colonization Society was organized in 1817, two years after black businessman Paul Cuffee (1759–1817) transported thirty-eight blacks to Africa at his own expense. President Bushrod Washington (1762–1829), Henry Clay (1777–1852), and John Randolph of Roanoke were among the society's prominent members. With aid from both the federal government and some state governments, the organization sought to establish a colony of free blacks in Africa. The first ten years of the organization's existence were its most effective. Some 12,000 blacks were returned to Africa. The motives for their return were varied; while some supporters of the program believed blacks were incapable of adjusting to Western civilization, others hoped returning African Americans would take a leading role in the evangelization of the continent. Southern blacks also viewed emigration as a desirable alternative to the oppression, exploitation, and violence they were forced to endure. An overwhelming majority of blacks in the North, however, opposed immigration.[48]

Support for African American emigration from the South seems to have peaked in 1879 and again in about 1890. The primary impetus for migration, according to August Meier, was economic. Though threats of mob violence and political repression did play some role, they were primarily used as rationalizations for a decision to emigrate.[49] Despite support for emigration among some southern blacks, an overwhelming number of readers who addressed their correspondence to the *Christian Recorder* during this period opposed emigration. In this they followed the lead of A.M.E. Bishops Benjamin Tucker Tanner and Benjamin F. Lee (1841–1926), both of whom served as editors of the *Christian Recorder*.[50]

Though Rudd may have spoken out against black emigration prior to the establishment of the *ACT*, he does not appear to have addressed the question until the early months of 1888. Internal evidence from the *ACT* indicates a newly conceived plan to establish a colony in South America for African Americans may have provoked Rudd's comments on the issue. In the winter of 1888, Rudd published a number of exchanges on the topic. Moreover, he began in his editorials to voice his opposition to the proposed exodus.

Though in the *ACT* Rudd gave the matter relatively little editorial coverage, he did periodically voice his disapproval of black proposals to exit the country. On one occasion he wrote, "The American Negro has felled the forests and moulded the bricks in all the Southland, he is a part and parcel of America's greatness. Any one who thinks that he is fool enough now to leave the monuments of his unrequited toil must be sadly deluded." He continued, "This talk of exodus makes us tired. The only exodus the American Negro needs is to exodus himself out of bed in the early morning, and save the money he earns. His other ills will disappear by this and the practice of virtue, quicker than any other way."[51]

On another occasion, Rudd printed an exchange from a publication entitled the *Pelican*. This article also seems to express Rudd's sentiments with regard to emigration. The *Pelican* contributor concluded that the South was the "place for the Negro: here he thrives and prospers, and, although in the past denied his political rights, by Southern Democrats, a change of sentiment, of progress, is rapidly breaking up these old ideas, and Southern Democrats are beginning to believe that the Negroes have rights which they are bound to respect, and, so believing, are declaring themselves in favor of according the same to them."[52]

In the 10 February 1888 issue of the *ACT,* Rudd voiced his opposition to a proposed scheme to establish a colony of African American pioneers in South America. He wrote, "The Exodus to South America, is like other panaceas for 'all ills,' it will not cure them, so the Negro who has a homestead and a mule in the South will stay there, and the one who has neither or its equivalent is too lazy or too careless to be a pioneer. Don't worry about the exodus."[53]

Rudd's experiences as an African American living in a Midwestern state, where blacks were relatively better positioned, socially and economically, no doubt influenced the editor's position on emigration. In other words, had Rudd lived in the Deep South, he may have been more keenly attuned to the hardships that made emigration a more attractive option for some southern blacks. Further, Rudd's editorial statements regarding the issue indicate his strong faith in the American economic system. He remained convinced, in part by his own life experience, that regardless of one's race, any enterprising individual willing to work could find success in America.

As mentioned, black migration to Africa was motivated not only by economic factors but also by the belief that American blacks would play a significant role in the evangelization of Africa. Though Rudd was a strong advocate for the evangelization of blacks in the United States, and though he voiced his support for the evangelistic work of Cardinal Lavigerie in Africa, the editor did not recruit missionaries for this cause.[54]

A fourth issue of racial justice taken up in the *ACT* was the manner in which prisons were operated in the South. Before the end of the Civil War, a two-tier system of punishment—one for blacks and one for whites—existed for criminals in southern states such as Georgia. The base for the punishment of black convicts was the plantation, so as not to interrupt the labor of the rehabilitating slave. Following the Civil War, southern states resorted to loaning out prisoners to private contractors, an arrangement that made it possible for states to raise much-needed revenue. Further, white Southerners found this labor pool to be cheap and reliable. Some employers even preferred prison labor to that provided by the free market.[55]

In the latter part of the nineteenth century, African American leaders worked to improve the treatment of inmates being held in these same institutions. It was an issue that black leaders cared deeply about because many of the inmates confined in southern jails were African Americans. For example, in Mississippi about 90 percent of the inmates were black, many of whom were children. Further, because of overwork, torture, and unsanitary living conditions, an alarming number of inmates in the state's lockups died while in custody. In 1887, 16 percent of Mississippi's prison population died.[56] In 1881 Arkansas reported an even higher death rate of 25 percent. A larger percentage of prisoners died while on lease to private companies working on selected construction projects. For example, as many as 45 percent of the prisoners building the Greenville (South Carolina) to Atlanta Railroad from 1877 to 1879 died, and their corpses were unceremoniously buried in levees and embankments along the way.[57]

Concern on the part of the nation's black leaders over the conditions of southern prisons was widespread. For example, T. Thomas Fortune's proposed Afro-American League sought to address the cruel treatment of those languishing in these institutions.[58] Though Rudd devoted relatively little attention to the plight of African American prisoners in the South, evidence from the *ACT* demonstrates that he did consider the state of southern prisons and the cruel treatment of black prisoners to be a question of justice. Speaking of manifestations of injustice, Rudd once labeled these penal institutions "Southern hell holes." He also found it intolerable that men and women were chained together and forced to work on southern roads and highways.[59] He further warned that the convict labor system in the South was "bearing sad fruit."[60]

Part of Rudd's objection to the southern penal system was related to the prisoner loan program. Though the practice had apparently been outlawed in some locales, inmates in southern states, including Tennessee, were being loaned out to various private individuals as an alternative labor pool. On one occasion, the editor of the *ACT* pointed out that 320 convicts from a single camp were pressed to work in such an arrangement. Rudd would have objected to this practice not only because of its resemblance to slavery, but also because of the degrading treatment some inmates were forced to endure.[61]

The Unjust Crop Mortgage System

After emancipation southern aristocrats retained their ideas as to how society should be organized. Because these same power brokers owned the land, blacks during the 1870s and 1880s returned to work for white land owners in an economic contract system that rendered them virtual slaves. Where this unjust economic arrangement prevailed, African American laborers were paid one-quarter to one-half of the year's crop of cotton or corn, and they were provided a home, fuel, and in some cases food. This contract system, however, worked to further impoverish black tenant farmers, who often found themselves in debt when their accounts were settled at the end of the crop year.[62] Rudd believed this contract system exploited African American renters. Like the editor's condemnation of southern prison conditions, his campaign against the crop mortgage system was probably part of the *OST*'s editorial agenda prior to the founding of the *ACT*.[63]

Rudd's opposition to the crop mortgage system placed him in company with other African American protestors. In November 1887, for example, Rudd printed an exchange that highlighted the injustices of the crop mortgage system as it was being practiced in the South. The article stated that plantation owners often paid their laborers in paper slips redeemable only at the plantation store. These plantation stores, in turn, significantly inflated the price of staple items, thus diminishing the sharecropper's profits.[64] In February 1888, Rudd printed an article discussing the issue. In this exchange the contributor explained how African Americans were having difficulty getting ahead because the crop mortgage system made it hard for them to secure a profit.[65]

Subsequent to Rudd's issuance of the call for the first Colored Catholic Congress, the editor of the *ACT* gave a number of reasons for assembling the meeting, one of which was the need to address the unjust crop mortgage system.[66] In August 1894 Rudd again voiced his opposition to this exploitive economic arrangement. He contended that blacks were not the only ones to suffer from the inequitable system:

> The crop mortgage system which we have inveighed in season and out is a very bad one for the producing farmer, no matter whether he be a land owner, a renter or only a common laborer. . . . Store orders and big charges give the store and shopkeeper the advantage over the consumer and they in turn lose largely to the outside whole-salers, because they must wait for the crop to ripen year after year before they can make settlement.[67]

Lynching and Justice

If space in editorials and exchanges is indicative of Rudd's priorities about justice and racial equality, the single most important issue addressed in the *ACT* was the escalation of vigilante violence against blacks. The most egregious incarnation of this violence was the practice of lynching. In the early years of the publication of the *ACT*, however, the editor rarely discussed mob violence or lynching. Like W.E.B. Du Bois (1868–1963), it appears Rudd's thinking on the issue went through a period of development. Prior to 1892 Rudd occasionally reported on lynchings occurring around the country. These accounts, however, were quite often exchanges from other newspapers. Rudd seems to have accepted the facts in these exchanges as they were reported. Moreover, Rudd did not as a rule object to the victims being denied due process, nor did he question their guilt or innocence.[68]

The justification given for the lynching of black victims often was an alleged sexual assault against a white female. But, as Ida B. Wells-Barnett argued, the charge of rape did not in fact appear in many newspaper reports. In those cases in which the charge of rape was leveled, the defendant was often exonerated.[69] Opposition to lynching, however, was not based merely on the guilt or innocence of the accused. Many in society opposed the barbarous practice because it denied the suspect the right to due process before the law. Both the Fifth Amendment and, by application, the Fourteenth Amendment were meant to ensure a person accused of a crime would have the right to hear the charges brought against them, to be tried in a court of competent authorities, to confront their accusers in a trial of proper proceedings, and to be freed unless found guilty.[70]

In the *ACT*'s articles on lynching prior to 1892, Rudd seldom contested the veracity of the assault charges brought against the accused. For example, in May 1888 Rudd printed an exchange entitled "Bad Man Lynched." This same article explained how a black victim had been killed because he had been preparing to commit a "nameless crime" against a young lady, Miss Smith.[71] On another occasion, Rudd printed the following exchange without comment, "John Humphreys, colored, was taken from jail at Asheville, N.C. and lynched for an outrage on a young white woman."[72] Finally, under the heading "A Wretch Lynched," Rudd detailed an account of an African American lynched near Donaldsonville, Louisiana, for an alleged attack on a young girl.[73]

Rudd's sensibilities to the injustice of mob violence more generally, and to lynching particularly, may have been stirred as early as the summer of 1891, when one of his traveling correspondents, Ed Reed, was nearly lynched in Water Valley, Mississippi. Rudd must have also been aware of the infamous lynching of Henry Corbin, a black man accused of killing a white woman and assaulting her daughter in nearby Oxford, Ohio, in January 1892.[74] Though prior to 1892 Rudd occasionally raised a cry to protest the practice of lynching, it was not until March of this same year that one is able to discern a change in Rudd's position on this important issue.

Internal evidence from the *ACT* reveals that Rudd became a vociferous antilynching activist following the murders of three black men in Memphis. On 9 March 1892 Thomas Moss, Calvin McDowell, and Will Stewart were taken from their jail cell at 3 a.m. and murdered by a vigilante mob. Stewart and McDowell were fatally shot, and McDowell's eyes were gouged out. The only crime committed by these men, according to Rudd, was the crime of "defending themselves."[75]

This violent act, perpetrated against men who had no prior criminal record, sent shock waves through the African American community around the country. For example, it was a watershed event in the life of Ida B. Wells-Barnett, in part because she knew the victims. Wells subsequently filled the columns of the *Free Speech* with editorials and antilynching tirades.[76]

In the spring of 1892 Rudd began to focus in a more systematic way on the injustice of mob violence and lynching. In March 1892, for example, the editor printed an exchange from the *St. Joseph Advocate* detailing the execution of ten black strikers in Arkansas who had been holding out for higher wages. After these victims were killed, their bodies were burned. This same article also mentioned the lynching of Ned Coy, who had been charged with assaulting a married woman, presumably white. According to the contributor of this exchange, the accused had been killed despite the lack of corroborating evidence against him.[77]

Like the African American citizens of Memphis, Rudd and Cincinnati's black community were disturbed by the lynchings of Moss, McDowell, and Stewart. Early in April a mass meeting was held in Cincinnati to protest the violence and to demonstrate the city's "heartfelt sympathies" and "deep distress" for the grieving survivors. A resolution was passed that included the assembly's approval for a circular that set aside 31 May as a day for fasting and prayer. The resolution also called for agitation through the press. It further proposed the sending of a delegate from every American city to Washington, D.C., in order that these selected representatives might present to the president and congress the grievances of black citizens. This group of delegates was also to communicate to the nation's leaders their deep frustration and to inform them that the country's African American population would "stand this treatment no longer."[78]

In April 1892 Rudd published a poem by A. W. Puller, pastor of the Zion Baptist Church. This poem gave voice to the sentiments of many of the Queen City's African American citizens.

O God our friend before our birth,
Our only source of true delights,
Our homes and all we have on earth
Are naught to us without our rights.

Injustice holds us in its power;
O come and help us here below!
And, in affliction's darkest hour,
The Negro shall thy goodness know.

The Negro race at thy command,
Have sprung from slav'ry and distress;

And though oppressed on every hand,
Ten million strong thy name we bless.

Our blood on ground we love is shed;
Our Nation will not hear our cry;
Our souls are filled with mighty dread;
O God of right to thee we fly!

While we unite to mourn our dead,
And pray for freedom's perfect day
Protect the orphans they have made
And wipe the widow's tears away.

Forgive we pray our cruel foes,
And lead them to a throne of grace;
And give us strength to bear the blows
White saints Inflict with masqued face

Our race by cords of love unite,
To plead the cause of those shot down
Gainst hatred strong help us fight,
And in the end our labors crown.

And when the war of Cast is o're,
And love shall flow from race to race
We'll praise our God forever more,
By every tongue in every place.[79]

Those who gathered in Cincinnati to declare their opposition to the Memphis murders attempted unsuccessfully to have the assembly's resolution printed in Cincinnati's white-owned newspapers. Black city leaders subsequently praised Rudd for his willingness to publish the resolution. The statement declared, "Though we are oppressed, starved and slain, yet we thank God that he has enabled us to own a paper among our race that will, and can plead the cause of our people. For when the white papers of Cincinnati refused to publish our sentiments Mr. Dan A. Rudd, editor and proprietor of the American Catholic Tribune stepped forward and said, 'Gentleman, I am a poor man, but I love my race. Give me your rejected manuscript and I will publish it and donate and mail five hundred copies free of charge.'"[80]

The African American community in Cincinnati remained agitated over the issue of lynching throughout the spring and summer of 1892. On 19 April of this same year, Rudd, S. J. Hunter, and W. B. Porter met to issue a call for a national black convention to be held in Cincinnati on 4–5 July 1892. The meeting was organized to "enlist the sympathy of all civilization on behalf of justice." As David Spalding has pointed out, the July convention was hastily called and poorly organized. Evidence from the *ACT* shows Rudd led the drive to organize the convention and served as the meeting's presiding officer. Perhaps due to poor attendance, the convention was changed to a mass meeting immediately prior to its commencement.[81]

In the months between the call for the 1892 convention and its subsequent gathering, Rudd continued to publish editorials condemning the practice of lynching. On one such occasion he explained that mob law posed more of a threat than "giant trusts and corporations." Rudd wrote:

> Whatever danger may lurk in these, it is not so imminent as the mob law that terrorizes the people by wholesale murders so brutal and shocking in their nature as to raise doubt in the minds of some, of the civilization of the American people. This thing cannot last. Justice must somewhere find the point of retribution. . . . If bad example continues to prevail, it will have a serious effect on the whole people and sooner or later inevitable dissolution, anarchy and consequent desolation will prevail. How long, O Lord, how long?[82]

In June 1892 a special memorial meeting was organized by black leaders in Cincinnati. The assembled citizens passed a resolution condemning lynching and the unequal prosecution of the law. This document read by Rudd, the chairperson of the committee on resolutions, stated the following:

> Whereas, in many parts of the United States, lawless mobs have made it a rule and practice, to take from the officers of the law, prisoners whose alleged offense against the State and society has never

been proven and executing said prisoners either by hanging, shooting, burning, skinning alive or disjointing and, Whereas, Certain States have encouraged this violence, the outgrowth of prejudice by passing laws that unjustly discriminate between the citizens thus violating the Constitution of the United States and Whereas, These unjust practices not only subvert the spirit and genius of American Government, but sow seeds of danger which must, if nurtured in the future as in the past, develope [*sic*] into Anarchy and destroy the Republic, be it Resolved, That we condemn as a crime against civilization the afore said mobs and unjust laws as well as the spirit that gives rise to them.

In conclusion, Rudd addressed these words to the gathered assembly: "In the name of the great God of all from whom justice must come at last, as come it will; we appeal to our fellow citizens, to give us a living chance in the race of life."[83]

A Mass Meeting Protesting Lynching

On 4 July 1892, the day of the Cincinnati antilynching convention, Rudd addressed the gathered assembly hoping to temper the crowd: "We need no dynamite. We are willing to trust to an enlightened common sense and to the judgment of men who must admit the justice of our demands." Despite Rudd's attempt to reign in the emotions of those in attendance, Mr. Merryweather, a refugee from Arkansas, took the floor predicting a time when the white race would receive "a baptism of blood." Rudd subsequently wrote, "Mr. Merryweather was so full of breathings of vengeance that when his time expired the convention refused to extend the limit."[84] A resolution was passed during this gathering which set forth the aspirations of the group. The document read, "We appeal to the American people in the imperial name of justice . . . We ask nothing of you in behalf of colored people, except the right to eat the bread our own hands have earned, to dwell safely in our homes, to pursue our vocations in peace, to be granted a fair and equal opportunity in the race of life to be protected under the law and to be judged according to the law."[85]

Following the mass meeting, Rudd kept up his campaign against the practice of lynching. Commenting on the proposed presentation of

"Uncle Tom's Cabin," which was to be displayed at the World's Fair in Chicago in 1893, he sardonically suggested a representation of a "few special scenes depicting the barbarities of the present."[86] In September 1892 Rudd criticized the American press and American public opinion. According to the editor, each respective group was guilty of obsessing over the outbreak of the disease of cholera, all the while ignoring a more deadly malady wrought by "American prejudice." He wrote, "Not less than twenty thousand Colored men have been murdered in cold blood by irresponsible scoundrels, in the last two decades."[87]

In August 1894 Rudd wrote, "All good people condemn the crime that gives excuse for the lynching murders that disgrace all America." He declared, on the other hand, that half the time the accused is innocent. Rudd concluded, "There is law enough for both of these classes of criminals. Public sentiment should compel its enforcement. For irresponsible people to smear human blood all over the country for alleged crimes . . . does not correct the abuses charged."[88]

Rudd's 1892 editorial campaign against the practice of lynching situates him among his peers in the black press of the period. A steady cry of protest against mob justice was raised by the nation's African American editors throughout the last fifteen years of the nineteenth century. Besides the vociferous campaign against the practice conducted by Ida B. Wells-Barnett, references condemning lynching can be found in other popular black publications of the day, including the *Christian Recorder* and the *A.M.E. Church Review.* In 1893, for example, the latter of these publications published the views of one contributor who recommended that African Americans band together to form a secret organization for self-defense.[89]

In like manner, Rudd's contemporary, Harry Smith of the *Cleveland Gazette,* wrote, "The wholesale lynching of Afro-Americans charged with crimes, from stealing a chicken up, goes on through out the south. The most barbarous are committed by 'southern chivalry.'"[90] In October 1893 Smith commented on the lynching of an African American man in Roanoke, Virginia. He wrote, "The poor Afro-American lynched, and whose body was riddled with bullets, then burned, is now generally acknowledged to have been innocent of the offense charged. The offense was striking down a woman and robbing her of $2.30. The woman was at her work next day as usual."[91]

Native Americans, Mexican Americans, and Chinese Americans

Rudd's campaign to end racial discrimination in America did not necessarily translate into a defense of the civil rights of other minority
groups. With regard to Native Americans, Rudd, in the pages of the *ACT,*
did not consistently advocate for their rights, nor did he always portray
them in a flattering light. In October 1887, for example, Rudd published
an exchange praising the exploits of Joe Hurt, who, the article claimed,
had killed 400 "hostile Indians." This same writer detailed an episode in
which Hurt prevailed upon 17 "copper colored savages" whom he subsequently scalped.[92] Similarly, in October 1892 Rudd printed an exchange
declaring that the "Digger Indians" of northern California did not possess "a single good characteristic." They were, according to this contributor, "swinish, dirty, indolent and sometimes ugly." The Native American
subject of this particular article was reportedly killed after bathing
because his fellow tribesmen did not recognize him after his bath.[93]

Why Rudd printed the above material in the *ACT* is a mystery. The
editor's negative stereotypical portrayal of Native Americans is incongruent
with his claims regarding the "Fatherhood of God and Brotherhood of
Man." How could a member of the Digger tribe not possess a single good
characteristic if he or she was a member of the human family and created
in God's image?

Two factors may explain why the above articles and others like them
appear in the *ACT.* First, Rudd was a man of his times; he was no less sus-
ceptible to negative stereotypes than other members of society. Given
Rudd's bias toward a Western view of civilization, it is possible to see how
he could have maintained negative stereotypical views of America's indige-
nous population. Second, and more practically, Rudd was a newspaper
man concerned with his business. He needed to fill his newspaper with
interesting and relevant material. At times he may have been guilty of not
carefully considering the contents of the exchanges copied by the *ACT.*

Despite the above problematic references, Rudd believed Native
Americans had throughout history been the victims of injustice. In 1889,
for example, the editor published Archbishop Ryan's remarks from the
prelate's opening sermon given at the lay congress held in Baltimore in
November of this same year. The archbishop identified Negro slavery

and the unjust treatment of the "Indians" as "great blots on our civilization."[94] More important, Rudd appears to have applied the Romantic apologetic for Catholicism to the "Indian Problem," just as he had done for the "Negro Problem." An exchange from the *Church News* published in the *ACT* declared, "The Church . . . is able to transform the hostile Indians into law-abiding and industrious men. . . . When we contemplate what the Church has done, and is doing, for the heathens, we cannot fail to conclude that she, and she alone, has properly interpreted the meaning of the command to teach all nations."[95]

The cause of a number of other marginalized groups in the United States, including Chinese immigrants, is not really seriously taken up in the *ACT*. Despite this fact, Rudd did on occasion publish accounts detailing the oppression of minority groups. For example, Rudd published an exchange that gave a brief account of two Chinese slave girls held in bondage in New York. Rudd's lack of comment on discrimination against Chinese immigrants may have resulted from his animosity toward this group of immigrants, which competed with blacks for low-skilled jobs.[96]

As an African American, Rudd was all too familiar with the indignities forced on people of color. From his early years in Springfield he worked to dismantle America's system of racial hierarchy in the hopes the door of opportunity would be opened for this country's black population. Rudd's Catholicism allowed him to imagine an equitable and harmonious society free from race prejudice. But despite the editor's adoption of the "Fatherhood of God and Brotherhood of Man" rhetoric, Rudd's church-centered vision of justice articulated in the *ACT* did not in any meaningful way address the concerns of other marginalized peoples of color, including Mexican Americans, Native Americans, and Chinese Americans.

CHAPTER 5

Beyond Concerns of Race

It hardly seems possible, that civilization would at this point of its development, brook for a moment the scenes that are being enacted in Ireland.

D. RUDD
7 OCTOBER 1887

Raising his "cry for justice," Rudd advocated for causes that stretched beyond the editor's campaign for racial equality. For example, he addressed the issue of women's rights. Rudd was equally concerned over the exploitation of American laborers. As a member of the Catholic Church, the editor was also aware of the injustices being faced by his coreligionists. In the *ACT,* therefore, Rudd spoke out on the contentious public school question. The editor's campaign for justice and full equality moved beyond domestic concerns as well. He followed the lead of many fellow churchmen in his support of the restoration of the temporal authority of the pope. And, embracing a position many Catholics in the United States would have held, the editor also spoke out in favor of granting home rule for Ireland. Finally, Rudd on a number of occasions condemned the injustices facing peoples of color both in Africa and Latin America. Especially important in this regard was the editor's fight against the African slave trade.

Justice and Equality for Women in the *ACT*

A new era of proscriptive pronouncements on the proper role of the woman in society was initiated at the close of the American Revolution. Barbara Welter has described the "cult of true womanhood" as it served to provide a model for the conduct of the ideal woman of the nineteenth century. Four virtues attended the life of the woman who had assumed her proper place: piety, purity, submissiveness, and domesticity. Anyone tampering with this gender construct was deemed an enemy of God, civilization, and the republic. A foundational tenet of these gender norms was the conviction that the woman's proper place was by her own fireside. From this vantage point, the true, pious woman could instruct her children and bring her men back to God. Those ascribing to this role for the ideal woman often viewed the campaign for women's suffrage to be potentially harmful both to the institution of the family as well as to society more generally.[1]

The social expectations governing the role of the woman in society were part of a wider domestic ideology espoused by a large segment of nineteenth-century Americans, Catholic and Protestant alike. An important proponent of Catholic domestic ideology was Bernard O'Reilly. This author's *Mirror of True Womanhood,* published in 1876, went through seventeen editions by 1892. In the pages of this volume, O'Reilly communicated gender norms held sacrosanct by many Catholics during the late nineteenth century. He believed the home to be the God-ordained sphere of influence for the woman. As the more virtuous of the two sexes, she was to bring her godly influence to bear on her husband and children within the home. On one occasion, O'Reilly wrote, "No woman animated by the Spirit of her Baptism . . . ever fancied that she had or could have any other sphere of duty or activity than that home which is her domain, her garden, her paradise, her world."[2]

Though O'Reilly may have been opposed by some writers, his was the majority opinion. During the Civil War, suffragists seeking a sphere of influence beyond the home were opposed not only by members of the Catholic hierarchy, but also by prominent Catholic women, including Ellen Ewing Sherman (1824–1888), wife of General William T. Sherman (1820–1891), and Madeleine Vinton Dahlgren (1825–1889), wife of Admiral John Dahlgren (1809–1870). James J. Kenneally seems to be correct in his assertion that many Catholics retained a more traditional and circumscribed view of the ideal woman, even as Protestants during this period gradually adopted more "reasonable sentiments" with regard to the place of the woman in society.[3]

Despite widely held societal convictions about the proper sphere of the woman, creative and visionary women in the Catholic Church had for years been assuming roles that tested the boundaries of contemporary gender expectations, such as women who assumed religious vows. Whereas the ideal woman of the nineteenth century was viewed as a paragon of piety and was expected to find her fulfillment in marriage and housekeeping, those who took religious vows were among the most liberated in America. Many were self-supporting, owned property, became well educated, and were otherwise free from both the dominance of a husband as well as the responsibility of motherhood.[4]

Gender and the Romantic Apologetic for Catholicism

Many Catholic leaders of this period applied the Romantic apologetic for Catholicism to the history of the gender. In James Cardinal Gibbons's *Our Christian Heritage,* for example, one finds a typical expression of the church's perspective on the elevation of the woman in Western society. Gibbons argued that in Greek culture the woman was kept in "perpetual bondage" and "unending slavery." In almost every nation of antiquity she was regarded as a "slave," an "instrument of man's passions" rather than his equal. Further, he affirmed, "Every impartial student of history is forced to admit that the woman is indebted to the Catholic religion for the elevated station she enjoys today in family and social life."[5]

Cardinal Gibbons wrote that women are the "peer of man in origin and destiny, in redemption by the blood of Christ, and in the participation of His spiritual gifts." Despite the equality implicit in the above citation, Gibbons subsequently clarified his position. He argued that women, though they possess equal rights, do not necessarily possess "similar" rights. Following this logic, Gibbons attempted to establish a distinct, albeit limited, sphere of influence for women. "To restrict her field of action to the gentler vocations of life is not to fetter her aspirations after the higher and the better," he added. Granting a woman "supereminent" rights instead of mere "equal" rights would endow her with a "sacred influence in her own proper sphere." Gibbons further observed that when women "trench on the domain of man," they should not be surprised if the honor once afforded them is diminished. Gibbons concluded by declaring "the noblest work given to woman is to take care of her children."[6] This same sentiment is echoed by Fr. William P. Cantwell, who wrote, "Woman is forcing herself out of her sphere, and precipitating a conflict which must hurl her back into the slough from which Christianity raised her."[7]

The Emergence of the "New Woman"

The last two decades of the nineteenth century were marked by conflict over the emergence of the concept of the "new woman." The new woman, educated and middle class, attended college, became involved in clubs, settlement houses, and politics. During this same period, women in large numbers began entering professions once held exclusively by males. Similarly, in the last two decades of the nineteenth century, women worked to secure the right to vote. By the 1890s, traditional domestic ideology concerning the role of the woman in society was slowly giving way as women both inside and outside the Catholic Church began asserting their rights.[8]

During this same transitional period, African American women across the denominational spectrum worked to win their rights as citizens and to gain a voice in their respective churches. For example, Evelyn Brooks Higginbotham, in her study of the National Baptist Convention, has detailed the influence African American women had on the development of the black Baptist church. She argued women contributed in varied but significant ways in the black church's quest for justice. They worked to eliminate racism from society and to end gender discrimination. In the process, women formed separate female conventions at the state, local, and national levels. These women advocated voting rights, equal employment, and educational opportunities. During this same period, they authored a biblically based theology affirming the value of women. In addition, in the late nineteenth century women made up the overwhelming majority of the teachers serving black pupils in schools across the South.[9]

In the A.M.E. Church, women also began exerting their rights as individuals. In the last few decades of the nineteenth century, some black women entered ministry. Amanda Berry Smith (1837–1915) was perhaps the best-known black woman evangelist of her era. Other courageous women in this denomination became ministers, ignoring an 1884 ruling forbidding the ordination of females. Women also made their influence felt by their work on women's missionary societies, which were established in congregations around the country. Other female groups exerting influence on the A.M.E. Church were the Women's Mite Missionary Society and the Women's Home and Foreign Missionary Society.[10]

By the 1890s members of the Catholic laity as well as some church leaders, including Archbishop John Ireland and the bishop of Peoria, John Lancaster Spalding (1840–1916), were challenging more traditional limitations placed on women in society.[11] Though Rudd on occasion did publish articles and exchanges echoing more traditional views about the primary role of the gender, his sympathies appear to have been with those church leaders who pushed for expanded rights and an enlarged sphere of influence for women.

That women were successfully assuming roles traditionally held by males was a fact celebrated by Rudd in many of the issues of the *ACT*. For example, in May 1887 Rudd mentioned the exploits of a teenage girl who, without assistance, managed a shop in Albany, New York. In July 1887 Rudd claimed the wife of Pennsylvanian John Murray was as good a blacksmith as he. In this same issue, he claimed the best horseback rider in Washington, D.C., was, in fact, a woman. In October 1889 Rudd informed his readers that a young woman, Mary Alexander, had scored higher on the civil service exam than anyone to date. In September 1891 Rudd praised the fine job being done by the female professors at Butler University in Indiana. Similarly, in March 1894 the editor of the *ACT* printed an exchange portraying the wives of France's entrepreneurs as the real brains and vitality behind the businesses of their husbands.[12]

Given the lack of editorial comment from Rudd on gender issues, clues as to Rudd's stand on the question of women's rights must be discerned primarily from the exchanges printed in the *ACT*. In July 1887 Rudd published a lecture delivered by Mary E. Britton (1855–1925), an African American educator, activist, journalist, and physician from Kentucky. In this lecture Britton argued that women, like their male counterparts, are uniquely gifted from birth by God. They by right, according to Britton, should make use of this giftedness beyond the sphere of the home and not merely content themselves with rearing talented children. Britton also argued, "every human being has a right to mark out his or her own destiny, subject only to those restraints of society which are applied to all alike." Further, Britton pointed out that those in the church guilty of subjecting women to a lesser position had "studiously avoided Christ and made much of Paul." She explained, "Christ inaugurated the reform and its progress has been the long continued efforts in Europe and America to rid the statute books of laws, made in the sole interests of men, and denying to wives and mothers their just rights." Further, she defended women's suffrage, declaring it "a Potent Agency in Public Reforms." Britton concluded, "Taxation without representation" is "tyranny."[13]

Evidence from the *ACT* reveals the fact that Rudd was sympathetic to Britton's advocacy for an expanded role for women in society. Rudd called Britton a "talented young lady and rising journalist."[14] Rudd also appreciated the work of suffragist Josephine St. Pierre Ruffin (1842–1924), a leader in Boston's Women's Club movement, a publisher, and an advocate of civil rights.[15] In March 1888 Rudd wrote:

> The ladies of the Bay State have a powerful and able advocate of woman suffrage in the person of Mrs. Judge Ruffin. She discusses all questions pertaining to the subject in a manner that shows that she has given the matter much consideration. She and Miss Britton of Lexington, Ky., would make a whole team for the female voters of the Hub city. The women up this way are getting very tired being help-mates to men. They are sighing for a change.[16]

Suffrage for Women

Many Catholic clergymen in the late nineteenth century were outspoken critics of women's suffrage. Protestant clergymen, on the other hand, were often more willing to support the voting rights of women.[17] Rudd appears to have supported women's suffrage. In December 1890 Rudd printed an exchange from the *Chicago Tribune* discussing the declining number of female voters in Boston. Rudd went on to declare that the reason for this waning of interest was the misuse of the ballot on the part

Mary E. Britton, educator, women's rights activist, journalist, and physician. (Courtesy of Special Collections Archives, Hutchins Library, Berea College.)

of a population seeking to "sweep 'Romanism' from the famed American Athens." This they could not do, according to Rudd, because of the wisely cast votes of Catholic women. Rudd went on to declare his conviction that women were "no more, nor less, intelligent than men." He stated he would not object to women voting. He further declared, "we understand the constitution of the United States, they have that right."[18]

In February 1890 Rudd published an article entitled "Sex Prejudice." The author of this exchange made the case for women's suffrage, further reasoning that a woman should be allowed to enter any field of her choosing. "Nor should the school teacher, clerk or saleswoman have to deduct a discount from her salary merely because she is a woman," the author concluded.[19]

Rudd's support of the enfranchisement of women in some ways mirrors the editorial stand expressed by Detroit's leading black newspaper, the *Plaindealer.* In March 1890, for example, the editor of the *Plaindealer* wrote, "Those who oppose woman suffrage are using the same argument that was used against the Afro-American when it was proposed to give him the right of suffrage." This editor argued that women have higher graduation rates and that their "average moral character" and "mental equipment" are "above men."[20]

If Rudd refused to forthrightly distance himself from the idea that the primary role of the woman was to manage the home, he seems, nonetheless, to have been convinced of her ability to contribute to the broader society. For example, he printed an exchange in February 1890 decrying the art craze among homemakers. The writer claimed, "The average American housewife can put her house in order, and minister to the needs of husband and children, read a dissertation on social reform or political economy, acquaint herself with congressional and legislative news" and spend less time decorating the home. In the same issue, Rudd printed an exchange from the *Queen Bee.* It read, "Do Not be afraid if your wife votes that you will loose your cook. The chances are that she may conduct a scientific cooking-school and feed you upon the results."[21] Further, in August 1890 Rudd printed an exchange that made the case that women should use their "moral sweetness and purity—to sweeten not only the home but society and government as well."[22]

With regard to questions concerning the proper role a woman should assume in society, Rudd seems to have adopted a stance closely allied with progressive Catholic women, including F. C. Farinholt, Mary A. Spellissy, and Katherine Mullaney. Spellissy, for example, argued the wife who "conforms her life to the couplet in Don Quixote and stays at home as if she were lame, is in danger of becoming morbid and a dullard, an uncongenial companion to her husband and an incapable as an advisor to her children." The aforementioned female Catholic activists promoted gender equality, a state of community relations that would allow women to assume an broader role in society. Among them were those who believed society would benefit from allowing women to vote. For example, Mary A. Dowd, bolstered by Archbishop John Ireland's address given at the Woman's Christian Temperance Union gathering in Chicago in September 1893, argued that the evils threatening the home made it necessary for women to exercise the franchise.[23]

If the editor did espouse a relatively enlightened position on gender equality, his decision not to seat women delegates at the first Colored Catholic Congress held in Washington, D.C., in January 1889, remains problematic. Rudd wrote prior to the congress, "While in the Call there is no clause prohibiting the attendance of female delegates, yet we do not believe that its signers thought it would be advisable to have women delegates at this, the initial meeting." He intimated the signers expected "the different sodalities and other societies of ladies would be represented by either their spiritual directors or by other of their gentlemen well-wishers."[24]

It must be kept in mind the decision not to seat women delegates is unremarkable for the time period in question. The German Central Verein, founded in 1855, was led by men until the creation of the German women's auxiliary in 1916. Similarly, the first meeting of the Catholic lay congress held in Baltimore in November 1889 had no female leadership or delegate representation. Finally, the National Baptist Convention, U.S.A. (NBC), formed in 1895, allowed the male delegates to represent black Baptist women until 1900. It was then that the Women's Convention of the NBC was formed.[25]

Though the decision to permit only male delegates to be seated at the first gathering of the Colored Catholic Congress was unremarkable, it is possible Rudd and the other organizers were reluctant to seat women delegates because it may have been objectionable to members of the Catholic hierarchy, including Gibbons and Elder. Rudd needed the approval of church leaders to carry out the congresses, and it is reasonable to assume he would have attempted to avoid any unnecessary controversy. Whatever the motivation, the decision not to seat women delegates at this important gathering demonstrates the fact that the ideal society called forth by an acknowledgment of the "Fatherhood of God and the Brotherhood Man," did not always fully consider the aspirations of one half of humanity.

Justice for Catholics on the Public School Question

As an active member of the Catholic press, Rudd did not fail to raise a voice of protest any time he believed his coreligionists were being treated unfairly. Most Catholics in the United States in the nineteenth century took issue with being forced to pay taxes to support public schools, which they believed to be Protestant centers of proselytization. Catholic leaders objected to the active role played by Protestants in the administration of tax-supported schools and disapproved of mandatory readings from the King James Version of the Bible. Catholic parents also resented the practice of having their children learn a Protestant version of the Ten Commandments or the Sermon on the Mount. Moreover, many in the Catholic Church believed the "watered down," "lowest-common-denominator" form of Protestantism promulgated in public school classrooms was simply not potent enough to stave off the significant threat posed to society by "materialism," "formal unbelief," and "secularism."[26]

Speaking of the public school question, John T. McGreevy argues that no issue in post–Civil War America so quickly "generated both anti-Catholicism and Catholic belligerence." In 1884 America's Catholic bishops formalized the Sacra Congregatio de Propaganda Fide instructions requiring the faithful to educate their offspring in Catholic schools. At the same time, many liberal national leaders viewed education as the means by which to produce loyal citizens. These same national leaders refused to acknowledge any sectarian bias in the manner in which liberal education was being promoted in the United States. According to McGreevy, however, the American educational system often did exhibit an inherent anti-Catholic animus.[27]

A survey of publications of the period shows Catholics viewed the school question to be a pressing issue of justice. Morgan Sheedy contributed an article to the *Catholic World* in August 1889 entitled "The School Question: A Plea for Justice," in which he articulated the main tenets of the Catholic position on the school question. He argued that it was a "natural and divine right" for parents to educate their children, and that to offer an education that was either godless or beholden to an "indefinite Christianity" in a nation of Christians was a position that "ought to be impossible of acceptance." Sheedy further argued that it would be unfair to create a system where "exclusive control and enjoyment of the school funds" was delegated to one class of the community. Forcing Catholics to pay for the education of their own children, as well as taxing them to support public schools from which they derived no benefit, was, he explained, "practically a double system of taxation." The existing system of education, which put much of the financial burden of state schools on the backs of Catholics, was, according to Sheedy, "the grossest injustice, to use a rather mild term."[28]

During the last decades of the nineteenth century, immigrants coming to the United States greatly increased the number of American Catholics. This influx led to debates as to the best way to accommodate their needs. The discussion over how to best care for these newly arrived immigrants was a principle concern for the Third Plenary Council of Baltimore in 1884. One strategy was to provide a system of parochial schools.[29]

The school question was deliberated among Catholics in the United States who disagreed as to the extent to which the church should adapt to American culture. On the one hand, Archbishop John Ireland and the Americanists believed immigrants should be mainstreamed into American society. On the other hand, Archbishop Michael A. Corrigan and his conservative allies remained skeptical of American culture and the advisability of the church accommodating to it. While Archbishop Ireland and Bishop John J. Keane believed the future of Catholicism was more promising in America than in the tradition-bound states of Europe, conservatives, including German Catholics, took a less sanguine view of American society and its compatibility with Catholicism.[30]

This same debate spilled over into discussions about the public school system. Conservatives such as Bishop Bernard McQuaid (1823–1909) of Rochester, New York, were outspoken advocates of independent parochial schools. German Catholics who sought to preserve their language and culture in their new home envisioned the parochial school as a means to this end. Similarly, Irish conservatives opposed the support of public schools because many believed these educational institutions promoted religious indifference. Moreover, conservative European Catholics found the use of public schools untenable because of the latter's view that the state rather than the institution of the family possessed the preeminent right to educate its youth.[31]

On the other hand, liberal American Catholics led by Archbishop Ireland did not view the public school as necessarily hostile to the faith. Ireland, for example, proposed a compromise with the state school system, an agreement modeled on the "Poughkeepsie Plan," which made the state financially responsible for the secular training of all students. After school hours, religion instructors would then enter these schools, the plan proposed, and instruct students according to their respective religious affiliation.[32]

Archbishop Ireland had proposed his controversial ideas about the potential for a partnership between the state and religious schools in a speech he delivered before the National Education Association on 10 July 1890 in St. Paul. Titled "The State School and the Parish School—Is Union between them Impossible?," Ireland's speech proposed the state pay for the "secular" instruction of those students in private religious schools as well as public.[33]

Ireland gave this speech during the same week the Colored Catholic Congress was gathered in its second meeting in Cincinnati. In fact, it is possible Ireland's commitment to speak before the teacher's convention in St. Paul on 10 July 1890 is what kept the prelate from traveling to the Colored Catholic Congress meeting in Cincinnati. It is also reasonable to assume Ireland's school speech received little coverage in the *ACT* because the July and early August issues of Rudd's newspaper were occupied with reporting the details of the second Colored Catholic Congress.

After Ireland's school speech, Rudd published the following comment from Memphis's *Adam, The Catholic Journal of the New South*: "Archbishop Ireland raised a hornet's nest around his ears by his recent utterances regarding a solution to the Negro problem, but it is nothing [compared] to the storm that his address at St. Paul on the school question aroused." Rudd responded, "And we regret to say that our esteemed

Southern contemporary did not publish the words of the great Archbishop on either question."[34] These above references make it appear that Rudd found nothing objectionable in the archbishop's assimilationist approach to the school question.

Rudd also published a speech given by Americanist Bishop John Keane, in which Keane proposed that instead of minimizing Christianity in the school system in order to make it acceptable to those "who have the least faith," an alternative plan should be developed. This plan would permit the states to have full control over secular training but allow each religious group to teach "Christianity freely and fully."[35] Again, this proposal, coming as it did from one in the liberal Americanist camp, drew no criticism from Rudd.

Rudd's apparent enthusiasm for Ireland and the Americanist approach to the school issue did not translate into opposition toward anti-assimilationist Catholics who remained skeptical of America's public school system. In 1889 Wisconsin passed the Bennett Law. This legislation mandated compulsory school attendance for children between the ages of eight and fourteen. It also mandated classes be taught in English. Those most opposed to this anti-Catholic school legislation were the anti-assimilationists who had little use for the public schools. Opponents of the Bennett Law had many allies within the church. Archbishop Michael Heiss (1818–1890) of Milwaukee, Bishop Kilian Flasch (1837–1891) of the diocese of LaCrosse, and Frederick Katzer (1844–1903), who would also serve as archbishop of Milwaukee, joined forces with Lutherans to oppose the legislation. Archbishop Ireland, on the other hand, would have had little problem with the legislation since it would have expedited the assimilation of the children of newly arrived immigrants.[36]

Rudd was friendly with conservative leaders in the Catholic Church who opposed the Bennett Law. In the *ACT* Rudd spoke out for the cause of these conservatives when he condemned the legislation. On one occasion he wrote, "The Bennett law is well understood as the tail-end of Boston bigotry that has been switching around the western side of Lake Michigan, hunting for a delayed blizzard."[37] Though it is conjecture, it is possible Rudd's comment on the "delayed blizzard" is a coy slight at Ireland, who had up to that time failed to condemn the Bennett Law. In short, Rudd seems to have been pulled in two directions on the public school question. Though he was a fan of Ireland and his proposals regarding the elimination of the color line, he was nonetheless sympathetic to Catholics who wanted to maintain their own religious schools.

Rudd, Justice, and the School Question

If Rudd cannot be definitively located in the assimilationist camp or the anti- assimilationist camp with regard to the school question, what were his views on this divisive issue? Rudd clearly believed it was important for all schoolchildren to receive a Christian education. Responding to a speech given by Rev. S. F. Scovel, president of Wooster College, Rudd wrote:

> Catholics are not the only people in the world, who are pleading for and demanding a Christian education for their children in this country . . . If this Republic is to stand, its children must have a good, practical, moral education, that is given hand in hand with the physical and intellectual. To teach correct morals entirely outside of the principals of Christianity, is impossible. Therefore children should have a Christian education.[38]

Rudd would have agreed with Catholic Americans, who overwhelmingly opposed secularized schools, schools they believed advanced "civic virtue" divorced from Christianity. He further believed the church should play an essential role in the moral education of children, printing an exchange by Fr. William Mullheron of Auburn, New York, in which Mullheron laid blame for many of society's ills at the feet of those who excluded God from the classroom and divorced religion from education. Among these ills were an increase in divorce and crime rates, incidents of suicide and insanity, and cases of "loathsome immorality."[39]

In July 1891 Rudd published the sermon of John Mackey, delivered at the laying of the cornerstone of the Holy Cross School in Cincinnati. In his homily, Mackey alluded to the injustices perpetrated on the state's Christian population by Ohio's educational system. He further emphasized the importance of religion and virtue in the education of a child. Like Sheedy, Mackey believed the current public education system bred crime.[40]

In Rudd's editorial, published in the same edition of the *ACT,* he offered qualified support for Mackey's views. Though he agreed with the main tenets of Mackey's argument, Rudd did not share the priest's fear that the two major political parties would avoid the divisive school issue in the upcoming gubernatorial election. He declared that he, himself, would send the gubernatorial candidates marked copies of the *ACT,* "that they may know that the Catholic body in the State of Ohio, as well as in the nation, demands the equal rights for which Reverend Father so manfully contends." In this same editorial response, Rudd wrote, "Rampant bigotry and intolerance are on the run, we purpose to keep these evils going, until the sense of justice and fairness of the people have righted the wrong that weighs so heavily upon the honest and intelligent Catholic portion of Ohio's citizenship."[41]

Many of the skirmishes in the battle over the school question occurred in Boston. In 1888 Rudd attacked Massachusetts's officials because he believed they were treating the city's Catholic population unfairly. Rudd labeled these state officials "puritanical bigots." Further, he observed their policies were opposed by Catholics and "all fairminded men of every denomination" on the "broad grounds of constitutional justice."[42] When the *Detroit Plaindealer* praised the Protestants of Boston for their position on the school question, Rudd reminded his counterpart from Detroit that "one half of the population of the city of Boston are Catholics. Have they no right to say what shall and what shall not be taught in the schools for which the[y] pay to support?" Rudd further pointed out that the "American spirit," lauded by the *Plaindealer,* was the same spirit that "debased and robbed the Negro," holding him "beneath every other race under the sun."[43]

With regard to the school question, Rudd argued that "parents have rights with which the State cannot interfere." He stated it was a "well-known fact" that "large classes of people" were paying taxes for schools they could not in "good conscience use."[44] He further claimed, "The foolish idea that children may be brought up to a high sense of moral manhood and womanhood, without having gone through a thorough and constant course of instruction in morals, while the other faculties are being trained, is sheerest nonsense." Addressing the editor of the *Springfield State Capital* of Illinois, Rudd wrote, "If the readers of our contemporary will but follow the advice of the Catholic Church, and see that no obstacles are thrown in the way of the moral education of children, it would be unnecessary within even another generation to ask, "what shall we do with our children."[45]

Though Rudd espoused a Catholic viewpoint concerning the need for religious training, this did not stop him from condemning the race discrimination infecting the nation's institutions of learning. In fact, Rudd drew parallels between the discrimination suffered by Catholics and by African Americans. On one occasion Rudd wrote the following:

> Let us define the injustice. Catholics are taxed to support the public schools whether they use them or not; this is the law and but little complaint is made, yet it is not just. The colored people are taxed and receive a benefit. But what right has the State to take money from both of these classes, and classes they are, and then refuse to give colored teachers places simply because they are colored?[46]

Moreover, Rudd's support of the Catholic position on the school question did not silence his criticism of the Catholic educational system. In August 1891 Rudd distinguished two "defects" in the operation of Catholic schools. The first involved the lack of a "common system of management"; the second involved the fact that these same schools were not "open to all races alike."[47]

Rudd and his white Catholic counterparts shared many similar convictions with regard to the nation's education system. There were, however, at times significant points of departure between his views and those of most white Catholics. For example, Rudd, like many of his black Republican peers, supported the Blair Federal Aid to Education Bill. This proposed legislation, drafted by Senate Republican Henry W. Blair (1834–1920) of New Hampshire, would have protected the political rights of African Americans while providing federal aid to improve the nation's schools, especially in the South.[48] Rudd's contemporary at the *Cleveland Gazette,* Harry Smith, editorialized on the proposed legislation in November 1889:

> The Gazette has so often spoken in favor of the Blair Education Bill, which will come before the Fifty-first Congress with better chances of passing than ever in its history, that its readers are familiar with its stand in favor of this great measure to secure national aid to education, particularly in the South. . . . Education for the masses, both white and colored, in the South is the thing most needed to bring about a change for the better in every avenue of Southern life.[49]

Rudd, like Smith, supported Senator Blair's legislation. In August 1887 the National Colored Press Association met in Louisville, Kentucky. During this meeting, Rudd proposed a resolution, stating, "Whereas, the census of 1880 shows a shocking state of illiteracy, therefore, be it 'Resolved, That we urge upon Congress the passage of the Blair Educational Bill.'"[50] As John McGreevy has pointed out, however, most Catholics did not favor Blair's educational initiative. They believed education policy needed to remain a local issue. Some Catholics may also have opposed the legislation because Blair was a Republican whose anti-Catholic sentiments were occasionally aired from the Senate floor.[51]

Economic Justice Concerns in the *ACT*

In the *ACT*'s editorials and exchanges Rudd enjoined America's pressing economic debates. During the 1880s and 1890s tens of thousands of this nation's unskilled workers, many of whom were Catholic, joined labor organizations to demand shorter workdays, higher wages, and a voice in the improvement of working conditions.[52] This era was marked with labor strife resulting in strikes and lockouts. Some of these disputes turned violent, including the Haymarket strike in Chicago in 1886 and the Homestead strike in Homestead, Pennsylvania, in 1892. In the closing decades of the nineteenth century, church leaders, including James Cardinal Gibbons, the head of the American Catholic Church, attempted to chart a moral course for the faithful. Cardinal Gibbons saw value in the bargaining power of unions and was successful in convincing Roman church officials that it would be a mistake to condemn the Knights of Labor.[53]

Social Catholicism was a late nineteenth-century phenomena that matured in the early decades of the twentieth century. No longer was it acceptable for Catholics in this period to merely conduct missions of mercy. Rather, those promoting Social Catholicism were convinced that the injustices of the age needed to be addressed at the foundational level.[54] The aims of Social Catholicism resembled in many ways those of the largely Protestant Social Gospel movement. A century after the beginning of the industrial revolution, both religious groups worked to ameliorate instances of injustice in the rapidly developing economies of Europe, as well as in the United States.[55]

After it was issued, Pope Leo XIII's 1891 encyclical, *Rerum Novarum,* became the foundational document of Catholic social thought. Leo XIII's adherence to "natural law" philosophy led him to recognize that many modern social arrangements predicated on individual self-interest violated the ideal communal pattern of societal relations. Those who appealed to Leo's work were doctrinal conservatives and social progressives. These same Social Catholics promoted new concepts for stewardship of private possessions. They stopped well short, however, of condemning the ownership of private property.[56]

Rudd, along with other Catholic leaders of the day, believed the Catholic Church would play an essential role in the establishment of a more just economic order. He published Pope Leo XIII's letter to the Kaiser of Germany on the occasion of the Berlin Labor Conference in the spring of 1890. In this correspondence, the pope explicated the important role religion and the church would necessarily fill in the "successful solution of the matter." Leo explained, "The religious sentiment, indeed, is the only thing that can give authority to law; and the Gospel is the only code containing the principles of true justice and those maxims of mutual charity which should unite all men as children of the same Father and members of the same family."[57] On another occasion, Leo declared the church to be the only power "competent to deal with the tremendous issues involved in the social and industrial movement."[58] In the same issue of the *ACT,* Rudd printed an exchange that argued the church was the "most faithful guardian of the rights of the wage earners." Speaking of the church, the editor further declared, "Her system of political economy is founded on the saying of her Divine Founder: 'The laborer is worthy of his hire.'"[59]

Rudd believed all members of the human race, whether they were capitalist or common laborers, were, indeed, members of the same family. In short, Rudd linked the egalitarianism inherent in his language concerning the "Fatherhood of God and Brotherhood of Man" to the issue of class.[60] In November 1889 Rudd gave voice to his sentiments on class relations when he published the platform of the first lay Catholic congress. The document read, "Another danger which menaces our Republic is the constant conflict between labor and capital. We, therefore, at all times must view with feelings of regret and alarm the antagonism existing between them.

. . . The remedy must be sought in the mediation of the Church through her action on individual conscience and thereby on society, teaching each its respective duties as well as rights."[61] Again in November 1890 Rudd discussed the rights of workers. He explained how capitalists were bound to "recognize the laborer as a co-worker, as one entitled to [the] reward of work. The worker was, according to Rudd, "to be treated not not [sic] as a machine, but as a man, justly, generously, kindly." Only this kind of treatment would bring a "solution of the labor trouble," Rudd reasoned.[62]

On at least one occasion, Rudd proposed a more equitable share of profits be allocated to the nation's working-class laborers. For example, the editor argued that though the duties of the nation's rail porters were "onorous" and their service "indispensable," their pay was but a "pittance." He continued, "If some of the money that is expended in high salaries and private cars for the chief officials of the Palace Car Companies should be given to this overworked class of men, who are really always obedient and obliging servants of the public, there would be much less cause for the spotters and detective system, used by millionaires who cater to the public comfort."[63]

Rerum Novarum was up to that time the Catholic Church's most decisive and comprehensive word on economic justice and class relations. The Catholic Church during this period maintained an aversion to liberal economic principles. Catholic leaders were convinced economic liberalism put workers at risk by subjecting them to the mercies of market forces. This aversion made it possible for Ultramontane Catholics to embrace a more social understanding of political economy. As a consequence, Catholic theologians including Italian Jesuit Matteo Liberatore (1810–1892) urged the formation of guilds for both workers and employers. Further, Liberatore attacked economic theory that was supported by unrestrained capitalism. During this period Catholic visionaries looked longingly at the Middle Ages as an ideal era, and one less possessed with the "pursuit of individual self interest."[64]

With the publication of *Rerum Novarum* the Vatican attempted to address systemic economic injustice and to improve the plight of urban industrial workers in Europe and in the United States. Rudd's distaste for systemic economic injustice, however, was probably most exercised by his opposition to the crop mortgage system. Though the editor of the *ACT* at times urged blacks to make their own way in the United States through thrift and hard work, he understood the systemic nature of injustice. Most assuredly he realized how America's sharecropping system disadvantaged African American farmers.[65]

Leo XIII's encyclical resonated with the editor of the *ACT*. Rudd printed *Rerum Novarum* in its entirety in five installments throughout the summer of 1891. Further, he enthusiastically endorsed the ideals promulgated in this encyclical. In August 1891 Rudd wrote the following:

> In this day of strikes and the oppression that causes them of the injustice of man to man, of prejudice, of murder and of violence, this great paper from the pen of the head of the Christian Church, is as refreshing as a summer shower and as strong as everlasting truth. . . . It would be almost a crime for one claiming to be interested in the condition of the poor, if he refused to at least read and study the treatise that covers so completely and fairly every phase of the question of equity as the Encyclical of Leo XIII.[66]

Rudd supported the primary principles set forth in *Rerum Novarum*, including the document's opposition to socialist economic theory. His views on socialist ideology were articulated in the *ACT* prior to 1891. In March 1887, for example, he published a refutation of Henry George's (1839–1897) "land theory," delivered by Father Higgins in Cincinnati. Higgins said misery and societal degradation were not the result of wealth but rather of the "dishonest methods of gaining it." Rudd subsequently editorialized: "After subjecting Mr. George's arguments to the test of logic, the lecturer established the true philosophical basis of property in general and of landed property in particular."[67]

Rudd, like the overwhelming majority of Catholics of the period, found Henry George's support of a confiscatory tax untenable. Nowhere in the *ACT* did Rudd show any sympathy for socialist ideology. On one occasion, Rudd attempted to persuade his readers that Henry George's economic theories mirrored the theories of German socialists and would, therefore, lead to the confiscation of "all productive industries."[68]

As noted above, a number of strikes and work stoppages occurred in the United States during the years of the *ACT*'s publication. Finding a solution as to how capital and labor might coexist peacefully and to the profit of both groups was a concern for Catholics and Protestants alike.

In 1889, for example, James Cardinal Gibbons published *Our Christian Heritage*. In the chapter titled "The Laboring Classes," he argued that "whoever strives to improve the friendly relations between the proprietors and the labor unions by proposing the most effectual means of diminishing and even removing the causes of discontent is a benefactor to the community."[69]

Despite Rudd's desire to see capital and labor working in harmony, the editor of the *ACT* supported the right of workers to organize into labor unions. In so doing, he followed the lead of both James Cardinal Gibbons and Archbishop Manning. Gibbons believed labor unions to be the "legitimate successors of the ancient guilds of England."[70] Subsequently, the right of workers to organize to secure better wages and working conditions was endorsed by Pope Leo XIII in *Rerum Novarum*.

Rudd's conviction regarding the right of workers to organize was also informed by his views on racial equality. His position on the matter was expressed in an official address to Catholics published by the delegates of the first Colored Catholic Congress in January 1889. The document read, "we appeal to all labor organizations, trade unions etc., to admit Colored men within their ranks on the same conditions as others are admitted." In May 1892 Rudd also commented on the meeting of what was to be Ohio's first chapter of the American Federation of Labor. The editor of the *ACT* offered praise for this organization because it made "no distinction to membership on account of color or nationality."[71]

The *ACT*'s editorial position concerning whether or not laborers should resort to the strike seems to intimate an ambivalence also articulated in *Rerum Novarum*. Following the lead of Catholic officials, Daniel Rudd seemed to be reluctant to endorse strikes. Perhaps he believed these labor stoppages held out little hope of negotiating divisive disputes on fair terms. On 16 June 1894 the *ACT* published an article celebrating the end of the coal strike, stating that this same strike had hurt all parties involved.[72] On occasion, however, Rudd seemed to favor the position taken by strikers. In July 1891 Rudd called attention to the detrimental impact that the notorious prison lease program was having on labor. Perhaps owing to his convictions concerning the ethics of the strike, Rudd would not comment on whether the striking miners in Tennessee were right or wrong. He did, however, recognize in this labor action the "knife of advancing civilization" cutting out the cancer that had been "gnawing at the very vitals of southern development."[73]

Rudd's experience of race discrimination sensitized him to the frustration felt by members of America's underclass. Those seeking to throw off oppression by violent or revolutionary means, however, found no sympathy with Rudd. Rudd believed in the inevitable advance of civilization and assigned to the church a vital role in its emergence. Speaking of African Americans, for example, the editor of the *ACT* wrote, "What benefit will it be to him politically to join in praising anarchy in America as against the Organization left by Christ himself and against which he declares 'The Gates of Hell shall not prevail.'"[74]

Rudd was skeptical of socialist economic theory, and sometimes he unfairly linked those promoting socialism with the anarchists who sought by violent means to overthrow the American capitalist system. As a result, Rudd took aim at Fr. Edward McGlynn, one of the most controversial and outspoken advocates for social justice in the late nineteenth century. Father McGlynn had become the pastor of St. Stephen's Parish in New York City in 1866, a position he held until 1886. He also had firsthand experience with poverty and human degradation. Subsequently, he became a supporter of New York City mayoral candidate Henry George. George believed the fundamental remedy to economic and social injustice was a single tax system, one which effectively disincentivized exploitive land speculation. This economic approach, however, threatened the right of individuals to own and make profit from their private property holdings. Because of McGlynn's endorsement of the single tax proposal, and his support of mayoral candidate Henry George, the priest was branded a socialist. He was subsequently excommunicated from the church, in part because of his refusal to submit to church authority.[75]

In June 1887 Rudd defended the pope's decision to excommunicate McGlynn, writing, "Well, the Church will go on in her work caring for the downtrodden and checking the march of anarchy, paganism and infidelity."[76] The above citation leaves one with the impression that Rudd failed to make a distinction between socialist economic theory and anarchist ideology. His negative appraisal concerning both seemed, nonetheless, to mirror the views held by many in the Catholic Church.

Justice for Ireland

On 8 April 1886, about four months before Rudd began publishing the *ACT,* Prime Minister William E. Gladstone (1809–1898), who led Britain's Liberal Party, rose in the House of Commons to present his Government of Ireland Bill, otherwise known as the "First Home Rule Bill." This watershed legislation involved the transfer of some power from the British ruling class to moderate representatives of Catholic Ireland.[77] Though many in Britain were divided over the issue, the Irish were not. They wanted to secure as much self-determination as could be won from Britain.[78] In fact, many more concessions were won by Ireland's population over the next forty years. The first Home Rule Bill demonstrates the rising influence of the Home Rule Party and the Irish nationalists led by Charles Stewart Parnell (1846–1891). By 1886 the party had worked its way from the periphery of British politics into a position of influence in Westminster.[79]

As might be expected, Rudd was in sympathy with the cause of his Catholic brothers and sisters living on the Emerald Isle. In the pages of the *ACT,* the editor advocated Irish home rule. Journalistic support for Ireland's self-determination was common among Rudd's peers in the Catholic press. Rudd joined other Catholic contemporaries, including S. B. Gorman, for example, in the promotion of an independent Ireland free from British oppression. In August 1887 Gorman contributed an article to the *Catholic World* in which he spoke out against the injustice of the oppressive coercion law of 1887. This same writer confidently affirmed Ireland would someday have self-government.[80]

Home rule for Ireland was a cause championed by many non-Catholics as well, and support for Irish home rule was a part of the Republican platform in the late 1880s. For example, Joseph Foraker, Republican governor of Ohio and U.S. senator, supported Irish home rule. In April 1887 Rudd praised Foraker's speech delivered at Ohio University, in which he declared that "the people of Ireland will sooner or later have home rule, in spite of all England can do, because it is the cause of liberty and the people." Rudd subsequently editorialized, "If the Governor could bring all in his party up to his own high standard of thinking, what a party he would lead."[81]

Rudd's support for Irish home rule placed him in the company of other prominent African Americans, including Frederick Douglass.[82]

Because a great many blacks remained loyal to the Republican Party during the last decades of the nineteenth century, Rudd could count on many sympathizers among delegates when he proposed the following resolution at the National Colored Press Association meeting in 1887:

> Whereas, the people of Ireland, like the American Negro, have been suffering and struggling under the injustice of man to man, and, Whereas, From every land where an Irishman is found there comes determination unconquerable, and liberal hands to aid in the freedom of the Emerald Isle; therefore, Resolved, That we send hearty greeting and warm congratulations to the sons of Erin for their matchless devotion to a noble cause.[83]

Presumably, many African Americans supported the cause of Irish independence because they could identify with the population of Ireland's struggle for civil rights and full citizenship. The linking of these two similar campaigns for justice goes back at least to the mid-nineteenth century, when Irish Nationalist politician Daniel O'Connell (1775–1847) vociferously condemned the institution of American slavery.[84] Subsequently, Rudd also drew a parallel between Ireland's struggle for independence and the plight of African Americans:

> It seems to us at this distance from the state of action, that if lost even to all sense of duty and fairness to their fellow men, common sense would teach the land-lords and the Government of England that they are sowing seeds that will eventually disrupt the kingdom. But then we do not need to go to Ireland to find cases of injustice. America is full of them as a hill is of ants.

According to Rudd, such injustices included the southern prison system, the crop mortgage system, and the discrimination routinely faced by black travelers in the South.[85]

Rudd joined other prominent African American leaders, including T. Thomas Fortune, in linking the African American quest for justice and freedom to the campaign for Irish home rule.[86] In June 1887 Rudd also published an article from the *Baptist Tribune*. One portion of this exchange acknowledged that blacks, Native Americans, and the Irish all suffered at the hands of oppressors. The editor of this journal further believed that the suffering of these three groups ought to bind them together in mutual sympathy.[87]

Rudd's support for Ireland's home rule remained strong even after Parnell's fall from grace occasioned the subsequent division of the home rule forces in 1890. In the spring of 1891, Rudd lamented the division of political allies who had for a long time been "so nearly united in the defense of Old Ireland." Rudd further wrote, "We trust, that the clouds which now hang so low and threaten to darken the pathway of those who fight for justice, will soon lift and show the silver lining."[88]

Rudd's campaign for justice on behalf of Ireland also led him to speak out against the English landlords' mistreatment of the country's inhabitants. For example, Rudd opposed the expulsions of Ireland's tenants from their homes. He also decried the fact that in Ireland 9,141 evictions were written in the month ending in June 1887. In February 1889, Rudd again took aim at Irish evictions.[89] Subsequently, he drew comparisons between Ida B. Wells-Barnett's expulsion from Tennessee and England's expulsions of Ireland's citizens.[90] After 1892, however, Rudd spoke little of Ireland's plight. Instead, the editor seemed to devote more and more attention to his antilynching campaign.[91]

The *ACT*'s Advocacy for the Temporal Authority of the Pope

The campaign for the restoration of the papal domains initially seized in 1848 from Pope Pius IX (1792–1878) by Italian nationalists and later retaken for the final time in 1870 by Victor Emmanuel II (1820–1878), the first king of united Italy, was yet another concern of American Catholics throughout the years of the *ACT*'s publication.[92] A number of the exchanges in the *ACT* condemned the Italian government's seizure of papal property. In November 1888 Rudd published an exchange explaining the "Vicar of Christ" had been "robbed sacreligious[l]y of his temporal domain and of the resourses of the Propaganda." This exchange further criticized the fact that the "insane Italian revolutionists [had] taken by force and fraud the patrimony of the Holy See," and had "unjustly" "deprived the Pope of his temporal crown as Sovereign of Rome," making him a virtual "prisoner of the Vatican."[93]

A pastoral letter penned upon the conclusion of the fifth Provincial Council of Cincinnati in 1889, and published in the *ACT,* expressed similar sentiments. The letter read, "It is a matter of history that [the pope] has been deprived of his temporal principality by violence. . . . Misrepresentation and fraud were used without scruple to mislead public opinion with regard to the disposition of the people of Rome, who had remained in the greater part faithful to their ruler, the Pope."[94]

Another article printed in the *ACT* highlighted a more recent injustice committed against the church by the Italian government. In May 1890 the *ACT* reported that a convent that had been the property of the Capuchins was seized and demolished by Italian authorities. The article labeled this seizure a "piece of the grossest injustice on the part of King Humbert and his minions."[95]

Rudd's position on the recovery of property seized by Italian nationalists from the papacy in 1848 put him at odds with some American Catholics who expressed support for the advocates of Italian unity. For example, Orestes Brownson maintained sympathy for the writings of other Liberal European Catholics, including Charles de Montalembert, Pierre-Suzanne-Augustin Cochin (1823–1872), Henri-Dominique Lacordaire (1802–1861), Bishop Felix Dupanloup (1802–1878), Lord Acton (1834–1902), Richard Simpson (1820–1876), and John Henry Newman (1801–1890). Brownson and other liberal Catholics believed that were the Vatican to maintain control of the Papal States, it would doom the pope's subjects to "hopeless slavery."[96]

In the *ACT*, Rudd also published a modest number of exchanges requesting redress for the Italian government's crimes against the pope and the Catholic Church. For example, at the first gathering of the Catholic lay Congress, held in November 1889, delegates voiced their demand for the "absolute freedom of the Holy See." This freedom was for those delegates "indispensible" for the "peace of the Church and welfare of mankind." These same representatives further demanded that the autonomy being sought be "respected by all secular governments."[97]

Though Rudd did not allocate a great deal of editorial space to this issue, he did call for the restoration of the pope's temporal power. In June 1891 the editor of the *ACT* wrote:

> The truth is that the head of the Catholic Church should not be subject of any but the God who created him. He is not free in the exercise of his duties, as spiritual head of the Church, as long as he is in a position to be robbed, insulted and abused by a government

that is not only inimical, to the Church but even opposed to every idea of Christianity and revealed religion . . . . nothing short of absolute independence will place the Pope in position to carry out his mission, as the vicar of Christ.[98]

Subsequently, Rudd reminded his Catholic readers that those who believed that the Catholic world had given up on the "idea of restoring the temporal power of the pope" were deceived. He argued that "Catholics are awake to the importance of this subject, and do not hesitate to say so upon every favorable occasion."[99]

Rudd's strong support of the Vatican may have been partially conditioned by Rome's history of advocacy on behalf of African Americans. Even as southern bishops like John England (1786–1842) of South Carolina were defending American slavery, Pope Gregory XVI's (1765–1846) 1839 encyclical, *In Supremo Apostolatus,* condemned the slave trade. Similarly, Rome's advocacy is evident in its efforts to get American bishops to address the needs of blacks following the U.S. Civil War. This advocacy on behalf of blacks was demonstrated in both the Second and Third Plenary Councils held in Baltimore in 1866 and 1884 respectively.[100]

The Exploitation of People of Color: An International Focus

In October 1889, Lincoln Valle, one of the *ACT*'s traveling agents, said of Rudd, "Mr. Rudd has devoted years of study to the questions that affect the Negro race in the United States, not only, but in all the world, and is therefore thoroughly competent to discuss them in all their bearings."[101] As implied in the above quotation, Rudd's "cry for justice" was not exhausted with his campaign for equality on behalf of African Americans. Evidence from the *ACT* reveals Rudd did on a number of occasions address the plight of oppressed peoples of color throughout the world.

Rudd's Campaign Against the African Slave Trade

Rudd's concern for international questions of justice is best illustrated by his coverage and subsequent involvement with Cardinal Lavigerie's antislavery campaign in Africa. The Catholic Church's fight against African slavery was led in large part by this same prelate. Rudd began reporting on the work of Lavigerie as early as July 1887. In November 1887 Rudd printed an encyclical from Pope Leo XIII praising Lavigerie's work on behalf of Africa's captives. Then in February 1888 he published an exchange from the *Ave Maria* praising the "great apostle of the anti-slavery crusade."[102]

Rudd began regularly reporting on the cardinal's efforts only after the editor became directly involved in the campaign to end the human trafficking of Africans. His interest in the cause seems to have been excited early in 1889. In the late spring of that year, he made reference to the upcoming gathering of an antislavery conference that was to be hosted by Lavigerie in Lucerne, Switzerland, in August.[103] In a subsequent issue of the *ACT*, he published a letter from Lavigerie to Archbishop Janssens of New Orleans. In the letter, the cardinal expressed a desire to see "some representatives of the Colored population of the United States" take part in labors that were intended to "benefit the continent of their origin."[104] Expressing a genuine concern to participate in the eradication of the African slave trade, Rudd, accompanied by his eastern agent, Robert Ruffin, traveled to Europe to attend the conference. This meeting, however, was subsequently postponed due to the elections in France.[105]

Despite the cancellation of the congress, the American delegation's meeting with Lavigerie made a deep impression on the editor of the *ACT*. Both Rudd and Ruffin were warmly received by the prelate. The editor reported that the cardinal placed one arm around Ruffin, the other around him, and then "stood silent for a moment almost overcome with emotion." Lavigerie then kissed them "as a father would kiss his sons," Rudd recalled. In one of their meetings with the cardinal, Rudd and Ruffin were consecrated to raise support in the United States for the ongoing campaign against slavery in Africa.[106]

The editor of the *ACT* enthusiastically embraced Lavigerie's work. Subsequent to Rudd's meeting with the cardinal, he wrote, "There is no doubt that the great Anti-slavery Crusade, which has been inaugurated by the eloquent Cardinal to combat this gigantic evil and which has already spread throughout Europe, will finally reach our own shores." He further noted, "there is no prospect of any permanent conquest to the Catholic faith until the crimes of an unnatural slavery be done away with."[107] The following month, the editor of the *ACT* wrote, "Those who have not followed the public prints closely may not be aware of the fact that a million of people are captured annually in Africa, and either die of ill treatment or are sold into slavery. It is against this horrid traffic that the Church is directing her forces."[108]

Rudd took seriously his commission from the cardinal, and he commenced his campaign on behalf of Lavigerie's work when he returned from Europe. In October he traveled to St. Louis, where he discussed the efforts of the cardinal with those gathered at St. Elizabeth Parish.[109] In the 9 November issue of the *ACT*, Rudd printed an engraving of the prelate along with the following appeal:

> The great apostle of Africa whose portrait appears above, has attracted the attention and enlisted the sympathy of all the civilized nations of the earth in his magnificent fight for Justice and Freedom for the poor African. To encourage his work, it is intended to form anti-slavery societies in all the states of this Union. It is right and proper that America, especially the United States of America should do something to requite the Negro for the wrong done him.[110]

Rudd's efforts on behalf of Lavigerie's campaign proved to be a major point of emphasis during the second Colored Catholic Congress, which was convened in Cincinnati in July 1890. For example, Rudd's formal call for the congress stated the assembly would continue the work of the first congress and also "take into consideration the great work of Cardinal Lavergerie in his efforts to abolish the African slave trade."[111]

In the opening address of the second Colored Catholic Congress, Rudd discussed his meeting with Lavigerie. The editor also gave an account of the cardinal's subsequent commissioning of him and Ruffin.[112]As is evident from the proceedings, the congress did discuss the work of the African prelate. For example, the final resolution of the second congress demonstrates both Rudd's influence on that gathering, as well as the importance placed on Lavigerie's campaign by the other delegates. The resolution read, "His Eminence Cardinal Lavigerie having appealed to all and especially the Colored people of the United States to make every sacrifice in aid of the benighted in darkest Africa, we, therefore ask that a practical plan be immediately prepared by the Executive Committee to assist His Eminence in his noble efforts to abolish the African slave trade."[113]

Peoples of Color in the Western Hemisphere

Though not a major issue for Rudd, the editor made a few passing references to the plight of Brazil's slaves. On one occasion, Rudd informed his readers that there were 700,000 slaves in the South American country. On another occasion, Rudd reported on the reluctance of Brazil's slaveholder's to free their charges. In May 1888 slavery was abolished in Brazil, and Pope Leo XIII issued his encyclical, *In Plurimis*, celebrating this momentous event. Rudd subsequently published an exchange announcing the emancipation of the nation's 1.5 million slaves.[114]

Rudd's concern over the exploitation of nonwhites residing beyond the borders of the United States is also revealed by his decision to print an exchange detailing the "ill treatment" of Mexico's agriculture workers living in the remote parts of this Central American country. The author of this article stated the "wretched peons hire themselves out as beasts of burden to whosoever desires to lease them." This same writer also argued that with a pay of four dollars a month, many of the "poor Indian[s]" were never able to get out of debt. The contributor further stated the offspring of the indebted laborers were being forced to work to fulfill the financial obligations of their parents.[115]

Finally, Rudd editorialized about what he considered to be unjust American colonial policies. On at least two occasions in the *ACT,* Rudd condemned American diplomatic policy as it related to people of color. For example, in May 1891 Rudd published an exchange revealing what he believed to be an underhanded U.S. plan to pit the nation of Haiti and the nation of "San Domingo" against one another in an attempt to secure a coaling station in the Caribbean for American ships.[116] Rudd wrote, "It is the same old story of the white man playing one Negro against another. . . . The truth is if the white man would keep his finger out of the West India pie, there would be fewer revolutions down there, and less room to charge the Negro with incapability of self Government."[117]

Beyond a critique of American foreign policy toward black-led governments in the Caribbean, the above citation is a forceful, frontal attack on whites guilty of thwarting the efforts of blacks. It is, perhaps, as strong a critique as any in the *ACT.* Rudd's criticism was aimed at those seeking to exploit divisions among blacks. The editor further resented the fact that people of color, after being thus victimized, were open to ridicule for their presumed incompetence.

Neither Rudd's advocacy for racial justice nor his attempts to draw attention to inequities beyond the issue of race would have made the editor's perspective unique. When he addressed the school question, however, he did so as a black Catholic. In other words, Rudd not only adopted a solidly Catholic position, but he also criticized Catholic school administrators he believed were guilty of discriminating against blacks. Similarly, when the editor of the *ACT* allied himself to the cause of his fellow religionists in Ireland, he did so with a genuine empathy for the oppression of the population, for he himself had suffered under the yoke of slavery as a youth in Bardstown. In short Rudd's cry for justice offered a unique perspective on the many complex issues confronting the disenfranchised in the final two decades of the nineteenth century.

CHAPTER 6

The Colored Catholic Congress
Movement, 1889–1894

The Colored man is naturally religious. He believes; but
"Faith without good works will not save us," say the doctors
of the Church. Let us be up and doing.

D. RUDD
21 SEPTEMBER 1888

Rudd and the Roots of the Colored
Catholic Congress Movement

It is impossible to discuss Daniel Rudd's vision of justice and equality
for African Americans without an examination of the Colored Catholic
Congress movement. In fact, this organizational initiative was an embod-
iment of Rudd's campaign for justice. Moreover, the decision to organize
this group of black Catholics allowed the editor to carry the work of justice forward by enlisting additional partners. For Rudd believed collective
action was the key to ameliorating the injustices confronting America's
black population.

Rudd strongly believed in African American agency. He was equally
convinced blacks ought to take a leading role in both defending the dignity
of the race as well as in protecting the group's civil rights. In April 1887

Rudd urged blacks to stand up for themselves.[1] On another occasion, Rudd praised the efforts of those who had agitated on behalf of blacks. At the same time, however, he also insisted that the "Colored people themselves must solve the Negro problem."[2]

The Colored Catholic Congress movement, founded by visionary Daniel Rudd, held five meetings in the nineteenth century. As a result of the organizational efforts of the editor of the *ACT,* the first Colored Catholic Congress met in Washington, D.C., in January 1889. With the support of Archbishop Henry Elder of Cincinnati, the congress met in Cincinnati in July 1890. A third congress was held in Philadelphia in January 1892. Following the third Colored Catholic Congress gathering, Rudd took a less active role in the organization he had created, focusing instead on his commission to write a book detailing the proceedings of the first three congresses.[3] The fourth Colored Catholic Congress was held during the World's Fair in Chicago in September 1893. It is unclear as to whether or not Rudd participated in the fifth, and the nineteenth century's final, meeting of this body, which was convened in Baltimore in October 1894.[4]

The Colored Catholic Congress movement appears to have been a hybridization of two movements. The first of these was the African American convention movement, which though established in 1830 had found its most recent manifestation in T. Thomas Fortune's call to create the National Afro-American League (NAAL).[5] The link between Rudd's Colored Catholic Congress movement and the African American convention movement was made by the editor himself. For example, in May 1889 Rudd discussed the historic character of the first gathering of the Colored Catholic Congress held a few months before in Washington, D.C. He said of the meeting, "It will stand as a buoy in the stream of progress, about which will cluster many pleasant profitable memories." In this same article, Rudd made reference to the first gathering of the African American convention movement, which had assembled in Philadelphia in September 1830. The editor of the *ACT* recalled with gratitude the work of the delegates to this previous assembly that had met almost sixty years earlier.[6]

A second source of inspiration for the Colored Catholic Congress movement was the Catholic congress movement begun in Europe and carried on by various national groups in the United States, including the German Catholics. Rudd's exposure to an American manifestation of these nationalistic congresses came by way of his encounter with the German Central Verein. Speaking before this assembly on one occasion, Rudd declared, "I have watched with intense interest the work of this great and broad-souled organization, because my race is about to engage in a work to help convert and educate those millions now in darkness."[7]

In June 1887 the *ACT* informed its readers that Fr. William Tappert of Covington, Kentucky, was in Chicago, "arraying for the great national Convention of German Catholics of America." In September 1887 Rudd traveled to Chicago in order to attend this gathering. The delegates to this meeting discussed a number of social issues, including membership in the Knights of Labor, education, and the German press. These were some of the same types of topics delegates to the Colored Catholic Congresses would subsequently address a little over a year later in Washington, D.C.[8]

In May 1887 Rudd proposed the idea of organizing an interracial congress for all English-speaking Catholics. Rudd wrote, "Let us have a great Congress of English-speaking Catholics. The Catholic Hierarchy of England, Ireland and America are deeply interested in this great movement. This will include all the races."[9] Though it is unclear why Rudd gave up on this particular idea, it is evident that by spring 1887 he was weighing the merits of Catholic collective action.

Through June 1887 Rudd continued to trumpet the need for black collective action. On one occasion, he contrasted the strength of Cincinnati's unified German population with the oppressed condition of the divided African American community. Rudd appealed to African Americans to unite in collective action. He urged, "Let us unite, brethren, in the interest of the American Negro; let us bind ourselves together, to act as a unit; let us agree that no public man or measure shall receive our consideration or support, that fails to take the view that we too, are a factor that may help or hurt. And when we are feared we will be respected."[10] In the above appeal, Rudd's faith in African American agency is once again articulated.

In the 17 June 1887 edition of the *ACT,* Rudd suggested the Afro-American League proposed by Fortune should be "[promptly] effected." He further urged his readers:

> Let us organize and convince parties that we, like other races, are susceptible to the influences which go to make them respected in a community. . . . Let us cultivate the same spirit of determined

agitation and unrest until the proper wholesome recognition comes.
. . . For more than two hundred and fifty years we have suffered
outrage and oppression from American law and pre[j]udice and it
is high time that we enter a protest. Let us come together then,
form this league and ere many days we may be sure of an awakening
among American politicians, statesmen and plain citizens.[11]

In July 1887, Rudd, bristling from an insult to blacks that had been
printed in the *Commercial Gazette,* again chided his target audience for
their lack of "race pride and cohesion."[12] In the editor's criticism of
African American collective action, he echoed the sentiments of Ida B.
Wells-Barnett, who had earlier declared blacks were a "disorganized,
divided mass of power and intellect."[13] Similarly, Rudd spoke out against
the "plantation philosophy," which, according to the editor, kept African
Americans divided. He wrote, "we are so dificult [*sic*] to convince of the
power of union and combination."[14]

Even as Rudd was urging African Americans to come together into
Fortune's proposed Afro-American League, the editor of the *ACT* was
paying careful attention to the deliberations of the German Central
Verein. In September 1887 Rudd attended the above-referenced German
Catholic congress meeting held in Chicago. Immediately following this
gathering, Rudd lamented, "The Germans are organized, the Irish are
organized, the Americans all, are organized except the poor black men."[15]
Rudd returned from Chicago more convinced of the potential of black
collective action. Following Rudd's return, he published the description
and constitution of Fortune's proposed Afro-American League. Moreover,
the editor once again endorsed the National Afro-American League. He
wrote, "We commend the views of Mr. Fortune as they are evidently in
the right direction."[16]

Rudd proposed the gathering of a congress of African American
Catholics in the 4 May 1888 edition of the *ACT.* He believed black
Catholics should strive to be the "leaven" of the race, raising the people
"not only in the eye of God but before men." In Rudd's proposal, he
also spoke of the merits of organization. "To personal worth, association
greatly adds," Rudd claimed. The editor of the *ACT* further trumpeted
the potential force of collective action. He wrote, "What a trifle is a drop
of rain! The terrible storms, however, which devastes [*sic*] towns, uproot
the sturdy oaks, sweep away the growing crops, and deal destruction on

all sides are but drops of rain united and pitted in the wild outburst of the elements." Rudd believed the leaders of the race should "gather together from every city in the Union in some suitable place, where under the blessing of Holy Mother, Church, they may get to know one another and take up the cause of the race." Rudd also speculated that such a meeting would involve addressing "questions directly affecting the race, irrespective of religion." He further presumed views would be exchanged and a united course of action adopted.[17]

In the 11 May 1888 issue of the *ACT,* Rudd urged his readers, both black and white, to express their opinions as to the merits of such a meeting.[18] He believed one of the "most important works" of the proposed congress would be to ascertain the exact number of black Catholics, "their avocations, their condition intellectually, morally and materially." Having accomplished this goal, Rudd stated the congress would next aim to "seek to better the condition" of these same individuals, thus bettering "all human conditions." In the next issue of the *ACT* the editor asked that the "prayers of the Catholic world" be raised on behalf of the proposed meeting.[19]

In June 1888 Rudd actively promoted the idea of holding a congress. At a gathering of the Catholic Young Men's National Union in Cincinnati Rudd discussed his proposed congress. The group answered approvingly with applause. Further, Fr. John Mackey, who would become associate editor of the *ACT,* offered the use of the cathedral for the proposed meeting. Rudd concluded, "Once more the falsehood that the Church abets discrimination is nailed."[20]

In the 8 June 1888 issue of the *ACT,* Rudd's article "The Proposed Congress of Colored Catholics: What Can It Do?" addressed the work Catholics would need to take up at the proposed meeting.[21] Tellingly, it speaks nothing of black Catholics getting to know one another, nor does it mention the delegates aiding members of the Catholic clergy in propagating the faith among African Americans. Instead, it emphasized another initial goal of the congress: bettering the condition of the race. In other words, the proposed congress was not merely concerned with sizing up the makeup of America's black Catholics, nor was it exclusively about converting blacks to Catholicism. Rather, it was about addressing issues of justice, about discovering the ways in which impediments to the recognition of the full equality of African Americans might be dismantled.

The goal of bettering the condition of the race seems to embody a more direct aspect of Rudd's campaign to promote racial justice. In the above-cited article on the congress, the editor began by declaring African Americans had "many grievances." He then explored a number of these existing injustices. For example, Rudd lamented the fact that blacks in the North as well as in the South were being barred from learning or practicing trades such as blacksmithing, wheel righting, carpentry, and bricklaying. Rudd also argued it was wrong for blacks to be denied factory work because of racial prejudice. Part of the dilemma for African Americans, according to Rudd, was the result of their being denied membership in trade unions. Consequently, he believed the congress ought to be invested with some authority. From this elected assembly a memorial on behalf of blacks could be addressed to Catholics in trade unions. In support of the memorial, Rudd proposed a "carefully selected" delegation from this same body be sent to the upcoming convention of the Knights of Labor in order to urge its adoption.[22]

With regard to issues the congress would address, Rudd stated that foreign mechanics from Ireland, England, Holland, and Germany were being routinely given preferential treatment over the country's African American population. The editor stated his conviction that the congress's work would capture the attention of Catholic bishops and priests who would in turn recognize the "injustice of robbing the Colored people of trades and factory work." At the same time, Rudd believed these same church officials would secure "every means in their power to destroy such a contemptible barrier." The above citation demonstrates the editor's convictions concerning the important role the Catholic Church would play in the campaign to achieve justice and full equality for African Americans.[23]

Another important goal of the congress was to promote black pride. In the 22 June 1888 issue of the *ACT,* Rudd wrote the following:

> We had watched for years the tendency on the part of some people to ignore the Negro as a man and citizen in the United States. We had noted the progress from other parts of the earth. We had seen that although our race had spent two and a half centuries here laboring without pay, when civilization had become civilized enough to let us walk about the country, our race had served so long, so faithfully, and received only kicks and robbery for reward, the robber spirit of caste discrimination, the crop-mortgage system, the prison labor

lease system, the unequal tax system, all kindred evils, remnants of a barbarous past, still stood Gibraltar like to bar our advancement; we thought that if we would turn the attention of our people to the moral truths and the exact equality of the human family before God, as taught by Holy Mother Church Universal that spouse of Christ our Lord would lift us as she has the mighty Caucassian [sic] race.[24]

Rudd went on to emphasize the achievements of blacks like Augustus Tolton, Frederick Douglass, and the Oblate Sisters of Providence. The recognition of the achievements of prominent African Americans is consistent with Rudd's commitment to justice and equality. In spite of claims to the contrary by critics of the race, Rudd was able to highlight individuals who had demonstrated remarkable achievements and virtue.[25]

In September 1888 Rudd discussed the church's missional efforts toward blacks. In this article, however, he once again emphasized the need for black Catholics to take up the work on their own behalf. Rudd wrote, "The proposed Congress is intended to to [sic] awaken the Negro Catholic to a sense of his duty. Important questions will be submitted and discussed. Steps should be taken to provide competent Catholic teachers to meet the growing needs of the Colored people in the South. . . . We must work ourselves if we expect to accomplish anything."[26]

The official call for the first meeting of the Colored Catholic Congress movement was issued in the 6 October 1888 edition of the ACT. Each Colored Catholic organization was entitled to one delegate for every "five-hundred members or fraction thereof." In order that delegates might be elected to attend the congress, the call urged the formation of black Catholic organizations. Parishes were also permitted to send one delegate. The official call for the congress was signed by Rudd, P. J. Augustine of Pennsylvania, Felix Pye, Henry L. Jones of Louisiana, Robert White, Robert L. Ruffin of Massachusetts, Charles H. Butler and W. S. Lofton of Washington, D.C., Wm. E. Blackstone of Ohio, Isaac Moten of Indiana, and John Page.[27]

In the official call for the congress, Rudd reasoned that "we have not as much information as we should have of the number, location and progress of the race in Catholicity." He further asked that black Catholics "do all in [their] power to aid in the conversion and education" of the race. Efforts to evangelize and instruct blacks seem to have introduced a somewhat modified agenda for the historic gathering. It is conceivable

Archbishop Elder or John Slattery desired to see this less controversial focus emphasized. It is also possible Cardinal Gibbons expressed concern over the possibility the gathering might agitate beyond the bounds of "wisdom, prudence, charity and discretion." In the end, Rudd did not mention the need to address the grievances of African Americans in the editor's official call for the first Colored Catholic Congress.[28]

As might be expected, in Gibbons's opening sermon to the congress the prelate made no reference to taking up the grievances of the race. Instead, he proposed the merits of discussing Christian education, temperance, and the "practice of economy." He further urged the assembly to "resolve to unite with your pastors in promoting every good cause, and to aid them in every possible way in the great work in which they are engaged."[29]

As the date for the meeting approached, it appears Rudd also avoided any suggestion that the congress would air the grievances of African Americans. Perhaps the editor adopted this approach because he feared that to do otherwise would have caused concern for church leaders who had sanctioned the meeting. Whether or not the more confrontational agenda, which included the airing of grievances, was approved by Gibbons, Elder, or Slattery is uncertain. What is clear is that delegates took the opportunity afforded them at the congress both to address discrimination and to appeal to Catholics to join the campaign for the social, moral, and intellectual uplift of the nation's blacks.[30]

In the 13 October 1888 issue of the *ACT*, Rudd again foregrounded the important role the church would play in the establishment of justice and the recognition of the full equality of blacks.

> The light of civilization of the present is so strong that no race can stand within its sun-like beams without improving in some particular. If we ask the cause of all this, the answer would be that it is one of the results of Christianity. . . . We submit the proposition that Christianity, in the breadth of her doctrines, has taught mankind the brother love, the justice and the intelligence to recognize, as far as is done, the absolute equality of one man with another, no matter what his race. But Christianity, pure and simple, is Catholicity; hence through the Catholic Church, which alone was commissioned to teach all nations, all this goodness has come.[31]

The First Colored Catholic Congress

On Monday, 1 January 1889, the delegates began arriving at St. Augustine's Parish in Washington, D.C. Spalding estimates eighty-five delegates attended the first meeting of the Colored Catholic Congress. When the doors were opened the crowds pressed in and filled every seat; those who could not find a seat gathered in the church's aisles. By the time the service began at 10:30 a.m., there was no remaining standing room. Augustus Tolton, the country's only openly recognized African American priest, celebrated High Mass.[32]

The honor of delivering the opening sermon fell to Cardinal Gibbons. In his homily, the prelate discussed the seamless character of the Catholic Church. Gibbons told the assembled body that the church "knows no North nor South." Not even the Civil War could divide her, the cardinal boasted. Most important, Gibbons declared the Catholic Church was a body that knew no "Jew, Greek, or barbarian." He argued, "Our Savior broke down the wall that divided men and made us one family; we know no race." Gibbons further declared that in the church there is "no distinction in church on account of race or condition." Evidence for the veracity of the cardinal's claim had been witnessed by the assembled delegates, according to Gibbons. For during the meeting, Tolton had offered up the "Holy Sacrifice" assisted by two white Josephite priests.[33]

Following Gibbons's sermon, W. H. Smith of Washington, D.C., stated the purpose of the gathering was not to carry on "doctrinal or theological discussion." These matters, Smith declared, would be taken up by duly appointed teachers of the church. Instead, the delegates had come to discuss the needs of African Americans and by "conference and consultation to try and devise ways and means of bettering" the condition of blacks, "both religiously and socially."[34]

The congress resumed its meetings on Wednesday morning at 10 a.m. On this second day, a committee of permanent organization was formed, and Rudd was subsequently elected president of the congress. Following his election, the editor spoke to the delegates. In his address, it is possible to discern both Rudd's strong support of black agency, as well as his commitment to a church-centered vision of justice. The equality presumed in the phrase "Fatherhood of God and Brotherhood of Man" provided the basis for the editor's understanding of justice. For

Rudd, it was the Catholic Church that represented the "only genuine effort to prove the fatherhood of God, and the brotherhood of man." Similarly, the editor of the *ACT* claimed "the fatherhood of God and the brotherhood of man are enunciated by the Catholic Church in no doubtful terms."[35]

The most important document produced at the first Colored Congress was its final resolution. This statement was subsequently disseminated across the country. The resolution of the first Colored Catholic Congress acknowledged the current state of injustice existing in society. It also declared that the "inalienable rights given to every man in the very dawn of creation . . . the sacred rights of justice and of humanity" were "still sadly wounded." Despite the present circumstances the resolution expressed the conviction that the Catholic Church would "by the innate force of her truth, gradually dispel the prejudices unhappily prevailing amongst so many of our misguided people." The document committed the delegates to work for the establishment of Catholic schools for African Americans. The resolution also called for the creation of literary societies to foster "social and intellectual improvement." Blacks were further urged to practice the "self-sacrificing virtue of temperance."[36]

In this same resolution African Americans sought redress for the many injustices forced upon them. For example, an appeal was made to labor organizations and trade unions to admit blacks. Businesses were also encouraged to hire African Americans. Similarly, the practice of renting poorly lighted, inadequately ventilated, and shabbily constructed tenements to blacks was condemned. This same resolution recognized the merits of industrial schools. It acknowledged the vital community role played by orphanages, hospitals, and asylums and praised the work of the "religious orders of the Catholic Church" laboring on behalf of the "African race." Finally, the resolution pledged a commitment to carry out the pertinent mandates of the Third Plenary Council (Baltimore III) held in 1884.[37]

Response to the Congress

In Rudd's mind the meeting of the first Colored Catholic Congress marked a pivotal moment in the history of the race. Further, he believed that the gathering evidenced the sincerity of the church's efforts on the part of the country's black population. Rudd remained convinced that a genuine "brotherly love" in society could only be attained through the efforts of the church. Justice would be established only when all groups of America's "heterogeneous population" were afforded the right to "move in the same plane" illumining the "many parts of a homogenious [*sic*] whole." Rudd observed that the Catholic Church presented a "common family" speaking a "common language," and that no "distinction on account of race or color" would be made.[38]

The fact that other Catholic and African American newspapers viewed the first Colored Catholic Congress meeting as important is evidenced by their coverage of the gathering. For example, the *Philadelphia Standard* observed that the meeting might teach politicians and humanitarian philanthropists that there was a way by which the "race problem" could be solved. This same writer declared the race question might be settled if the white race would begin to treat blacks as "dear brothers in the Lord."[39] The *Catholic Standard* (presumably the same publication as cited above) informed its readers most of the 200 delegates to the first Colored Catholic Congress held in Washington, D.C., hailed from the South, but the North and West provided the spokespersons for the gathering. The newspaper also claimed "immense good" would result from future meetings of this organization.[40]

After the congress, the *Chicago Conservator*, a black publication, reported that the Catholic Church was "determined to make a spirited struggle for converts to its faith." A contributor to this same publication reasoned this initiative would be successful because, though other denominations were guilty of maintaining the color line, the Catholic Church was not.[41] Following the congress, black Protestant newspapers also reported on the historic meeting. On one occasion, Rudd printed an exchange from the A.M.E. Zion Church's *Star of Zion*. The contributor to this publication contrasted the Protestant Church's treatment of blacks with that of the relatively progressive Catholic Church. The former fostered a "spirit of caste," the latter, "as a rule," showed "little race prejudice." This same publication further noted that whites and blacks worshipped together in the Catholic Church without the "slightest apparent friction."[42]

Given the success of the first gathering of the Colored Catholic Congress movement, Rudd and its leaders decided to continue the work of the assembly. Four additional congresses were held, though it appears Rudd took an active leadership role in only two of the subsequent meetings, the one he hosted in Cincinnati in 1890 and the one held in Philadelphia in 1892. In his analysis of the congress movement, Davis observes that beginning with the second gathering of the Colored Catholic Congress the assembly began addressing more "substantive issues." He further points out that after its 1889 meeting delegates began thinking in terms of cohesive action and permanent organization. He also discerns a "certain radicalization" of the movement after its initial meeting. More important, as black Catholic leaders worked collectively to address the concerns of their constituents, Davis identifies the emergence of a "black Catholic theological consciousness."[43]

The Second Colored Catholic Congress

The delegates to the second Colored Catholic Congress gathered for the celebration of the Solemn High Mass at the Cathedral of St. Peter in Chains in Cincinnati at 9 a.m. on 9 July 1890. Slattery subsequently reported about 125 delegates in attendance. Given the absence of Archbishop Elder, Fr. John Mackey, the pastor of the Cathedral of St. Peter in Chains, delivered the opening sermon. Mackey had already joined Rudd on the staff of the *ACT* by this time, having assumed the duties of associate editor of the newspaper in May 1889.[44]

It will be recalled that in Mackey's sermon delivered to the delegates of the second Colored Catholic Congress, the priest voiced his opposition to "amalgamation." A careful reading of the *ACT* suggests Mackey's out-of-place comments were made in response to Archbishop Ireland's 4 May speech delivered only two months earlier. Though in his opening address Mackey made no direct reference to Ireland's speech, it is evident the Cincinnati priest opposed the archbishop of St. Paul's call for the immediate recognition of the full social equality of blacks.[45]

Though Mackey opposed Ireland's complete obliteration of the color line, he did, nonetheless, employ Rudd's rhetoric concerning the "Fatherhood of God and Brotherhood of Man." Moreover, Mackey assured the delegates that the Catholic Church would champion the cause of blacks by defending their rights, including the right to learn and practice all trades, to sit at the table of gentlemen in public hostelries, to attend Catholic parish schools, and to be accepted into Catholic charitable confraternities and benevolent societies.[46]

Some of the assembled delegates, euphoric over Ireland's previously published remarks on social equality for blacks, must have been put off by Mackey's opening address. Delegates Charles Butler and William S. Lofton cast doubt on the associate editor's more sanguine portrayal of the church's relationship to its black members. Particularly, Butler and Lofton took issue with Mackey's claims regarding black access to Catholic schools. Though there is no indication in the *ACT* that the delegates expressed a direct rebuttal to Mackey's comments regarding "amalgamation," there is evidence to suggest Mackey was forced to retreat some from his previously outlined, more circumscribed platform of social equality.[47]

On the second day of the meeting, Archbishop Elder offered encouraging words to the delegates assembled "not as a race but as equals." Bishop John Ambrose Watterson (1844–1899), of Columbus, Ohio, and Bishop Camillus Paul Maes (1846–1915), of Covington, Kentucky, also addressed the assembly on the second day. In an article penned for *Donahoe's Magazine,* Slattery detailed the speeches given by Elder, Watterson, and Maes. He did not, however, record the remarks of the African American speakers, including Rudd, Lofton, and Butler. This omission leaves one with the impression that the Josephite may not have held these three black congressional leaders in high regard. Or perhaps his refusal to publish their speeches was because Lofton's and Butler's remarks were more critical of the church's efforts on behalf of blacks.[48]

On the second day of the meeting of the Colored Catholic Congress, William S. Lofton spoke. In his address, Lofton declared blacks would "hail the dawn of that day when Justice will hold the field a conquerer [*sic*]." The delegate further named a number of allies who had joined the African American campaign for justice. Not surprisingly, first on his list of names was Archbishop Ireland. In this same address, Lofton placed great importance on education. He stated it was second only to a person's need to know God. Lofton acknowledged some Catholic missionaries were prejudiced against blacks. He told the assembled delegates the "Catholic layman or Missionary who refuses to do what is in his power for the conversion of the Negro, simply to humor a petty prejudice, [should] blush with shame before God and man." Later in this same address, the Washington, D.C., native illumined the need to make available industrial education for blacks. Moreover, the delegate argued Catholics had given little attention to the issue of black education. Lofton concluded, "we value our religion and Catholic training; we marvel that Divines of the church do not support their teaching by having Catholic Colleges and schools open their doors to at least those of our Colored children who are well behaved and able to pay."[49]

Charles H. Butler, a clerk in the U.S. Treasury Department's Division of Appointments and also a native of the nation's capital, read a paper at the congress. He prefaced his remarks with praise for the work of Archbishop Ireland. Such a statement must have been perceived as a rebuttal to Mackey's more conservative stand on social equality for blacks. Butler spoke to the fact that many African Americans were being lost to the church every year due to the small number of Catholic schools willing to admit black students. This same speaker called for the establishment of a "Catholic National High Industrial School" in Washington, D.C., a gesture Butler believed would "remedy a great injustice and secure to our holy mother many of her children." Butler, a strong advocate of vocational training, observed that "Industrial Education is the great need for our boys it will give them the most complete control of their faculties will make them alert, accurate, ready physically as well as mentally for the performance of the duties of life." Butler further speculated that the racial prejudice plaguing blacks might well be the result of their inability to secure more prestigious jobs.[50]

Tellingly, the most rousing speech delivered at the gathering of the second Colored Catholic Congress was offered by a priest from John Ireland's archdiocese, Fr. Harrison who served as rector of the cathedral located in St. Paul, Minnesota. In his speech, Harrison spoke of the "absolute religious equality" existing in the church. He told the assembled delegates that "there are no such persons as Colored Catholics." He contended, "In matters of race the Church is color-blind." Harrison's position paralleled Ireland's more controversial stand on social equality. The applause that greeted Harrison following his address lasted several minutes. Harrison's speech on the "problem of social equality" almost certainly placed Mackey in a rather uncomfortable position.[51]

Though he did not record his speech in the *ACT*, Rudd subsequently editorialized on Harrison's address. Rudd's vision of justice was supported

by a version of social equality akin to what Harrison and Ireland had promulgated. As to the issue of full equality and justice for blacks, it is likely
that Harrison's comments best expressed the sentiments of the congressional delegates. Rudd wrote, "Father Harrison made a speech that will
ring in the ears of the foolishly prejudiced for many a day. He could fill
any hall in this city with Colored people any time he might find it con-
venient to pay us a call." Slattery also commented on Harrison's rousing
speech: "In his speech, [Harrison] *out-Irelanded* Archbishop Ireland
himself."[52]

On the final day of the meeting, a set of resolutions drafted during
previous sessions was read to the delegates. These resolutions embodied
practical steps that, if implemented in society, would have allowed blacks
to more fully experience the equality Rudd was promoting. In these resolutions a commitment was made to provide African Americans with
religious education. Also, delegates were asked to advise governing
authorities as to the protection of the civil rights of all citizens. Further,
trade unions were called on to admit blacks, and storekeepers were
encouraged to hire African American clerks. A resolution condemning
the African slave trade was also read. Finally, a statement promising "filial
obedience" to the church was offered, along with a commitment to
recruit men and women to fill the ranks of the clergy. These resolutions
were approved prior to the adjournment of the meeting. Philadelphia
was chosen as the host site of the third Colored Catholic Congress, which
was to be held in January 1892.[53]

Following the second congress, Rudd was confined to his bed for
several days because of illness. The nature of the malady is unclear. It is
reasonable to assume, however, that the stress of organizing and hosting
such a gathering, combined with the criticism he was reported to have
received during the meeting concerning the quality of the *ACT,* were
contributing factors.[54]

The official statement of the second Colored Catholic Congress was
not published by Rudd until 30 August 1890, about six weeks after the
adjournment of the gathering. Rudd observed that the second congress
had put forward the delegate's "simple, straightforward," and "respectful"
demands, claiming as they did the "rights of simple but complete justice
whether in Church or State." Catholics were addressed directly in the resolution. The document read, "We ask more particularly of our Catholic

brethren that the teachings of the Church, Who, in her expansive charity embraces equally and to the fullest extent all the sons of Adam whether collectively or individually, be cheerfully and thoroughly practiced."[55]

The statement adopted by the second congress in many ways resembled the justice priorities expressed in the resolutions passed in the first congress. For example, there was in the statement adopted in Cincinnati an appeal to open schools for African Americans. There was also a call to open trade unions, as well as a plea for white business owners to hire black laborers. The document also created a committee to look into the establishment of agricultural and industrial schools. The statement recognized the work of Cardinal Lavigerie and called for a plan to aid the prelate in his efforts to abolish the slave trade. Further, the resolution adopted at the second Colored Catholic Congress urged Catholics to uphold in "every way" the work of the colored sisters, especially with regard to the "preservation and education" of black orphans. The document endorsed the virtue of temperance. Also, working men were encouraged to join approved industrial leagues and workingmen's clubs. Young men were further encouraged to form conferences of "St. Vincent of Paul." Tellingly, the resolution expressed its "deep and lasting appreciation" for the "kind words" spoken on behalf of blacks by the "most sincere champion of the race," Archbishop Ireland.[56]

Slattery's account of the Second Colored Catholic Congress included a report on the delegates' alleged dissatisfaction with the quality of Rudd's newspaper. He reported that the *Tribune* was the object of much discussion in which the assembled delegates severely criticized the *ACT*'s "make-up, matter," and "poor paper." Slattery further noted that Rudd had promised to improve the paper. The Josephite hoped this improvement would be accomplished after Rudd moved the paper to Philadelphia. In its new location, Slattery believed the "talent and energy" of Fr. Patrick McDermott would ensure the *ACT* would "become a source of incalculable good to the negro race." Rudd made mention of these discussions neither in the *ACT* nor in his subsequent book on the congresses.[57]

Slattery's criticism of the *ACT* is puzzling because there had been no prior indication that the newspaper failed to meet the expectations of its subscribers. In fact, during the first gathering of the Colored Catholic Congress the *ACT* was praised by delegates for its "useful and entertaining reading."[58] Moreover, the *Journal*, which was subsequently established by those reported to have been disappointed with the quality of Rudd's newspaper, does not appear in any way to eclipse the *ACT.* Lackner has speculated that Slattery's displeasure with the *ACT* may have had more to do with the fact that the Josephite exercised no control over it. That Rudd's newspaper offered competition to the two Josephite publications, *St. Joseph's Advocate* and the *Colored Harvest,* may have also created animosity between him and Slattery.[59]

In August 1890 Rudd urged his readers to begin organizing the next meeting of the Colored Catholic Congress, which was to be hosted by Fr. Patrick McDermott in Philadelphia, in January 1892. The details of the congress held in Cincinnati become clearer in later issues of the *ACT.* For example, because of his comments during the meeting in the Queen City, W. J. Smith of Washington, D.C., earned himself the title "Radical Smith." Reflecting on his contribution to the gathering, Smith recalled how he had told the assembled delegates he was there "as a Catholic and a Colored man, a Catholic in every sense of the word." He further recalled how he had informed the delegates that "the Catholic Church had able defenders and needed no defense at his hand." Rather, he had come to Cincinnati to "speak for his race," which was being "discriminated against." For Smith's part, he was following the advice of Archbishop Ireland, who had prior to the second congress urged each delegate to contend for their rights until every right had been secured "as a Catholic and a man."[60]

Following the second gathering of the congress, neither Rudd nor Slattery recalled any action on the part of the delegates that one might construe as radical or unduly critical of the Catholic Church. There is, however, evidence to suggest while in Cincinnati members of the second congress, emboldened by Archbishop Ireland's public comments on social equality and the rights of African Americans, did in fact more freely voice their grievances against the Catholic Church. Evidence of the radicalization of the congress movement can be discerned in an article by C. H. Butler, in which he defended the "manly manner" of the delegates who "demanded equal and impartial justice from the hands of their white fellow Catholic laymen at Cincinnati." Butler's comments appear to have been given to assure dissatisfied black Catholics residing in Washington, D.C., that the delegates sent to represent them did, in fact, express the black Catholic community's frustration over the church's discriminatory practices.[61]

Plans for a Third Meeting

A gifted cadre of black Catholic leaders was called on to plan the third meeting of the Colored Catholic Congress. Pennsylvania's congressional delegate, P. J. Augustine, appears to have headed up the effort. In the gathering's planning phase, Rudd likely served only in an advisory capacity. It may have been that Rudd chose to work in the background because of the friction between the *ACT*'s editor and the Pennsylvania delegation. It will be recalled that the first edition of the *Journal,* Philadelphia's rival black Catholic newspaper, was published only weeks after the conclusion of the third congress. Rudd must have known for some time prior to the upcoming congress that Catholic leaders in Philadelphia were planning a rival newspaper. To Rudd's credit, he continued to cooperate with these delegates.[62]

Prior to the meeting in Philadelphia, the editor of the *ACT* was asked by the executive committee to recruit delegates from the southern and western parts of the country.[63] In July 1891 Rudd bemoaned the fact that in the two previous congresses New Orleans, Mobile, Florida, and the Far Western states had little if any representation at all. Rudd further explained that he would soon be visiting principal southern points for recruiting purposes.[64] Departing for New Orleans on 9 August, he particularly wanted to make certain that the region, with its 75,000 black Catholics, was represented in Philadelphia.[65]

On Thursday evening, 13 August, in New Orleans's St. Alphonsus Hall, Rudd addressed a small crowd on the "necessity of being represented at the coming congress." He urged his hearers to "grasp the opportunity that presented itself to better [their] condition," an opportunity Rudd believed was extended by the Catholic Church. The *ACT* subsequently reported that Rudd spoke on "Catholicity and its benign influence on the Negro." He urged his audience to compare the "work of the other churches to that of the one Catholic and Apostolic church." The editor of the *ACT* further boasted that the church "knew no color, no race, no nationality."[66]

Taking into account the fact Rudd himself reported the event in the *ACT,* it nonetheless appears he was well received by his audience. The newspaper subsequently reported his address was frequently interrupted by applause. Rudd's visit to New Orleans was unexpectedly cut short by "important business." The editor failed to disclose the nature of the business, but he did promise to go back after a few days.[67]

The official call for the third Colored Catholic Congress was issued 24 November 1891. Delegates were expected to bring the following information with them:

> *What is the estimated Colored population of your city or county?*
> *What is the estimated Colored Catholic population?*
> *How many children attending Sunday School or Catechism classes?*
> *How many Catholic schools in your city?*
> *How many children attending Parochial School?*
> *What faculties are there for the education of boys over twelve years?* [68]

In December of the same year, Rudd looked forward to the coming assembly and expressed his desire to see the congress "extend somewhat" the power of the executive committee. Further, he outlined his ideas for the agenda, highlighting the need to discuss the establishment of schools, the work of the "Colored clergy and Colored Sisters," "uniformed and benevolent societies," as well as the need to establish industrial schools. Rudd also argued the "duty" of the congress moved beyond the spiritual welfare of black Catholics. He stated the congress should "see that avenues now barred against . . . be thrown open." Rudd concluded his editorial by suggesting "zeal, prudence, humility, energy, courage and determination" ought to "characterize every word and act" of the delegates. [69]

The month before the proposed meeting Rudd traveled to Washington, D.C., to meet Lofton. In all likelihood the two men met in order to work out details for the upcoming congress. Rudd appears to have been quite impressed with Lofton's preparations. The editor wrote, "If the Congress is not a success, he must not be blamed, for he has written personal letters to every dignitary in the land, [he] also has sent 12 copies of the case to each member of the executive committee." He also commented on the "young gentlemen of push and energy . . . deeply interested in the Congress." [70]

A Third Gathering of the Colored Catholic Congress

On 5 January 1892, in the city of Philadelphia, Archbishop Ryan gave the opening address before the delegates gathered for the third Colored Catholic Congress. The archbishop appears to have attempted to reign in expectations regarding any immediate acknowledgment of the full social equality of blacks. Ryan recalled the slow progress made by the church in its efforts to abolish slavery. The recognition of the equality of blacks would also take time, he suggested. In this same address, the archbishop explained that the assembled delegates had, in fact, achieved political equality. He further stated "other equalities" must be worked out "in God's own time." He told the assembled delegates not to expect too much to be "performed at once." "A betterment of your condition, to be permanent, must come gradually," he continued. The gradualist approach articulated in the speech seems to run contrary to the spirit of Ireland's call for the immediate elimination of the color line.[71]

Ryan's opening address may have been intended to discourage delegates from voicing their criticisms of the Catholic Church, but the criticisms came. For example, Charles H. Butler's resolution, which was adopted by the assembly, detailed the church's discriminatory behavior toward its African American members. Whereas in 1884 Baltimore III had prescribed religious training for Catholic children, Butler claimed blacks had been "deprived" of educational opportunities due to the "unjust discrimination made against colored children."[72] The normally diplomatic Rudd who had earlier been unanimously elected as national lecturer for the congress also delivered a critical paper condemning the practice of denying blacks admittance into Catholic secondary schools. The affected youth, Rudd claimed, too often "become lukewarm or drift away from the safe guidance of the church" because they are forced into public schools to finish their training.[73]

There were two main issues addressed by the delegates to the third Colored Catholic Congress. The first was the establishment of a permanent congressional organization. The second was the campaign to build industrial and vocational schools for African Americans. The permanent congressional organization was to be a source of the ongoing implementation of the designs set forth in the congress. It would serve as an umbrella organization covering the activities of the various parish societies that had sent delegates to the meeting. Fredrick McGhee (1861–1912), the first black admitted to the bar in the Upper Midwest, and an emerging leader of the Colored Catholic Congress, wanted an executive board to be formed that would then choose this executive council. Each society was to pay a tax into the executive council based on the society's membership. McGhee also wanted to establish a building and loan association to aid in the construction of black institutions and churches. A resolution for the establishment of a permanent congressional organization was approved at the third meeting of the Colored Catholic Congress.[74]

A second key issue taken up by the delegates to the third congress was the need to secure vocational training for blacks. To this end, William Easton, a delegate from Texas, emphasized the importance of establishing "industrial" schools. This same southern delegate proposed that the building of churches for black Catholics be temporarily halted in order that the "energies of the people" might be "devoted solely to this great project."[75] Similarly, President James A. Spencer (1849–1911), who had previously served in the Reconstruction legislature in his home state of South Carolina, encouraged the delegates to be "contented with the present number of churches" established for "special use" of black Catholics. The South Carolinian urged them instead to push for the building of schools to benefit the race. He declared blacks wanted to be "placed on an equal footing with all other classes of American citizens," a practice Spencer argued was the way in which the church always treated the "races of men." This same speaker highlighted the need to establish the "most sacred unity of Christian brotherhood among her children." He further anticipated the day when the "sacred mission of the Church would be realized, practiced as preached, and her children made to feel that brothers" they were, whatever their "color or nationality."[76]

In an apparent attempt to expand educational opportunities for blacks, Delegate Robert N. Wood of New York sought to form a committee of three to investigate charges that blacks were being discriminated against by Catholic schools and other institutions. The proposal was approved. Delegate Fredrick McGhee also spoke out against school segregation. He stated that though "common equality of man" was like the "enchanted palace" told of in fairy tales, the segregated school system fostered among whites the "irreligious, ignorant, blind," and "unjust prejudice." Moreover, the delegate from St. Paul was concerned with the widely held belief that blacks were inferior to whites. In defense of African Americans, he called on the words of one of the "foremost champions of the Negro cause," Archbishop Ireland, who had earlier declared that the difference between the races was "the merest accident of color." The third congress adjourned on 7 January 1892, naming Pittsburgh as the site for the fourth congress to be held in September 1893. Intuiting the significance of the proceedings, President Spencer offered a resolution to have the delegates share the expense of a publication detailing "present and proceeding" congresses. The congress movement turned to Rudd to carry out this task. Consequently, in 1893 Rudd published his first book, *Three Afro-American Congresses*.[77]

The *Journal*: A Rival Newspaper

Immediately following the third congress, a number of prominent delegates from Philadelphia began publishing a rival black Catholic newspaper, the *Journal*. The first issue of this newspaper, published by Thomas W. Swann and Sam B. Hart, appears to have been issued 14 February 1892, only a month after the adjournment of the third congress. A number of prominent black Catholics who took part in the congresses contributed to the publication of the *Journal*, including Arthur Arnott, Martin J. Lehman, Stephen Davis of Philadelphia, and Charles H. Butler of Washington, D.C. It is possible the establishment of the *Journal* strained relations between Rudd and his congressional counterparts. This may have been the reason Rudd was less active in subsequent congresses.[78]

The Fourth Colored Catholic Congress

The fourth gathering of the Colored Catholic Congress was held in Chicago in 1893. The Colored Catholic Congress and the lay Catholic congress both held meetings during the Columbian Exposition. Despite the fact that Rudd had a hand in drafting what has been called the "most important document" of the fourth congress, it appears the editor assumed a less active leadership role. This may have been due in part to Slattery's lack of faith in Rudd. Prior to the gathering, the Josephite had penned a letter to William J. Onahan, the leader of the lay Catholic congress movement. In this correspondence, Slattery had agreed that neither Rudd nor Fr. Tolton would be suitable choices for addressing the lay congress on behalf of the race. There is no indication, however, that other black Catholics shared Slattery's low opinion of these two accomplished leaders.[79]

Rudd published an announcement for the upcoming meeting of the fourth Colored Catholic Congress, which was to be held on 4–8 September in Chicago's Columbus Hall.[80] He viewed the gathering as an unprecedented opportunity for black Catholics. The editor voiced his hope that the proceedings would be as "dignified as those of the past," declaring that "prudence" should be the motto. For blacks, Rudd stated, the church was the "safest guide," their "only hope." In the 19 August 1893 issue of the *ACT*, Rudd further speculated that the congress of colored Catholics would be the "largest and most harmonious of the series."[81]

On the question of racial discrimination, Butler and his congressional cohorts were not appeasers. And yet it is possible to discern in Butler's congressional address a movement away from his 1890 endorsement of Ireland's bold calls for the immediate obliteration of the color line. For example, while in Chicago the Washingtonian emphasized the distinction between the terms "civil equality" and "social equality." He reasoned full social equality was "as distasteful to the negro as to the white." In this same address, Butler's primary goal seems to have been a more modest one, to merely ensure that blacks would not suffer discrimination in public facilities and would have an equal chance to secure jobs and other opportunities.[82]

W. S. Lofton and James A. Spencer also addressed the fourth gathering of the Colored Catholic Congress. Lofton urged employers to give the black man the chance to "earn the bread by the sweat of his brow." Spencer gave an apology for the establishment of African American churches, though he again reiterated the fact that building black schools might be a more pressing priority.[83]

The most important document produced at the fourth congress was the final address issued to fellow Catholics. Rudd was one of the eight black Catholic leaders who signed this resolution. An important feature of the document, according to Cyprian Davis, was its balance between expressions of loyalty to the Catholic Church and its condemnation of the racism among the church's bigoted members. In the final address, reference was made to the findings of the committee on grievances that had been established during the gathering of the third congress in Philadelphia in 1892. Hope for the conversion of white Catholics was expressed for those who had "departed from the teaching of the Church" and had "yielded to the popular prejudice."[84]

The Fifth Colored Catholic Congress

It is unclear whether or not Rudd attended the fifth Colored Catholic Congress, which met in Baltimore on 8–11 October 1894. In the last extant issue of the *ACT,* however, Rudd printed an announcement for the upcoming meeting. W. S. Lofton was designated acting president of the assembly. The Mass was said by Fr. Charles Uncles at St. Francis Xavier's Church, the oldest official black parish in the country. That Uncles was invited to celebrate Mass may be an indication of Slattery's influence on the meeting.[85]

Slattery's opening address to the delegates of the fifth Colored Catholic Congress reveals the unflattering paternalistic tendencies of a man otherwise praised for his diligent work on behalf of blacks.[86] In this speech, however, Slattery claimed "the colored man need[ed] encouragement to well-doing, to ambition," in order that he might rise above his "degrading circumstances."[87] African Americans were not on the same moral footing of independence as whites, he continued.[88] On the other hand, Slattery attacked whites for their "ostrich-like" attitude toward blacks. Further, he praised African Americans for the "great deal of quiet push" he detected in the race. In this same speech, the Josephite warned the black delegates against too much activism. "Time and Silence," according to Slattery, were "two powerful factors" working in favor of blacks. He told the delegates that "they had everything to gain by patient forebearance [*sic*], and much to lose by hurry and temper."[89]

During this meeting, delegates called for the establishment of an industrial school. A follow-up committee was commissioned to look into the purchase of 250 acres of land for the purpose of building a university with an attached industrial school. A speech by Fr. John De Ruyter, a Josephite, condemned the discriminatory practices of labor unions. The priest intimated that it would take the power of the Catholic Church to overcome organized labor's hostility toward blacks. President Lofton also addressed the assembled delegates of the fifth congress. Given the teachings of the Catholic Church, Lofton stated that he expected to see caste distinction banished. Concerned with the limited economic opportunities afforded blacks, he further hoped to see a reduction in immigrant labor.[90]

The findings of the grievance committee that had been established during the third congress to investigate discrimination in the church were also the subject of considerable discussion in Baltimore. Generally speaking, the bishops had reported that blacks were not discriminated against by any rule of the diocese. If discrimination had occurred, the report stated, it was at the parish level and was unsanctioned by the bishop. In the end, a delegation was authorized to lay these same grievances before the bishops meeting in Philadelphia. The fifth congress adjourned on 11 October 1894.[91] No record of a response exists.

Both Davis and Spalding have observed a number of factors that may have contributed to the collapse of the congress movement. It is reasonable to assume the growing militancy of the movement, combined with the church's increasing mistrust of lay initiatives, may have led to the collapse of the Colored Catholic Congress movement. Perhaps racial bias and apathy for the plight of African Americans also contributed to the movement's demise. Some delegates, on the other hand, may have recognized the futility of their efforts and lost interest. Though members of the movement attempted to hold subsequent congresses after 1894, the Colored Catholic Congress movement did not assemble again until its reemergence in 1987.[92]

The Success of the Congresses

After the fifth congress adjourned in October 1894, black Catholic leaders were unable to persuade church officials to sanction another meeting of this body. Though congressional leaders, including Rudd, Lofton, Butler, Spencer, and McGhee, did much of the organizational work for these gathering, they coordinated their efforts with white church officials. Moreover, in a church with a relatively fixed hierarchal leadership structure, members of the movement were, no doubt, reluctant to push ahead without the support of key church officials. As the unofficial head of black missional efforts in the United States, John Slattery had more of a say in whether or not the movement would receive the sanction of church leaders. His influence may have carried even more weight since he was a financial supporter of the congresses.[93]

The Colored Catholic Congress movement was a unique and vital lay initiative. Its emergence offered proof that a black Catholic community existed. Though there were few black priests, there was a cadre of gifted black leaders among the members of this body. Similarly, these gatherings forged a movement that was both intellectual and social. In the congressional meetings key ideas and strategies were debated, and the groundwork was laid for black Catholic movements of more recent times. Finally, as Cyprian Davis has pointed out, the Colored Catholic Congresses were more of a sign of lay involvement in the work of the American church than any other lay initiative in the nineteenth century.[94]

Rudd's involvement in the Colored Catholic Congress movement declined following the third gathering of this body in 1892. The editor of the *ACT*'s commitment to equality for African Americans, however, never waned. After his departure from the organization he had founded, Rudd continued his campaign for racial justice in American society. The editor of the *ACT* worked to promote his church-centered approach for achieving a state of race relations, inspired as he was by his unwavering belief in "the Fatherhood of God and Brotherhood of Man." In December 1892 Rudd wrote the following:

> Anyone who has read history and given ear to the inevitable conclusions that grow out of its teachings can see at a glance that in the Catholic Church alone is the only permanent advancement to be made. She alone advances steadily, and in her upward flight, carries with her all the races of mankind on an equal footing. There is no hope for us outside her portals even in a temporal sense. All other friendships are ephemeral and must vanish.[95]

Despite Rudd's efforts with the *ACT* and the Colored Catholic Congress movement, justice, and the full equality it implied, would remain for African Americans in the late nineteenth century only a hopeful vision. As Jim Crow became more ensconced in American society, Rudd could no longer depend on the American Catholic Church to be a reliable ally in the quest for racial justice. Though Rudd remained a Catholic until his death in 1933, he was let down by his church and its leaders. Sometime after the collapse of the *ACT,* Rudd looked elsewhere for a more promising path forward. In his later life, he promoted a prescription for racial uplift that closely resembled Booker T. Washington's economic self-help approach.

CHAPTER 7

Daniel Rudd's Post-*ACT* Years in the South

*The Colored People themselves must solve the Negro prob-
lem. Upon their shoulders rests the well-being of their race.*

D. RUDD
6 APRIL 1888

The Collapse of the *ACT* in Detroit

Daniel Rudd skillfully led the *ACT* through a number of setbacks and
difficulties on its way to financial viability. For example, in December
1890, about a month before Mackey's departure from the *ACT,* Rudd
decided to open a newspaper branch office and printing facility in
Chicago. The newspaper's Chicago plant was located at 283 South Clark
Street, Room 14. This new venture was short-lived, however. In January
1891 the *ACT* reported that a fire had badly damaged the facilities. Rudd
later seemed to suggest the fire may have been an act of vandalism. Why
Rudd chose not to comment more extensively on the fire is unclear.[1]

Rudd's *ACT* reached as many as 10,000 subscribers at its zenith in
1892.[2] This number seems remarkable when measured against other
notable black newspapers of the period. For example, the *Christian
Recorder* at its peak reached only 8,000 subscribers.[3] Another well-known
black newspaper, the *Chicago Conservator,* could boast of a circulation of

just over 1,000.[4] But despite the remarkable success of the *ACT,* it wouldn't last.

Subsequent to Rudd's move from Cincinnati in 1893, he established the headquarters of the *ACT* at 37 Mullett Street in Detroit. Rudd's new base of operation was located between St. Antoine and Hastings streets, in the city's fourth ward, near St. Mary's Hospital and Detroit College of Medicine.[5] After securing a location for the headquarters of his printing operation, Rudd continued to demonstrate his ingenuity. For example, he produced the electricity for his own printing shop and planned to provide electricity for "this entire section of the city."[6] As a dedicated Catholic, Rudd would have no doubt found a home parish. Which parish Rudd attended while residing in Detroit is not known, however. He may have attended St. Mary's, a German parish located a couple of blocks away at St. Antoine Street and Monroe Avenue. It is also possible Rudd attended one of the neighborhood's English-speaking churches, either St. Aloysius, located on State and Washington streets, or St. Peter and Paul, located at Jefferson and St. Antoine streets.[7]

Neither Rudd's name nor the name of the *ACT* is listed in Detroit's 1896 city directory. No resident appears to have been living at 37 Mullett Street after 1895. This may mean the facility was sold and not occupied or, more likely, the property had been abandoned. Rudd's name again appears in the 1897 edition of Detroit's city directory. Here he is listed as the proprietor of the *ACT.* By this time, Rudd was residing at 469 Monroe Avenue in the city's seventh ward, between Orleans and Dequindre streets, about five blocks away from his previous Mullett Street address. The last year Rudd was listed in the city's directory was 1897.[8]

The collapse of Rudd's newspaper in 1897 is likely attributed to one or more of the following four factors. First, the *ACT* was forced to compete with a number of new black newspapers established in Cincinnati in early 1891; second, the establishment of Philadelphia's black Catholic newspaper, the *Journal,* appears to have resulted in the *ACT* losing as many as 3,000 subscribers; third, the collapse of the *Detroit Plaindealer* in 1892 may have encouraged Rudd to move his newspaper to Detroit. Here he may have mistakenly thought he could capture a significant share of the advertising dollars once controlled by the failed newspaper. Finally, the above adverse factors were, no doubt, exacerbated by difficulties associated with the economic recession, which began in 1893.

The decline of the *ACT* probably commenced sometime before the economic recession began in 1893. In fact, Rudd's local black subscription base may have been threatened as early as the summer of 1891. For example, in June of that year Rudd reported Cincinnati would soon be welcoming a number of new black political newspapers.[9] The next month, Rudd announced the arrival of the first of these anticipated publications, the *American.*[10] In April of the following year, one of Rudd's journalistic associates, William H. Anderson, editor of the *Detroit Plaindealer,* began publishing a Cincinnati edition of his well-known newspaper. Employing two of Rudd's former agents, William F. Anderson and W. S. Tisdale, the *Detroit Plaindealer's* editor, attempted to establish a subscription base in Cincinnati.[11] A subsequent threat to the *ACT's* newspaper market share in Cincinnati may have also come from another of Rudd's close associates, Charles W. Bell. In September 1892, Bell's *Ohio Republican* made its debut in the Queen City.[12]

Though it appears that a decreasing market share and stiff competition for advertising dollars available to black newspapers in Cincinnati threatened the *ACT,* an even more profound blow to Rudd and his newspaper came with the establishment of a rival black Catholic newspaper, the *Journal,* in 1892. Despite Rudd's periodic claims that the *ACT* was the only black Catholic journal owned and published by colored men, other black Catholic publications were established during this period, including the *Journal* of Philadelphia, published from February 1892 to September 1892, and the lesser-known *Colored American Catholic,* published in New York City in the summer of 1888.[13]

Though the impact of the *Colored American Catholic* on the *ACT* seems to have been negligible, the *Journal,* on the other hand, threatened Rudd's national subscription base. Particularly vulnerable would have been Rudd's subscribers living in large urban centers on the East Coast, near Philadelphia. The *Journal* began publication 14 February 1892, subsequent to the meeting of the third Colored Catholic Congress. This newspaper was published in Philadelphia by Thomas W. Swann and S. B. Hart. Though its publication was relatively short lived, it appears to have existed long enough to do irreparable damage to Rudd's national subscription base.

Following the establishment of the *Journal* in February 1892, Rudd's *ACT* appears to have experienced difficulties in its marketing operation.

For example, in 1891 the newspaper reported no fewer than fifty-five marketing visits to various cities around the country. In 1892, however, this number dropped to twenty-one. More tellingly, the circulation of the *ACT,* which was reported to have been as high as 10,000 in 1892, dropped to 7,000 in 1893. In May 1892 the *Journal* claimed 3,000 readers, the same number of readers the *ACT* is reported to have lost. Though the link between the establishment of the *Journal* and the crippling of the *ACT* cannot be proved conclusively, it is certainly plausible.[14]

The collapse of the *ACT* appears to have been linked to Rudd's ill-fated decision to move the paper to Detroit. Willging and Hatzfeld reported that Rudd may have moved the *ACT* because of a drop in the number of its subscribers.[15] It is reasonable to assume that Rudd carefully calculated this move prior to his departure from Cincinnati. The question is then begged, Why Detroit? Rudd had visited the city in the fall of 1887.[16] In June 1889 Rudd announced a planning meeting of a group charged with organizing the Catholic lay congress that was to be held in Detroit.[17] In the next issue of the *ACT,* Rudd wrote: "We are much pleased with our visit to the beautiful city of Detroit. The people are hospitable and full of American vigor. Rt. Rev. Bishop Foley, and Mr. W. M. O'Brien has our thanks for kindness to this paper. Editor Hughes of the *Michigan Catholic* showed us the city and suburbs in an afternoon drive."[18]

Despite Rudd's positive appraisal of the city, it seems unlikely that this alone would have led Rudd to move the *ACT.* Moreover, Leslie Woodcock Tentler has pointed out that neither Bishop Foley nor the clergy in his diocese are known to have spoken publicly on the matter of race. She also has suggested that relations between the Catholics and African Americans in Detroit were especially antagonistic, this given the fact that the two groups competed for jobs and housing. More tellingly, Irish Catholic toughs occasionally terrorized African Americans living in the section of the city largely inhabited by blacks. In turn, by the 1890s African Americans in the city often sided with those who opposed foreign immigration. Some even lent their support to the virulently anti-Catholic American Protection Association. Further, by the mid-1890s William H. Hughes, longtime editor of the *Michigan Catholic,* seems to have associated himself with groups hostile to the issue of African American equality. In 1893, for example, the same year Rudd moved the *ACT* to Detroit,

Hughes, who was an anti-integrationist, even came close to condoning the practice of lynching.[19]

There is no record in the *ACT* of any attempts made by church leaders to influence Rudd to move the newspaper to Detroit. If Rudd would have been concerned primarily with exploiting a new local black Catholic market, or moving to a location with a larger black population, he would not have chosen Detroit. In 1900 only 4,129 blacks lived in Detroit, compared to 14,498 in Cincinnati. Moreover, given their relatively large black Catholic populations, New Orleans, Baltimore, New York, Philadelphia, or St. Louis would have been much more attractive host cities.[20]

It appears that Rudd's decision to move the *ACT* to Detroit was primarily motivated by business considerations. Detroit was Michigan's major urban center at the end of the nineteenth century; it also served as the hub of publishing in the state.[21] The major black newspaper of the region during this period was the *Detroit Plaindealer*. The success of black newspapers depended largely on the publication's ability to sell subscriptions. But the *Plaindealer* was particularly successful in attracting local advertisements.[22] Most black papers, on the other hand, could not count on a robust advertising income because of the relatively small number of African American entrepreneurs.[23] In the spring of 1893, the *Plaindealer* ceased publishing its paper. It is possible Rudd moved his *ACT* to exploit a vacuum created by the collapse of this Detroit publication.[24]

There are wide variations in the reported size of the *ACT*'s subscription base after its move. Some sources speculate that the newspaper reached as many as 7,500 subscribers from 1894 to 1897. Given the circumstances of Rudd's move, this number seems remarkably high. Other sources judge the number of subscribers to have been much smaller, as few as 1,000 over the last three years of its publication.[25] In the last extant issue of the *ACT*, Rudd listed only two traveling agents, Isaac Moten and William Ervin. This number is down from the three listed in February 1892. It appears, then, that after the move to Detroit, the newspaper lost subscribers and subsequently would have had difficulty covering its operational expenses.[26]

By the time Rudd printed the first edition of the *ACT* from Detroit in December 1893, an economic recession had tightened its grip on the country. It wasn't until late 1897 that the U.S. economy began to slowly improve. Before the end of this economic depression, however, 16,000 businesses had failed, 500 banks had closed their doors, and one-fourth of the nation's railroads were bankrupt. During this same economically depressed period, the nation's unemployment rate hovered around 10 percent.[27] The high rate of unemployment meant millions of the nation's citizens struggled to meet financial obligations, and available disposable income became scarce. These adverse economic conditions made it difficult for Rudd, then in Detroit, to resurrect the struggling *ACT*. Despite the adverse economic climate created by the recession of 1893, some of the city's black newspapers, including the *National Independent* (1891–1903) and the *Detroit Advocate* (1891–1901) survived.[28] It appears, therefore, that the economic depression of the 1890s only partially explains the *ACT*'s collapse. The competition by local black newspapers in Cincinnati, the establishment of the *Journal* in 1892, and an ill-conceived decision to move the newspaper to Detroit, all combined to seal the fate of the *ACT*.

The Move South

Rudd is not listed in the U.S. Census of 1900. His whereabouts from 1898 to 1910 is a mystery yet to be solved. Sometime before 1910, Rudd moved to Boyle Town, Mississippi (currently known as Boyle), just south of the town of Cleveland, in Bolivar County. Here Rudd would have been hard-pressed to find advocates for his ideals on social equality and racial justice. In the Jim Crow–era South many whites believed blacks to be inferior. Members of the dominant racial class, therefore, refused to use the same dishes or to wear clothing previously worn by African Americans. Blacks were considered unclean, lazy, irresponsible, childlike, and lacking moral inhibitions. Formal law forbade interracial marriage, and society prohibited sexual intercourse between members of the two races. African Americans were also expected to assume a deferential manner when conversing with whites. Moreover, many whites in the South were unswervingly committed to the idea that a racial caste system would continue indefinitely.[29]

In 1903 the citizens of Mississippi elected one of the period's most bigoted politicians, Gov. James Kimble Vardaman (1861–1930). In 1907 Governor Vardaman declared, "If it is necessary every Nigger in the state will be lynched, then it will be done to maintain white supremacy."[30]

Following Theodore Roosevelt's visit with Booker T. Washington in the White House, Vardaman declared the White House was so "saturated with the odor of the nigger that the rats have taken up refuge in the stable."[31] Vardaman's racially charged rhetoric certainly did not hurt him politically; in fact, it may have helped him get elected. The year Rudd left Mississippi, 1912, Vardaman won a U.S. Senate seat in a landslide victory that gave him seventy-four of the state's seventy-nine counties. [32]

Given the views of many whites in the Magnolia State, one might wonder why Rudd chose to leave the relative safety of the North to take up residence in Mississippi. It may have been that he followed the thousands of other Midwestern laborers who traveled to the Mississippi/Yazoo Delta region to work seasonally in the region's lumber mills.[33] It is also possible that Rudd was attracted to Bolivar County, Mississippi, because of Booker T. Washington's infatuation with the Yazoo Delta region of the state. In 1910 Washington wrote of this area: "There, if anywhere, I believe, the black man is going to finally get on his feet, or finally perish."[34]

The Mississippi Delta at the turn of the century was a frontier region with booming towns full of people seeking to make good on the American dream. In the decades following the Civil War, this area of the Deep South attracted land speculators, farmers seeking cheap land to plant cotton, and entrepreneurs who recognized that money could be made logging the region's first growth timber. The community's development was further encouraged by the completion in 1884 of the Louisville, New Orleans, Texas Railroad.[35]

While residing in Bolivar County, Rudd worked as a lumber mill manager and boarded with Aaron and Katie Smith. This African American family appears to have been one of the region's many blacks who owned farms. For whom Rudd worked during his years in Mississippi is yet to be established. In 1894 Mr. Cafin erected a spoke mill near Boyle. By 1900 the area boasted a number of lumber mills. In 1908 the Peavine Cooperage Company, a subsidiary of the Ozark Mills Company headquartered in St. Louis, moved to the area and opened three mills with the capacity for loading sixty train cars per day. Given the fact that the Peavine Cooperage Company was the largest lumber mill in operation in the area, it is possible Rudd worked for this firm.[36]

A New Start in Arkansas

Rudd's post-*ACT* years in the South bring to light an accomplished man whose genius and talents seem to have been only partially revealed during the years he published his newspaper. In 1912 Rudd and a Mr. Stewart, perhaps one of Rudd's fellow employees, were recruited by Scott Bond, a wealthy African American farmer and entrepreneur, to come to Madison, Arkansas, in order to establish a sawmill. A devastating flood had inundated Bond's farms near Madison, and the community was depressed economically. Bond, who owned large quantities of timber reserves on the St. Francis River, wanted experienced hands to handle his new venture. Rudd must have been a rather desirable catch for Bond, demonstrated by the fact that he committed to bringing both he and Mr. Stewart in from Mississippi.[37]

If living as a black man in Mississippi had been difficult, Rudd's move to Arkansas did not significantly improve his living conditions. It is true that following the emancipation of the nation's slaves in 1865 many blacks viewed the state as a land of opportunity. But as early as 1891 a separate coach law was passed in Arkansas curbing the civil rights of blacks. More Jim Crow legislation was passed in 1903. From 1889 to 1918 there were 214 lynchings in the state; 85 percent of the victims were black.[38] Rudd's station as a second-class citizen in Arkansas stemmed not only from his racial status but also from his Catholicism. This placed Rudd in the nondominant culture with respect to his religion as well. Only 1.26 percent of Arkansas's residents were foreign born. The only religious diversity to speak of in the state was between Protestant groups. Catholics were sometimes stigmatized as devils by Arkansas' Protestants. Moreover, the KKK attacked and harassed not only blacks living in the state but also Catholics.[39]

It is unclear how Rudd met Bond. It may have been that the two met through Booker T. Washington. Scott Bond was a member of the National Negro Business League (NNBL), which was founded by Washington in 1900. Bond traveled to New York in 1902 to attend the annual meeting, and while there he gained a pledge from Washington to visit Arkansas's St. Francis County. In 1903 Washington held the annual NNBL meeting in Little Rock, and following that meeting Bond played host to Washington in his Madison home. In 1911 Washington visited Madison again, and thousands came to this small town to hear the "Wizard of Tuskegee" speak. At the time, Rudd resided in Boyle Town, Mississippi. It may have been that Rudd traveled to Madison to hear Washington lecture and met Bond at this time. Given that Rudd was recruited to join Bond's enterprises in 1912, this last scenario seems plausible.[40]

Despite the amazing business success of Scott Bond, Arkansas was a dangerous place for African Americans at the turn of the century. For example, near Elaine, Arkansas, in southern Phillips County, over two hundred blacks were killed in a series of racial disturbances in 1919.[41] It is also true that though the conflicts between Bond and his white neighbors at times were drastically played down in the Bond biography, evidence from this same text reveals that the black entrepreneur was sometimes harassed by whites jealous of his business success.[42]

After Rudd's move to Madison, Arkansas, he boarded with Scott Bond's son and daughter-in-law, Theophilus and Viola. Rudd, who was about fifty-six in 1912, was an accountant for the Bond family, as well as a superintendent for a number of his employer's businesses, including Bond's gravel operation and lumber mill.[43]

While Rudd was supervising Bond's gravel operation, the former *ACT* editor approached Bond with a rough sketch of a loading device made of cables and blocks, which Rudd believed would make the loading of gravel onto rail cars faster and more efficient. Subsequently, Rudd was involved in the negotiations for the erection of a plant based on his design. Because the timber specifications could not be met by local mills, Rudd was also called on to locate the timber and supervise the cutting of the required oversized boards. After the plant was completed, the machinery boasted the capacity to load a railroad car with gravel in only seven minutes; further, the plant had the capability of loading 800 cubic yards of gravel per day. During this same period, Bond signed a contract with the railroad company to supply it with $20,000 worth of gravel.[44]

Rudd also served the Bond family as a business adviser while in Madison. Rudd and Stewart had been with Bond for about a year when in 1913 a flood again inundated the area, destroying the farm's newly planted crops. At the time, Rudd and Stewart were overseeing Bond's sawmill. Bond decided to replant but became demoralized when he discovered his fields were infested with cutworms. Confiding in Rudd and Stewart, he declared, "I am practically at a loss what to do." Rudd responded, "Let's shut the mill down the logs won't rot in the river. Let's take the hands and go and make a crop. The farm is the foundation of the saw mill, the store and everything else." Despite Bond's initial objections, Rudd prevailed and the fields were planted a third time. The heat slowed the progress of the cutworms, and it looked as if the fields would produce a large crop. An early frost, however, hurt the yield. As it turned out, a meager harvest was gathered, "very little corn" and only 250 bales of cotton.[45]

Rudd's Biography of Scott Bond

While residing in Madison, Rudd put his journalistic skills to work. The former editor of the *ACT* partnered with his subject's son, Theophilus, in the publication of the biography of Scott Bond. The title of this biography is *From Slavery to Wealth: The Life of Scott Bond: The Rewards of Honesty, Industry, Economy, and Perseverance* (1917). Published two years after Booker T. Washington's death, Rudd's book offered its readers an individualistic, economic, self-help prescription for racial uplift very similar to that found in Washington's own autobiography, *Up from Slavery.* Rudd's journalistic experience and the fact that he is listed as primary author of the biography suggest he was the writer of the manuscript. Moreover, Rudd's detailed accounts of his own conversations with Bond suggest the same. Theophilus, who had more formal education than Rudd, likely provided stories and served as an informant to the latter. To get the information for the book, Rudd interviewed his subject, sometimes allowing Scott Bond to tell his story in the first person.[46]

Throughout Rudd's career he worked for the recognition of the full equality of blacks. Like other nineteenth-century African American leaders, he encouraged blacks to take responsibility for their own destiny, urging them to find work, save money, and educate their children. A proponent of vocational education, he also anticipated key components of Booker T. Washington's platform. But this was only one aspect of Rudd's message. In the *ACT,* Rudd promoted the Catholic Church as the essential force that would necessarily lift blacks from the low station they held in American society. Further, Rudd's self-help message was given alongside an aggressive editorial campaign defending the dignity

Scott Bond, a wealthy black Arkansas farmer/merchant for whom Rudd worked in Madison, Arkansas. Rudd coauthored his biography. (Courtesy of the Arkansas History Commission.)

and the civil rights of blacks. In this last respect, Rudd's message in the *ACT* more closely resembled that of post-Reconstruction Frederick Douglass. But as race relations in the country deteriorated around the turn of the century, many blacks, including the former editor of the *ACT,* placed their faith in Washington's more pragmatic self-help message.

Rudd and Booker T. Washington's Self-Help Philosophy

Booker T. Washington was the most influential African American leader of his generation. He was catapulted into national prominence in 1895 after delivering a speech that became known as the "Atlanta Compromise Address."[47] Washington sought to help blacks living in an era rife with anti–African American sentiments. In this racially charged climate, the

"Wizard of Tuskegee" attempted to recover for blacks whatever gains could be secured. Whenever possible, Washington curried favor with whites in positions of power, especially if he believed they could help him further his racial agenda. Instead of placing the blame for the plight of African Americans on white racism, Washington urged blacks to take responsibility for their destiny and to seek progress through education and economic prosperity. Whereas Frederick Douglass and Ida B. Wells-Barnett had primarily condemned the unjust prejudice of whites, Washington chose to address his Jeremiadic warnings to negligent blacks he believed were failing in their duties of "Christian Citizenship." By this he hoped to spur members of his race to walk the road to economic success, a path he was convinced would lead to eventual respectability and equality.[48]

Washington advocated a concrete program for black advancement that included industrial education and the promotion of business. In short, the pragmatic Washington was willing to trade black acquiescence in disenfranchisement and some measure of segregation in return for a chance to share in the economic prosperity northern investment would bring. Though Washington privately worked to combat lynching, disenfranchisement, peonage, educational discrimination, and segregation, his critics have observed that his public statements on civil rights vitiated his purposes.[49]

Though in the Bond biography it is impossible to definitively disentangle Rudd's views from those of his subject, it is clear that Rudd would have gravitated to certain key aspects of Washington's plan for racial uplift.[50] For example, he had always been a strong believer in black agency, and Washington's self-help program placed the responsibility for success and progress on the individual. He also would have supported Washington's promotion of the equality of economic opportunity. Moreover, Rudd believed if African Americans were given a level playing field, they would in the end advance, eventually winning the respect of whites.

Rudd's portrayal of Scott Bond made the wealthy Arkansas farmer/merchant a model of Washington's self-help program. In a section at the end of the biography entitled "A Look into the Future," Rudd claimed the race would not "retrograde." The former editor of the *ACT* offered Bond as proof of this fact. Bond, like Washington, urged blacks to remain in the South. The wealthy Arkansas farmer and merchant insisted

Fredrick Douglass *(left)* and Booker T. Washington were both important leaders in the campaign for black civil rights, even if much has been made of their contrasting approaches for reaching similar but elusive objectives. (Douglass photo courtesy National Archives and Records Administration. Washington photo courtesy Library of Congress.)

on one occasion that the South, especially Arkansas, was the best place in the world for the poor, hence for the "Negro." He further claimed hard work "overcomes all" and urged a positive approach to the problems facing African Americans.[51]

Though Rudd's biographical subject sometimes acknowledged blacks were the victims of race prejudice, he claimed it was largely the poorer class of whites who were to blame. For example, after a conflict with local whites attempting to keep Bond from erecting a lumber mill, he declared, "I would be glad to have the reader note here that the sentiment of the class of white people who oppose me, was not the sentiment of cultured refined white people of the South." Despite the opposition of some whites, Bond placed the responsibility for success on the individual. He neither recognized nor took aim at the South's structural pattern of racial prejudice.[52]

Rudd portrayed Bond as a man convinced one could succeed in business regardless of skin color. Bond, like Washington, believed racial equality held sway in the field of economics. Bond pointed out, for example, the following:

> I was wonderfully surprised after I had entered the mercantile business to learn how broad the commercial world was. The basis of fairness to all mankind that could furnish the intellect and the ability, including the financial part of it. When these things were at hand I found that it was left to the individual to succeed or fail. The poor white man's chances and opportunity along these lines are just as great as the rich white man and the Negro's chances and opportunities are the same as other men's. The commercial world knows no color and has no pets. The great earth, mother of all people, is acquainted with all her children; she neither knows them by color nor sex.[53]

Washington, Bond, and, apparently, Rudd found in the era of Jim Crow that in the business world a vehicle existed that could potentially lift African Americans to their ultimate goal, full racial equality. Over time, Rudd became convinced that the earth as the foundation of this economic system was colorblind and had "no pets." The language in the previous quotation suggests the unity of the human family, but the mother of all races of people in this new formulation was Mother Earth, and not the Catholic Church, as it had been in Rudd's earlier writings.

There are a number of points of continuity between Rudd's statements in the biography and his campaign for justice in the *ACT*. For example, in the 25 August 1886 edition of the newspaper, Rudd condemned the "invidious discrimination and hateful caste prejudice" he claimed was "ever bobbing up to thwart the Negro in his manly efforts to make himself an honest and upright citizen."[54] Three decades later, in his biography of Scott Bond, Rudd again spoke out against racial discrimination. He noted the negative impact that prejudice had on the economy of the nation. Rudd estimated the "loss to progress thus caused averaged not less than $100 per capita per annum of the total Negro population." This forfeiture also could be measured in the loss of "morale" in the citizenry of the country, according to the editor.[55]

In the biography of Scott Bond, Rudd condemned the practice of denying blacks membership in labor unions. He had done the same in the *ACT*. Rudd also echoed the *ACT*'s earlier "cry for justice" when in 1917 he spoke out against the crop mortgage system and the practice of racial segregation. Further, in the Bond biography Rudd at times expressed some of his prior directness. For example, he reasoned that if blacks continued to progress through "efficiency," "thrift," and "continuity," African Americans in the future would be able to "demand" rather than "plead" for a "place in the sun."[56]

As is evident from Rudd's biography of Scott Bond, the former editor's promotion of race pride did not end with the collapse of the *ACT*. Rudd argued that white impressions of blacks were inaccurate. He supported his apology for African Americans, stating that in the community in which he lived, Madison, Arkansas, blacks and whites were generally "hard working" and "industrious." In 1917 he detailed how in the surrounding region there were places where one could travel for miles on joining farms owned by blacks. Rudd further argued that African Americans in the United States owned $500 million worth of real estate, an amount he claimed was increasing each year. The editor concluded, "Little more than fifty years ago the Negro was a slave. Now he is a citizen, counting his wealth in millions."[57]

Rudd's previous campaign to open the doors of opportunity to African Americans seeking to improve their station by securing gainful employment continued in his biography of Bond. For example, in its pages the former editor of the *ACT* pointed out that blacks would have been of far more service to the country had whites not constructed a "wall of prejudice" barring entrance into the "fields of skilled labor." Rudd further decried the practice of labor unions, which he claimed operated on the premise "no nigger need apply." Moreover, Rudd's desire to see African Americans create their own opportunities through hard work and the virtues of "honesty," "industry," "economy," and "perseverance" shared many commonalities with the message of Booker T. Washington.[58]

Though Rudd's desire for full racial equality had remained consistent throughout his journalistic career, the sociopolitical context in America had changed after the collapse of the *ACT.* Conditions for blacks in the United States had gotten much worse. Similarly, few Catholics Rudd encountered in the South would have held the same relatively high opinion of blacks expressed by more progressive church officials decades earlier. Given these exigencies, evidence from the Bond biography suggests that Rudd by 1917 had become convinced that the best way for blacks to secure equality and racial justice was to follow the example of successful African Americans like Scott Bond, who had earned, through financial success, some measure of respect from whites. Speaking of the African American mind-set, Rudd wrote the following:

> He knows every child of every citizen of this great democracy has a right to aspire to every position that is open to the child of any other American citizen and he knows that aspiration is crushed beneath a wall of prejudice that he cannot scale; certainly not at present. Hence he thinks he is not being fairly dealt with. He also thinks that if like Scott Bond, he can show a clean character and a good bank account, backed by large holdings of real property he may then look forward to those things guaranteed by the laws of his country.[59]

As is apparent from the examples cited above, a good deal of continuity exists between the issues of justice previously raised by Rudd in the *ACT,* and those addressed in his biography of Scott Bond. There is in the work of the later Rudd, however, apparent development in perspective with regard to the most promising method for achieving racial justice and equality in society. Absent from the Bond biography, for example, is any reference to the role the Catholic Church would play in the ushering in of a casteless society in America. This church-centered approach had been a critical aspect of Rudd's "cry for justice" during the years of the *ACT*'s publication. Given that this was Scott Bond's story, however, one would assume Rudd would have kept any views about the Catholic Church to himself, especially since Bond was Protestant, a member of the Missionary Baptist Church. Surprisingly, in the biography the author leaves little room for the lifting force of Christianity more generally. He instead promotes Booker T. Washington's gospel of wealth and self-help in its place.

The biography of Bond also illustrates the extent to which Rudd moved away from another earlier position on a key justice question. Early in Rudd's journalistic career he remained convinced of the potency of black suffrage. During the period in which he published the *ACT*, Rudd argued that the "elective franchise" ought to be protected by the federal government.[60] Similarly, in the Bond biography Rudd acknowledged that the right to vote had been seized from blacks by "violence as well as legal subterfuge." At the same time, however, he reasoned that following the Civil War, those who sought to give blacks voting rights "did not take into consideration the fact that the ex-slave was not fully prepared for that advanced step. They expected too much in so short a time." Further, Rudd seems to have internalized the Washingtonian program for self-help when he declared that following the disenfranchisement of blacks an enlightened Washington instituted a "New era" for blacks, one which provided a proper foundation for advancement. This school of men, Rudd observed, claimed "efficiency and thrift would be the proper foundation upon which to build . . . that ownership of some of this world's goods would go a long way towards removing the stumbling blocks from the pathway up."[61]

Though Rudd endorsed Washington's self-help platform generally, at times his stand seems directly at odds with the early Rudd. For example, in the biography of Scott Bond, Rudd recognized the staggering economic cost incurred by the nation as a result of race prejudice. This position appears consistent with the Rudd of the *ACT* era. In this same biography, however, Rudd labeled the segregation of the Jim Crow era a "blessing in disguise." The former editor of the *ACT* reasoned race segregation taught the black man to "take an introspective view of himself to see whatever heights he may aspire." By thus "flocking by himself" he would recognize that "the force" necessary to attain these heights came from within. The systemic character of race injustice railed against by the early Rudd is minimized if not completely unacknowledged in the biography's prescription for black self-help.[62]

Rudd and the NAACP

Throughout the period of Washington's ascendancy, conditions for blacks grew even worse. This fact coupled with the reform currents set in motion during the Progressive Era prepared the way for the emergence of the National Association for the Advancement of Colored People (NAACP).[63] Rudd's affiliation with the NAACP in the years following the writing of his biography of Bond also makes it difficult to determine the extent of his level of commitment to Washington's self-help program. The NAACP had been founded in 1909 in response to dissatisfaction with the accommodationist approach promulgated by Washington. The NAACP was committed to twin convictions: the basic rights of citizenship were being denied to blacks, and agitation was required to win them. The NAACP set to work, therefore, to halt the stripping away of human rights, a practice that had accelerated since the end of Reconstruction. This same organization brought together a number of groups in common cause, including the remnants of the Niagara movement, the settlement house workers, muckrakers, labor progressives, and "race scientists." Among other goals, this organization set out to improve conditions for blacks, including the abolishment of forced segregation. This same organization worked to promote racial equality in educational opportunities, as well as the promotion of full franchisment.[64]

The NAACP was successful in winning the hearts and minds of blacks dissatisfied with Washington's accommodationist approach. In January 1918, John Shillady, a social worker and specialist in the administration and fiscal management of social service organizations, took over. In the subsequent six months the NAACP grew from 7,000 to 36,000 members. Shillady also presided over the organization's first book publication, *Thirty Years of Lynching in the United States 1889–1918*. Over the next year, membership in the NAACP soared to 90,000. This increase occurred as a result of a number of factors, including the Sharecropper's War, race riots in the cities of Chicago, Omaha, Tulsa, Charleston, and Knoxville, as well as an increase in the number of lynchings. It is plausible, given Rudd's interest in the NAACP, that he himself may have joined the organization during this critical period in race relations.[65]

In May 1919 Rudd wrote to John B. Morris (1866–1946), bishop of Little Rock, requesting that the former editor be appointed a diocesan representative to the upcoming national convention of the NAACP.[66] The meeting, which was held in Cleveland, was better attended and lasted longer than former gatherings. Thirty-four states were represented in the assembly by the organization's dramatically expanded membership. Absent from the meeting were the NAACP's white leaders.[67]

Bishop John Hurst (1863–1930), the thirty-sixth bishop of the A.M.E. Church, set the tone for the convention in his address to the delegates. Hurst explained how blacks had been lulled to sleep under the delusion that if they quit vociferously advocating for their rights and kept on working, justice would eventually be meted out to them. The author, however, pointed out that the South had renewed its assaults on the black man with every step forward. Moreover, Hurst urged delegates to die if need be in the fight for their rights.[68]

Organizers of the Cleveland NAACP meeting apparently invited Rudd to be a presenter at the gathering. His recent completion of the biography of Bond, his years as a journalist, his agricultural experience, as well as his expertise as a lumber mill manager, would have made him an attractive presenter. When Rudd received the invitation, he must have sought help to fund the trip back to Ohio. Morris refused Rudd's request to be allowed to represent the diocese, but the bishop forwarded sixty dollars to him to help with traveling expenses. In a letter to Rudd, Morris also reminded Rudd that he had "great personal confidence" in him.[69]

On the third day of the gathering, Rudd was among the presenters called on to discuss "The Negro in Labor and Industry" and the "Rural Conditions on Labor." Neither in the *Cleveland Gazette* nor in the NAACP's publication, *The Crisis,* is any record given of the nature of Rudd's talk. Sentiments expressed at the Cleveland meeting, however, run counter to some of the tenets of Washington's philosophy communicated in Rudd's biography of Bond. For example, though Bond espoused Washington's ideas regarding blacks seeking their fortunes in the South, this was not the majority opinion among delegates at the NAACP gathering in Cleveland. Professor George A. Towns of Atlanta, speaking on the evening after Rudd's talk, posed the question, "Shall we stop this migration north, with the shameful waste it leaves in its wake?" The resounding answer from his audience of delegates was, "No!" Moreover, Towns detailed the discrimination routinely practiced against blacks in the South, declaring, "If you're as wise as Socrates and as good as Jesus, you can find ten chances a week for being lynched in Georgia."[70]

On the same day that Rudd addressed the assembly, delegates passed a resolution requesting, as a prerequisite to affiliation, that the American Federation of Labor demand the brotherhoods of railway engineers, trainmen, and firemen stop barring blacks. Another speaker proposed a "constructive program" that included a call for "decent housing," "fair wages," "decent school provisions for colored children," and "justice in every court." At this same meeting, delegates called for the end of Jim Crow legislation on the nation's buses and trains.[71]

The resolutions proposed in the Cleveland meeting of the NAACP are consistent with Rudd's more aggressive editorial campaign from a quarter century earlier. It remains unclear, however, whether Rudd's earlier commitment to activism was somewhat muffled in Bond's biography, or if Rudd's commitment to direct activism underwent something of a renewal in light of the continued violence toward blacks in the months leading up to "Red Summer."[72]

Sometime prior to 1920, Rudd went to work for another successful black farmer-merchant, John Gammon Sr., who lived in Marion, Arkansas. Why Rudd left Bond's employ as a lumber mill manager is unclear. A decline in timber production during this period in the state's history may have necessitated the move. It is also possible John Gammon knew Rudd because the Gammon and Bond families were related.[73]

In the years following emancipation, John Gammon and his brother Ambrose joined five other families and purchased land in the Arkansas wilderness just north of the city of Marion. The families worked together to establish an independent black community called "Gammonville." John's son, John Gammon Jr., remembered Rudd as being "highly intelligent," "adept at handling machinery," "handsome," and "fluent in several languages."[74]

While in Gammon's employ Rudd served as an accountant.[75] It is possible Rudd also worked as a teacher in the community during his years in Marion. On Rudd's death certificate his occupation is listed as "Teacher."[76] Both Bond and Gammon supported the establishment of black schools. Though it is possible that Rudd taught school while in the employ of Scott Bond, there is no mention of it in Bond's biography. If Rudd did teach school, it seems more likely he would have done so while in the employ of Gammon. Gammon had, in fact, established a school for blacks in the Gammonville community. There is also a possibility that the former editor may have taught at the historic Marion Colored High School, built in 1924 with monies from the Julius Rosenwald fund. This historic institution was constructed in the neighboring black community of Sunset just north of Marion. The Marion Colored High School was one of the only black secondary schools in the region, and students traveled from other states, including Mississippi, Tennessee, and Missouri to receive a secondary education there.[77]

The former editor of the *ACT*'s relationship to the Catholic Church remained steady throughout the last years of his life. While in the employ of Gammon, it is possible Rudd attended Crawfordville's Sacred Heart Mission Church, or Forest City's St. Francis of Assisi Parish. It is also possible Rudd attended one of a number of Memphis's city parishes.

Rudd's relationship with Morris, his bishop, appears to have remained strong as well. In Morris's reply to Rudd's request to represent the diocese at the Cleveland meeting of the NAACP discussed above, Morris communicated his confidence in Rudd. Subsequently, Rudd petitioned Morris in the hopes that he would be sent to represent the diocese at the black Catholic laymen's convention held in Washington, D.C., in 1920. Morris denied the request, however, because the diocese had fewer than 500 black Catholics and so was not qualified to send a delegate. But, six years later, Morris appointed Rudd to represent the black Catholics of Arkansas at the Eucharistic Congress, which was to be held in Chicago. The late appointment, however, precluded Rudd's attendance.[78]

Rudd made his home in eastern Arkansas until 1932, when he suffered a debilitating stroke.[79] After nearly four decades living in the South under the dehumanizing shadow of Jim Crow, Rudd returned to the home of his youth, Bardstown. He took up residence on Chestnut Street, only a few blocks north of the Basilica of St. Joseph Proto-Cathedral. On 3 December, at about 4:30 a.m., the former editor of the *ACT,* who had been battling symptoms of senility, passed away. The visionary's hope that he would live long enough to see in the United States the establishment of a just society free of racial prejudice also died. Rudd was seventy-nine at the time of his death. He was laid to rest at St. Joseph Cemetery in consecrated ground alongside his Catholic brothers and sisters. [80]

CONCLUSION

A Justice Seeker's Legacy

Biographers have published works on the lives of a number of Rudd's contemporary black journalists, including T. Thomas Fortune, Ida B. Wells-Barnett, Frederick Douglass, Bishop Benjamin Tucker Tanner, and Bishop Henry McNeal Turner (1834–1915). To date, however, no biography has been penned on Rudd, despite the fact that his newspaper was among the most widely distributed black newspapers of its era. Perhaps the editor's relative obscurity is due in part to his religious affiliation. For, as a black Catholic, Rudd remained a relative outsider among his mostly Protestant peers. Though the editor of the *ACT* was concerned with the same grievances as other civil rights leaders, his polemical church-centered approach for attaining racial justice in America would have been unpalatable for many blacks.

Rudd was a remarkable man of action and a strong believer in the power of black agency. His accomplishments extend across a wide number of fields, including politics, business, journalism, education, and church work. Though he was born a slave, he made the most of each opportunity afforded him. He managed to get an education and learn a trade; he built a successful printing business, employing along the way several African American printers. Rudd, like Booker T. Washington, was a believer in vocational training. For this reason, the former editor established a printing school in each of the facilities he managed. Moreover, as a teacher Rudd planted his ideals in the minds of those who would live to witness the casting off of the demeaning and stifling yoke of Jim Crow legislation.

Rudd's accomplishments as a newspaper man are impressive as well. He envisioned and built a successful nationally circulated newspaper, the *ACT*. In its pages the editor lifted a cry to defend the dignity and civil rights of African Americans. At its zenith, Rudd's publication boasted a readership of 10,000.

Rudd was an active Republican during his early years in Springfield, Ohio. Upon his move to Cincinnati, he was named among the city's leading black citizens and civil rights leaders. As is evident from his newspaper, Rudd worked across denominational lines to promote racial justice. While residing in Cincinnati, the editor of the *ACT* also established the Colored Catholic Congress movement, an organization that has served as an example for twentieth-century black Catholic groups seeking to advance the cause of African Americans. Moreover, it appears Rudd was the primary impetus in the creation of the important lay Catholic congress movement.

The ambitious and multitalented Rudd charted a new course following his move south. He managed a lumber mill in Bolivar County, Mississippi, and worked for Scott Bond. While in Bond's employ, the aging Rudd designed a gravel-loading machine that appears to have earned Bond tens of thousands of dollars. Rudd also coauthored a biography of Bond's life.

Despite this former slave's many accomplishments, none is more inspiring than Rudd's church-centered cry for justice. For as Jim Crow cast its benighted shadow over the South in the last two decades of the nineteenth century, many Catholics seemed unwilling to stand for the truth of the gospel. Yet during these dark days, Rudd, with the inspiration of a prophet, enthusiastically and courageously proclaimed what he believed to be the cardinal truth of the Catholic Church: the "Fatherhood of God and Brotherhood of Man."

NOTES

PREFACE

1. David Spalding, C.F.X, "The Negro Catholic Congresses, 1889–1894," *Catholic Historical Review* 55, no. 3 (October 1969): 337–357.

2. Cyprian Davis, *The History of Black Catholics in the United States* (New York: Crossroads Publication Co., 1990).

3. Joseph H. Lackner, S.M., "Dan A. Rudd, Editor of the *American Catholic Tribune,* from Bardstown to Cincinnati," *Catholic Historical Review* 80, no. 2 (April 1994): 258–281; Lackner, "The *American Catholic Tribune* and the Puzzle of Its Finances," *Records of the American Catholic Historical Society* (Spring/Summer 1995): 1–24; Lackner, "*The American Catholic Tribune:* No Other Like It," *U.S. Catholic Historian* 25, no. 3 (Summer 2007): 1–24.

INTRODUCTION

1. *ACT,* 12 January 1889, 4. Rudd was also hosted by this same president following the Catholic lay congress in November 1889. *Philadelphia Tribune,* quoted in "For Two Christians," *ACT,* 21 December 1889, 2.

2. "Full Text of a Paper," *ACT,* 30 January 1892, 2.

3. "Full Text of a Paper," 2.

4. "Full Text of a Paper," 2.

5. "Full Text of a Paper," 2.

6. "Full Text of a Paper," 2.

1 • DANIEL RUDD AND THE ESTABLISHMENT OF THE *AMERICAN CATHOLIC TRIBUNE*

1. V. P. McMurry and C. F. Crews, "Kentucky, Catholic Church In," *New Catholic Encyclopedia,* 2nd ed. (Detroit: Gale, 2003)146–149.

2. Nelson County, Kentucky, Cemeteries, Nelson County Public Library, Bardstown, 4:58; *Nelson County Kentucky 1870 Federal Census* (Nelson County Genealogical Society, 2001), 1:157; *Nelson County Kentucky 1880 Federal Census* (Nelson County Genealogical Society, 2001), 10; Joseph H. Lackner, S.M., "Dan A. Rudd, Editor of the *American Catholic Tribune,* From Bardstown to Cincinnati," *Catholic Historical Review* 80, no. 2 (April 1994): 265. In 1840 Charles Haydon owned only two slaves, one male between the ages of fifty-five and one hundred, and one female between the ages of ten and twenty-four. See *1840 Federal Census Nelson County Kentucky* (Nelson County Genealogical Roundtable, n.d.), 78. In 1852 Charles and Matilda were party to the sale of a fifty-eight-acre parcel of property located about one mile east of Bardstown and owned by Edward and Ann Smith. This could have been

the property where Eliza lived at the time of her marriage to Robert in 1831 (Nelson County Deed Book, 21:51, Nelson County Court Records, Sutherland Building, Bardstown, KY).

3. Sarah B. Smith, *Historic Nelson County: Its Towns and People* (Bardstown, KY: Nelson County Genealogical Roundtable, 2008), 381.

4. Gilbert J. Garraghan, *The Jesuits of the Middle United States* (Chicago: Loyola University Press, 1983), 2:293.

5. The Family Chart of Charles Haydon, Haydon Family Genealogical File, Genealogy Room, Nelson County Public Library, Bardstown, KY; Federal Census of 1870, Nelson County, Kentucky.

6. Nelson County, Kentucky, Cemeteries, 4:58.

7. Nelson County Deed Book, 21:378–379; Slave Data Base for Nelson County, s.v. "Charles Lemons," Genealogy Room, Nelson County Public Library, Bardstown, KY. For further discussion of the cholera epidemic, see "Bishop Benedict Joseph Flaget," *Diocese of Bardstown Bicentennial Booklet 1808–2008* (2008): 6.

8. Inventory and Appraisement of the Estate of Richard Rudd, Nelson County Court Records, Sutherland Building, Bardstown, KY.

9. Patricia Craven and Richard Pangburn, *From Out of the Dark Past: Their Eyes Implore Us: The Black Roots of Nelson County, Kentucky* (Bardstown, KY: Nelson County Genealogical Roundtable, 2009), 82.

10. Daniel and two of his brothers would also subsequently work as sextons in the church. *ACT,* 3 June 1887, 2; Lackner, "Dan A. Rudd," 265; Nelson County Black Baptisms, s.v. "Daniel and Delores Bohn," Genealogy Room, Nelson County Public Library, Bardstown, KY.

11. Record of the Personal Property of Charles Haydon, Will Book, 9:494, Nelson County Court Records, Sutherland Building, Bardstown, KY; Lackner, "Dan A. Rudd," 264–265; J. Winston Coleman Jr., *Slavery Times in Kentucky* (Chapel Hill: New York; Johnson Reprint Corp., 1970), 57 61. Rudd's siblings and their respective ages in 1858 were listed as follows: Charles Henry, twenty-six; Anice, twenty-four; William, twenty-two; Sarah, twenty; John, eighteen; Catherine, sixteen; Josephine, fourteen; Madison, twelve; Isabella, ten; Frank, eight; Daniel, four; and Charles, three (Nelson County, Kentucky, Cemeteries, 4:58).

12. Lackner, "Dan A. Rudd," 264–265.

13. Marion B. Lucas, *A History of Blacks in Kentucky: From Slavery to Segregation, 1760–1891,* 2nd ed. (Frankfort: Kentucky Historical Society, 2003), 43.

14. George P. Rawick, ed., *The American Slave: A Composite Autobiography* (Westport, CT: Greenwood Publishing Co., 1972), 16, 26.

15. Rawick, *The American Slave,* 44.

16. Among Catholic liberals who opposed slavery were Orestes Brownson (1803–1876), founder of *Brownson's Quarterly Review*; John Baptist Purcell (1800–1883), archbishop of Cincinnati; Fr. Edward Purcell (1808–1881), the prelate's brother, who served as editor the *Cincinnati Catholic Telegraph;* and Bishop Sylvester H. Rosecrans (1827–1878), Archbishop Purcell's auxiliary.

17. John T. McGreevy, *Catholicism and American Freedom: A History* (New York: W. W. Norton & Co., 2003), 13, 36, 75–88. Rosecrans was appointed archbishop of Columbus, Ohio, in 1868. He served in this position until his death in 1878. Satish Joseph claims that the Purcell brothers' antislavery sentiment was a minority opinion

among Catholics. Further, Joseph argues that the Purcells called for the immediate emancipation of the nation's slaves. The two brothers promulgated their controversial campaign against human bondage in their publication, the *Catholic Telegraph*. Despite the Purcells' conviction regarding the fundamental unity of the human family, they retained the belief that blacks were inferior to whites. In this same article, Joseph points out that the Purcells' campaign against slavery was primarily motivated by the brothers' support of white laborers. Moreover, the Purcells were opposed to racial integration. Satish Joseph, C. Ss. R., "Long Live the Republic; Fr. Edward Purcell and the Slavery Controversy: 1861–1865," *American Catholic Studies Journal of the Catholic Historical Society* 116, no. 4 (Winter 2005): 25–54; Davis, *The History of Black Catholics*, 65; Francis Patrick Kenrick, "On Slavery" (1841), quoted in *Creative Fidelity American Catholic Intellectual Traditions,* ed. Scott Appleby, Patricia Byrne, and William L. Portier (Maryknoll, NY: Orbis Books, 2004), 167–170.

18. C. Walker Gollar, "Catholic Slaves and Slaveholders in Kentucky," *Catholic Historical Review* 84, no. 1 (January 1998): 42–62.

19. Gollar, "Catholic Slaves and Slaveholders in Kentucky," 44.

20. Federal Census of 1870, Nelson County, Kentucky, 157; Federal Census of 1880, Nelson County, Kentucky, 10.

21. Commissioner's Report of the Slaves of R. Rudd Appraisement & Allotments, Nelson County Court Records, Sutherland Building, Bardstown, KY.

22. Gollar, "Catholic Slaves and Slaveholders in Kentucky," 53–61.

23. Clayton E. Jewett and John O. Allen, *Slavery in the South: A State-by-State History* (Westport, CT: Greenwood Press, 2004), 104–105; Coleman, *Slavery Times in Kentucky,* 54–56; Lucas, *A History of Blacks in Kentucky,* 42; Jewett and Allen, *Slavery in the South,* 105.

24. Jewett and Allen, *Slavery in the South,* 107; Rawick, *The American Slave,* 2, 13, 18; Coleman, 64.

25. Jewett and Allen, *Slavery in the South,* 107; Rawick, *The American Slave,* 2, 14, 74.

26. Jewett and Allen, *Slavery in the South,* 105; Rawick, *The American Slave,* 5, 18.

27. *ACT,* 3 June 1887, 2.

28. John Hope Franklin and Alfred A. Moss Jr., *From Slavery to Freedom: A History of African Americans,* 7th ed. (New York: McGraw-Hill, 1994), 134–135; Rawick, *The American Slave,* 3, 15, 21.

29. Rawick, *The American Slave,* 71.

30. Davis, *The History of Black Catholics,* 98.

31. Gollar, "Catholic Slaves and Slaveholders in Kentucky," 48–49.

32. *ACT,* 3 June 1887, 2.

33. Lackner, "Dan A. Rudd," 266.

34. Garraghan, *The Jesuits of the Middle United States,* 325–326.

35. Garraghan, *The Jesuits of the Middle United States,* 327–329.

36. As many as 180 soldiers were baptized during the college's military period, and many of these on their death bed. See Garraghan, *The Jesuits of the Middle United States,* 327–330.

37. Garraghan, *The Jesuits of the Middle United States,* 330.

38. *ACT,* 3 June 1887, 2.

39. Kentucky's slaves officially won their freedom on December 18, 1865, after the state legislature approved the Thirteenth Amendment.

40. Rawick, *The American Slave,* 3, 6; Franklin and Moss, *From Slavery to Freedom,* 137.

41. *ACT,* 12 September 1891, 2.

42. Lackner, "Dan A. Rudd," 266.

43. "The Race Problem," *ACT,* 29 April 1893, 2.

44. David A. Gerber, *Black Ohio and the Color Line, 1860–1915* (Urbana: University of Illinois Press, 1976), 31.

45. Lackner, "Dan A. Rudd," 268. This same year, a large number of blacks traveled to Springfield, Ohio, to work in the homes of well-to-do white residents. Whether Daniel's sister-in-law, Jemimah, came to Springfield to work as a domestic remains unclear.

46. Jack S. Blocker, *A Little More Freedom: African Americans Enter the Urban Midwest, 1860–1930* (Columbus: Ohio State University Press, 2008), 70; *The Heart of Springfield 1873–1974,* Fisher Family Library and Archives, Clark County Historical Society, Springfield, OH (a booklet with a time line of significant events in the history of the city).

47. Willard D. Allbeck, *Springfield in the 1870's* (Springfield, OH: Clark County Historical Society, 1977), 2.

48. *ACT,* 14 March 1891, 2.

49. Davis, *The History of Black Catholics,* 164; Lackner, "Dan A. Rudd," 268; *One Hundred Seventy Five Years of Struggle: A History of Black People in Springfield, Ohio* (Springfield, OH: n.p., n.d.), 83; Allbeck, *Springfield in the 1870's,* 9.

50. *Springfield City Directory* (Springfield, OH: Swartz & Co., 1876), 209.

51. William M. Rockel, *20th Century History of Springfield and Clark Co. Ohio and Representative Citizens* (Chicago: Biographical Publishing Co., 1908), 575–576.

52. *Manufacturers and Merchants of Ohio* (New York: International Publishing Co., 1886), 129.

53. See "What Other's Say of Us," *ACT,* 17 June 1887, 2; *Springfield City Directory* (Springfield, OH: T. H. Edwards & Co., 1877–1878), 16; *Springfield City Directory* (Cincinnati, OH: Williams & Co., 1883–1884).

54. M. Edmund Hussey, *1999 Sesquicentennial Directory St. Raphael Catholic Church* (Springfield, OH: St. Raphael Catholic Church, 1999), 8–11.

55. Gerber, *Black Ohio,* 54–57.

56. Hussey, *1999 Sesquicentennial Directory,* 11.

57. "Springfield, O.," *ACT,* 30 November 1889, 2; *ACT,* 12 September 1891, 2.

58. August Meier, "Frederick Douglass's Vision for America: A Case Study in Nineteenth-Century Negro Protest," in *Along the Color Line: Explorations in the Black Experience,* ed. August Meier and Elliott Rudwick (Urbana: University of Illinois Press, 2002), 4–27.

59. Meier, "Frederick Douglass's Vision for America," 7, 21, 24. Though Douglass did, especially in the 1850s and immediately following the Civil War, speak of the merits of racial solidarity, industrial education, and the need for middle-class respectability, he was always explicit as to his desire for full equality. His posture toward the dominant culture was consistently confrontational rather than publicly accommodating.

60. Lackner, "Dan A. Rudd," 268, 276–277. There are competing claims as to when the *Ohio State Tribune* was established. An exchange in the March 16, 1888, edition of the *ACT* suggests the date for the establishment of this publication was January

1886. There are no extant copies of the newspaper publications Rudd founded prior to the *ACT.* Lyle Koehler, *Cincinnati's Black Peoples: A Chronology and Bibliography, 1787–1982* (Cincinnati: University of Cincinnati, 1986), 87. Koehler erroneously reports Rudd founded the *ACT* in Cincinnati in 1884. Felecia G. Jones Ross follows him in this error. See Felecia G. Jones Ross, "Democracy's Textbook: A History of the Black Press in Ohio, 1865–1985," in *The Black Press in the Middle West 1865–1985,* ed. Henry Lewis Suggs (Westport, CT: Greenwood Press, 1996), 243–246.

61. "Public Meeting of the Black Citizens of Springfield," *Springfield Republic,* 13 April 1882, 2.

62. Lackner, "Dan A. Rudd," 268. This case came about in Springfield at the start of 1881–1882 school year when blacks were denied entrance into the all-white Shaffer Street School. A division occurred in the black community as to whether to push for equal facilities or to push for integration of the city's schools. Those who favored integration, including Rudd, filed suit in federal court to test the constitutionality of race segregation. Because the plaintiffs did not base their case on the essential inequality of the separate schools, the case did not get past the District Court of Cincinnati. The unfavorable judgment against those pressing the Gazaway case was handed down in November 1882. See Gerber, *Black Ohio,* 198.

63. Lackner, "The *American Catholic Tribune* and the Puzzle of Its Finances," 28–29.

64. The date of this dissolution was 10 July 1888. "Dissolution of Co-partnership," *ACT,* 20 July 1888, 3.

65. *Williams' Cincinnati Directory 1886* (Cincinnati: Williams & Co. Proprietors, 1886), 1754–1755.

66. *Atlas of the City of Cincinnati, Ohio* (New York: E. Robinson, 1883–1884), plate 1. The ward boundaries change each year. The ward locations cited in this chapter correspond to the 1880 and 1890 assessments. Simon J. Bronner, ed., *Lafcadio Hearn's America: Ethnographic Sketches and Editorials* (Lexington: University Press of Kentucky, 2002), 87; Nikki Taylor, *Frontiers of Freedom: Cincinnati's Black Community, 1802–1868* (Athens: Ohio University Press, 2005), 186.

67. *Atlas of the City of Cincinnati,* plates 2, 5; *Williams' Cincinnati Directory 1887,* 1434; *ACT,* 7 October 1887, 2.

68. *Atlas of the City of Cincinnati,* plates 2, 5.

69. Lackner, "The Foundation of St. Ann's Parish, 1866–1870: The African-American Experience in Cincinnati," *U.S. Catholic Historian* 14, no. 2 (Spring 1996): 17.

70. *Woodstock Letters: A Historical Journal of Jesuit Missionary and Educational Activities* 46, no. 2 (1917): 406.

71. Stephen Hahn, *A Nation under Our Feet: Black Political Struggles in the Rural South from Slavery to the Great Migration* (Cambridge, MA: Harvard University Press, 2003), 219–220.

72. Franklin and Moss, *From Slavery to Freedom,* 242–244.

73. Robert H. Zieger, *For Jobs and Freedom: Race and Labor in America since 1865* (Lexington: University Press of Kentucky, 2007), 59; Franklin and Moss, *From Slavery to Freedom,* 251.

74. Rayford W. Logan, *The Betrayal of the Negro from Rutherford B. Hayes to Woodrow Wilson* (originally published as *The Negro in American Life and Thought: The Nadir, 1877–1901* (New York: Collier Books, 1965), 23–47.

75. Logan, *The Betrayal of the Negro,* 97.

76. Douglas A. Blackmon, *Slavery by Another Name: The Re-Enslavement of Black Americans from the Civil War to World War II* (New York: Doubleday, 2008), 93.

77. Franklin and Moss, *From Slavery to Freedom,* 238.

78. Franklin and Moss, *From Slavery to Freedom,* 262.

79. Stephen J. Ochs, *Desegregating the Altar: The Josephites and the Struggle for Black Priests, 1871–1960* (Baton Rouge: Louisiana State University Press, 1990), 99, 134.

80. Dolores Egger Labbe , *Jim Crow Comes to Church: The Establishment of Segregated Catholic Parishes in South Louisiana* (New York: Arno Press, 1978), 27; Similarly, James B. Bennett has argued that by the 1920s the pattern of voluntary segregation in New Orleans's parishes was made mandatory. James B. Bennett, *Religion and the Rise of Jim Crow in New Orleans* (Princeton: Princeton University Press, 2005), 9, 210.

81. See Charles A. Simmons, *The African American Press: A History of News Coverage during National Crises, with Special Reference to Four Newspapers, 1827–1965* (Jefferson, NC: McFarland & Co., 1998), 5.

82. Armistead S. Pride and Clint C. Wilson, *The History of the Black Press* (Washington, DC: Howard University Press, 1997), 13.

83. Many of those who believed in the inferiority of ethnic groups believed that over time the strongest races would assume their dominance. These Social Darwinists applied Charles Darwin's (1809–1882), scientific evolutionary theories to human social groups, including racial groups. Actually, Darwin refuted the idea of the multiplicity of human species. Further, he did not believe that one race was superior to another. English philosopher Herbert Spencer applied Darwin's evolutionary theories to racial groups in society. It was Lewis Henry Morgan (1818–1881), however, who popularized social evolution in America as an explanation of human development. He theorized that societal development occurred in three stages: "savagery," "barbarism," and "civilization." See Philip Dray, *At the Hands of Persons Unknown: The Lynching of Black America* (New York: Random House, 2002), 95. See also Frederick E. Hoxie, *A Final Promise: The Campaign to Assimilate the Indians, 1880–1920* (Lincoln: University of Nebraska Press, 1984), 17–18. See also Logan, *The Betrayal of the Negro,* 268–269.

84. "Public Meeting of the Black Citizens of Springfield," *Springfield Republic,* 13 April 1882, 2.

85. *ACT,* 1 April 1887, 2.

86. Some sources claim Rudd continued to publish the *ACT* in Detroit through 1899. This is unlikely, as Rudd is not listed in Detroit's City Directory after 1897. Eugene P. Willging and Herta Hatzfeld, *Catholic Serials of the Nineteenth Century in the United States: A Descriptive Bibliography and Union List,* 2nd ser., pt. 12 (Washington, DC: Catholic University Press, 1966), 80; *ACT,* 17 January 1891, 2; *ACT,* 24 January 1891, 3.

87. *ACT,* 31 January 1891, 2.

88. *ACT,* 4 February 1893, 2.

89. "The National Afro-American Press Association," *ACT,* 12 August 1893, 1.

90. "Convention of Catholic Editors and Publishers," *ACT,* 10 May 1890, 3; "Catholic Editor's Meet," *ACT,* 9 May 1891, 2; "The Pope and the Press," *ACT,* 10 May 1890, 1; *ACT,* 1 June 1889, 2. In July 1887 Rudd printed an exchange from the *New Orleans Democrat* featuring this same quotation. Rudd may have borrowed this quote directly from the above southern publication (see *ACT,* 15 July 1887, 2.

91. Simmons, *The African American Press,* 15, 21.

92. Ross, "Democracy's Textbook: A History of the Black Press in Ohio, 1865–1985," 244–246. It is likely Ross underreported the number of black papers established in this time period. Rudd, for example, announced the arrival of a new political newspaper, the *American,* in June 1891. Ross failed to mention this publication. Professor Charles W. Bell addressed the second Colored Catholic Congress in July 1890. At this same meeting Rudd pointed out that Bell held the distinction of being the only African American writing instructor in the country currently teaching in a white school. Bell also wrote the "Our Colored Citizen's Column" for the Cincinnati *Commercial Gazette.* See Koehler, *Cincinnati's Black Peoples,* 86.

93. Lackner, "Dan A. Rudd," 277. This publication was possibly the *Columbus Observer.*

94. *Columbus Observer,* quoted in "Columbus, O.," *ACT,* 16 March 1888, 2.

95. *ACT,* 9 August 1890, 2. In this edition Rudd reprinted an editorial from the first edition of the *ACT* dated August 22, 1886.

96. *Times Star,* quoted in "Development of Africa," *ACT,* 19 July 1890, 2.

97. *ACT,* 9 August 1890, 2.

98. The religious order she founded, the Sisters of the Blessed Sacrament for Indians and Colored People, was established in 1891.

99. Prior to the Civil War, the Oblate Sisters of Providence, led by Mother Mary Elizabeth Lange (1784–1882) and Sulpician priest Fr. Jacques Hector Nicolas Jourbert, worked among blacks in Baltimore. Similarly, the Sisters of the Holy Family, led by Henriette Delille (1813–1862) and Juliette Guadin, worked among African Americans in New Orleans. The Mill Hill Fathers arrived in the United States in 1871 to work among blacks. This was a religious order founded by Cardinal Herbert Vaughan (1832–1903). Vaughan was the vice president of St. Edumund's College in England at the time the order was founded. The Congregation of the Holy Ghost (Spiritans), arriving in the United States in 1872, also achieved some progress with regard to their efforts to evangelize African Americans. See Davis, *The History of Black Catholics,* 99–100, 125–126, 131–132, 133–136.

100. Joseph H. Lackner, "The *American Catholic Tribune*: No Other Like It," paper presented at the American Catholic Historical Association Meeting, University of Dayton, April 23, 2005, Dayton, OH, photocopy, pp. 1–2. The above material was edited out of the subsequent article published by Lackner under the same title in 2007.

101. *ACT,* 30 December 1887, 2;

102. M. Torrensdale to Father Hudson, 11 January 1887, transcript in the hand of M. Torrensdale, Hudson Papers, University of Notre Dame Archives, South Bend, IN.

103. *ACT,* 1 August 1891, 2; *ACT,* 4 March 1887, 2.

104. *ACT,* 18 April 1891, 2. In March 1887 Rudd announced his plans to visit the southern cities of Knoxville, Chattanooga, Atlanta, Macon, Augusta, Savannah, and Charleston. There is, however, no record of these visits in the *ACT.* It is reasonable to assume Rudd would have made some reference as to the particulars of these visits had he, in fact, made them (see *ACT,* 18 March 1887, 2).

105. Lackner, "The *American Catholic Tribune* and the Puzzle of Its Finances," 30.

106. *ACT,* 2 September 1887, 2.

107. *ACT,* 26 January 1889, 2.

108. "The Cincinnati Editor of the *Plaindealer* Says," *ACT,* 17 December 1892, 2; "A Helping Hand," *ACT,* 21 December 1889, 1.

109. *ACT,* 2 March 1889, 2.

110. See "Editor Mention," *ACT,* 25 November 1887, 2. Archbishop Elder's endorsement can be found on the editorial page of the *ACT.*

111. "A Few Samples of Many," *ACT,* 7 October 1887, 3. This donor was from Cincinnati.

112. "Washington C.H., O," *ACT,* 24 February 1888, 2.

113. Lackner, "The *American Catholic Tribune*" (2005), 4–5.

114. Ross, "Democracy's Textbook," 249.

115. *Globe-Republic,* 10 June 1885, 1, quoted in Lackner, "Dan A. Rudd," 278; *Commercial Gazette,* quoted in "What Others Say of Us," *ACT,* 17 June 1887, 2.

116. Wendell Phillips Dabney, *Cincinnati's Colored Citizens, Historical, Sociological and Biographical* (New York: Negro Universities Press, 1970), 121–123.

117. "Ruffin Club," *ACT,* 10 February 1888, 1; "City and Vicinity," *ACT,* 27 May 1887, 3; "The Ruffin Club Election," *ACT,* 10 February 1888, 1; "Ruffin Club," *ACT,* 3 June 1887, 2; Dabney, *Cincinnati's Colored Citizens,* 122.

118. See "The *American Catholic Tribune,*" *ACT,* 2 September 1887, 2.

119. "The Colored Man in the Popular Magazines," *ACT,* 6 April 1889, 2.

120. *ACT,* 4 May 1889, 2.

2 • A NEW CIVILIZATION BASED ON THE FATHERHOOD OF GOD AND THE BROTHERHOOD OF MAN

1. Rudd printed an article estimating that there were 200 black papers in the spring of 1891. See "The National Afro-American Press Convention," *ACT,* 11 April 1891, 2.

2. "The Negro Planter in the Common School," *Southern Planter and Farmer* 37 (April 1876): 253; quoted in H. Shelton Smith, *In His Image, but . . . Racism in Southern Religion, 1780–1910* (Durham: Duke University Press, 1972), 267.

3. "The Congress Proceedings," *ACT,* 19 July 1890, 1.

4. Edmund Clarence Stedman, "Christophe," *Century* 23 (November 1881): 34–35; quoted in Logan, *The Betrayal of the Negro,* 269.

5. August Meier, *Negro Thought in America, 1880–1915: Racial Ideologies in the Age of Booker T. Washington* (Ann Arbor: University of Michigan Press, 1963), 54.

6. "The Nonsense of It: Adam Again Talks Foolishness," *ACT,* 4 February 1893, 2; *Boston Pilot,* quoted in "Interviews," *ACT,* 9 August 1890, 1.

7. *Chattanooga Justice,* quoted in *ACT,* 22 July 1887, 2.

8. *ACT,* 17 February 1888, 2.

9. *Cincinnati Post,* quoted in "'The Post' Our Friend," *ACT,* 21 September 1889, 2.

10. *ACT,* 19 July 1890, 2.

11. See *ACT,* 4 May 1889, 2. *ACT,* 30 November 1889, 2; "Good Words," *ACT,* 24 January 1891, 2; *ACT,* 4 May 1889, 2; "Same Old Falsehood," *ACT,* 22 July 1887, 2.

12. Charles Carroll, *The Negro a Beast* (Salem, NH: Ayer Co., 1991), 87–90.

13. Smith, *In His Image, But,* 154–164.

14. "A Neat New Church," *ACT,* 24 December 1892, 1; *ACT,* 19 July 1890, 2.

15. The first to label this concept may have been Thomas E. Wangler in his article "John Ireland's Emergence as a Liberal Catholic and Americanist: 1875–1887," *Records of the American Historical Society of Philadelphia* 81 (June 1970): 67–82.

16. In the early extant issues of the *ACT,* Rudd employed an artistic representation to illustrate his belief in the universality of the Catholic Church. On the editorial page in both of the first two extant issues of the newspaper (18 and 25 February 1887), Rudd included a sketch of the pope surrounded by four adoring children. Two of these children are clearly white, one is clearly of African origin, and the other appears to be a native of the New World. Below this sketch are the words "The Church the mother of all."

17. "Good Words," *ACT,* 24 January 1891, 2.

18. *ACT,* 31 August 1888, 2.

19. "Good Words," *ACT,* 24 January 1891, 2.

20. "Good Words," *ACT,* 24 January 1891, 2.

21. *ACT,* 13 January 1888, 2; *Negro American,* quoted in "The Negro and the Catholic Church," *ACT,* 11 May 1888, 2.

22. *ACT,* 9 September 1887, 2.

23. *ACT,* 23 September 1887, 2.

24. "Good Words," *ACT,* 24 January 1891, 2.

25. Patrick W. Carey, ed., *American Catholic Religious Thought: The Shaping of a Theological and Social Tradition* (New York: Paulist Press, 1987), 15–24.

26. *ACT,* 16 November 1889, 2.

27. See *Christian Recorder,* 1 May 1890, 1.

28. "To Be Well Shaken before Taken," *ACT,* 15 April 1887, 2.

29. *ACT,* 16 December 1887, 2.

30. *ACT,* 13 April 1888, 2.

31. Fr. Jaime Luciano Balmes, *Protestantism and Catholicity Compared in Their Effects on the Civilization of Europe* (Baltimore: John Murphy Co., 1861), 27.

32. "The Colored Man in the Popular Magazines," *ACT,* 6 April 1889, 2.

33. *ACT,* 13 April 1888, 2. See also Balmes's treatment of private judgment's usurpation of lawful authority (Balmes, *Protestantism and Catholicity,* 26).

34. *ACT,* 23 December 1887, 2.

35. *ACT,* 4 April 1891, 2; *ACT,* 13 January 1888, 2.

36. *Church News,* quoted in "The Teacher of Nations," *ACT,* 15 June 1889, 1.

37. François Pierre Guillaume Guizot, *The History of Civilization in Europe: From the Fall of the Roman Empire to the French Revolution,* trans. William Hazlitt (New York: J. B. Alden, 1893), 138.

38. Guizot, *The History of Civilization,* 264.

39. Guizot, *The History of Civilization,* 272–273.

40. Balmes, *Protestantism and Catholicity,* 115, 419.

41. Wangler, "John Ireland's Emergence," 67–82.

42. *ACT,* 18 May 1888, 2.

43. "The Catholic Congress Photographed," *St. Joseph's Advocate,* no. 2 (April 1889): 606; "The Catholic Congress," *Catholic World* 49, no. 289 (April 1889), quoted in *ACT,* 20 April 1889, 1.

44. "The Catholic Congress," *Catholic World* 49, no. 289 (April 1889), quoted in *ACT,* 20 April 1889, 1.

45. "Leo XIII. on Human Liberty," *ACT,* 24 August 1888, 1.

46. Portier has acknowledged Slattery's appropriation of the Romantic apologetic for Catholicism in the latter's work on behalf of African Americans. The same historical

hermeneutic is also present in the work of the men active in the Colored Catholic Congress movement. See, for example, the speeches of R. L. Ruffin and archbishop Henry Elder, delivered at the first meeting of the congress. "Washington D.C. Catholic Congress," *ACT,* 12 January 1889, 1; Daniel Rudd, *Three Catholic Afro-American Congresses* (New York: Arno Press, 1978), 24–25; See also William L. Portier, "John R. Slattery's Vision for the Evangelization of American Blacks," *U.S. Catholic Historian* 5, no. 1 (1986): 19–44.

47. *ACT,* 31 August 1888, 2.

48. *ACT,* 18 May 1888, 2.

49. *Commercial Gazette,* quoted in "What Others Say of Us," *ACT,* 17 June 1887, 2.

50. "Lexington, Ky.," *ACT,* 3 June 1887, 2.

51. "Lexington, Ky.," *ACT,* 3 June 1887, 2.

52. *ACT,* 7 October 1887, 2.

53. *ACT,* 25 May 1889, 2.

54. *ACT,* 25 May 1889, 2.

3 • ARCHBISHOP JOHN IRELAND'S MASTERLY PLEA FOR JUSTICE

1. Daniel Rudd to Archbishop Henry Elder, 3 May 1888, transcript in the hand of Daniel Rudd, Historical Archives of the Chancery, Cincinnati.

2. "Editorial Mention," *ACT,* 25 November 1887, 2.

3. "Ratified in New York," *ACT,* 2 March 1889, 2.

4. Thomas Burke served in Chicago. *ACT,* 29 November 1890, 3.

5. *Catholic Standard,* quoted in "The Holy Father's Appeal," *ACT,* 17 January 1891, 1.

6. "The Church Our Hope," *ACT,* 10 January 1891, 2.

7. *Catholic News,* quoted in "The Doom of Slavery," *ACT,* 10 August 1889, 1.

8. *ACT,* 31 August 1888, 2.

9. *Philadelphia Tribune,* quoted in "For Two Christians," *ACT,* 21 December 1889, 2.

10. *Ave Maria,* quoted in *ACT,* 21 December 1889, 2.

11. *Philadelphia Tribune,* quoted in "For Two Christians," *ACT,* 21 December 1889, 2.

12. There are two different spellings for the name in the article. I have chosen the one most likely correct.

13. *Commercial Gazette,* quoted in "No Color Line for Them," *ACT,* 15 November 1890, 2.

14. "C.K. of A.," *ACT,* 15 November 1890, 1.

15. *St. Paul Literary Northwest* (May 1892), quoted in James H. Moynihan, *The Life of Archbishop John Ireland* (New York: Harper & Brothers, 1953), 229.

16. See "An Episcopalian View," *ACT,* 16 December 1893, 1; Also see "How They See It," *ACT,* 4 February 1893, 1.

17. William L. Portier, "John R. Slattery's Vision for the Evangelization of American Blacks," 24; Marvin R. O'Connell, *John Ireland and the American Catholic Church* (St. Paul: Minnesota Historical Society Press, 1988), 61–87.

18. O'Connell, *John Ireland,* 268. The *Northwest Chronicle* was published in St.

Paul 1867–1900. Act III was the law Homer Plessy and the Citizens Committee of New Orleans sought to overturn, resulting in a critical Supreme Court battle in 1896: *Plessy v. Ferguson* (*Northwestern Chronicle*, 11 April 1890, 9 January 1891); quoted in O'Connell, *John Ireland*, 268.

19. St. Peter Claver Church would be the only black parish established during Ireland's tenure in St. Paul (see O'Connell, *John Ireland*, 268). "Colored Catholics in St. Paul," *ACT,* 19 April 1890, 2.

20. "Colored Catholics in St. Paul," *ACT,* 19 April 1890, 2. In the pages of the *ACT* Rudd showed little interest in the evangelization of Africa.

21. "Colored Catholics in St. Paul," *ACT,* 19 April 1890, 2.

22. "Colored Catholics in St. Paul," *ACT,* 19 April 1890, 2.

23. "Colored Catholics in St. Paul," *ACT,* 19 April 1890, 2.

24. "Colored Catholics in St. Paul," *ACT,* 19 April 1890, 2.

25. "Colored Catholics in St. Paul," *ACT,* 19 April 1890, 2.

26. James H. Moynihan incorrectly asserts that Ireland delivered his controversial sermon at St. Augustine in Washington, D.C., in April 1890 (see Moynihan, *The Life of Archbishop John Ireland*, 228). Michael J. Walsh to the editor of the *Catholic Mirror*, 5 May 1890, Baltimore, quoted in "Archbishop Ireland and the Negro Press Comments," *ACT,* 17 May 1890, 2. Ireland's controversial St. Augustine speech calling for the recognition of the social equality of blacks is not included in *The Church and Society*, a two-volume set of the prelate's collected works published in 1904. It may be that Ireland's ideals concerning the color line articulated in his 1890 speech were by 1904 even more out of step with national sentiment. Leo XIII issued his condemnation of Americanism in his papal letter *Testem Benevolentiae*. John Tracy Ellis, *American Catholicism*, 2d ed. (Chicago: University of Chicago Press, 1969), 120.

27. "There Is No Color Line," *Catholic Mirror*, 10 May 1890, 5; also quoted in "Washington, D.C.," *ACT,* 10 May 1890, 2. See also Morris J. MacGregor, *The Emergence of a Black Catholic Community: St. Augustine's in Washington* (Washington, DC: Catholic University of America Press, 1999), 135–136.

28. "There Is No Color Line," *Catholic Mirror*, 10 May 1890, 5.

29. "There Is No Color Line," *Catholic Mirror*, 10 May 1890, 5.

30. "There Is No Color Line," *Catholic Mirror*, 10 May 1890, 5.

31. "The Colored Problem," *Catholic Mirror*, 10 May 1890, 4; also quoted in "Archbishop Ireland and the Negro Press Comments," *ACT,* 17 May 1890, 2.

32. *ACT,* 10 May 1890, 2. The enlightened stand taken by Ireland on the race question did not preclude his ill treatment of other minority groups—for example, Native Americans and emigrant Ruthenian Uniates. See O'Connell, *John Ireland*, 268–269.

33. Albert Whitman, "Archbishop Ireland on the Color-Line," *Christian Recorder*, quoted in *ACT,* 21 June 1890, 2.

34. *People's Advocate*, quoted in "Rome's Bid," *ACT,* 24 May 1890, 2.

35. *Catholic Mirror*, quoted in "Archbishop Ireland and the Negro Press Comments," *ACT,* 17 May 1890, 2.

36. *Catholic Columbian*, quoted in "Archbishop Ireland and the Negro Press Comments," *ACT,* 17 May 1890, 2.

37. *New Orleans Pelican*, quoted in "Archbishop Ireland and the Negro Press Comments," *ACT,* 17 May 1890, 2.

38. *Chicago Conservator,* quoted in "Archbishop Ireland and the Negro Press Comments," *ACT,* 17 May 1890, 2.

39. *New York Age,* quoted in "Archbishop Ireland and the Negro Press Comments," *ACT,* 17 May 1890, 2.

40. *Washington Bee,* quoted in "Brave Defense," *ACT,* 24 May 1890, 2.

41. "Archbishop Ireland and the Negro Press Comments," *ACT,* 17 May 1890, 2.

42. *New York Tribune,* quoted in "Echoes Awakened," *ACT,* 14 June 1890, 2.

43. Albert Whitman, "Archbishop Ireland on the Color-Line," *Christian Recorder,* quoted in *ACT,* 21 June 1890, 2.

44. "More Thoughts on the Colored Problem," *ACT,* 14 June 1890, 2.

45. Patrick J. Ryan to Michael Augustine Corrigan, 20 May 1890, transcript in the hand of Patrick J. Ryan, Special Collections, Archdiocese of New York Archives, St. Joseph's Seminary, Yonkers, NY. See also Moynihan, *The Life of Archbishop John Ireland,* 228.

46. Mackey served as the associate editor of the *ACT* from May 1889 to January 1891. His main contribution to the newspaper appears to have been a set of serialized articles on the sacraments (see "Colored Catholics," *ACT,* 20 April 1889, 1). No reference is made to Mackey's partnership with the *ACT* in the prelate's obituary. See Gary Agee, "The Reverend John M. Mackey and Daniel A. Rudd in the Second Colored Catholic Congress," research paper, University of Dayton, 2003, pp. 6–8; "Colored Catholics," *ACT,* 20 April 1889, 1; *ACT,* 20 July 1889, 2.

47. Spalding, "The Negro Catholic Congresses," 344.

48. Lackner, "The *American Catholic Tribune*" (2005), 4.

49. "Washington, D.C.," *ACT,* 10 May 1890, 2.

50. "The Congress," *ACT,* 19 July 1890, 1.

51. "The Congress," *ACT,* 19 July 1890, 1.

52. Rudd, *Three Catholic Afro-American Congresses,* 127.

53. "The Negro Problem," *ACT,* 24 January 1891, 1.

54. "The Negro Problem," *ACT,* 24 January 1891, 1. Ireland's relatively enlightened position on this last question distinguished him from other liberals, including Slattery and Mackey.

55. "The Negro Problem," *ACT,* 24 January 1891, 1.

56. "The Negro Problem," *ACT,* 24 January 1891, 1.

57. *ACT,* 2 May 1891, 2.

58. "Pentecost at the Cathedral," *ACT,* 30 May 1891, 3.

59. "Civil Rights," *ACT,* 28 November 1891, 2.

60. "Washington, D.C.," *ACT,* 19 December 1891, 2.

61. *Journal,* 6 August 1892, 2.

62. Here Rudd appears to have appropriated an ecclesiological model articulated by Isaac Hecker in the latter's *The Church and the Age.* In this same text, Hecker discusses the presence of "bad Christians" in the church. The author defines these "bad Christians" as those who are "deaf to the word of God," who listen to their temper, and otherwise follow their passions. Hecker, therefore, speaks of the need of ongoing "reform" and "revolution" in the church. See Isaac Hecker, *The Church and the Age* (New York: H. J. Hewitt, 1887), 222–226.

63. *ACT,* 14 September 1888, 2.

64. *ACT,* 1 April 1887, 2.

65. *ACT,* 25 May 1888, 2.

66. "Caucasians Must Rule," *ACT,* 14 September 1889, 2.

67. "Caucasians Must Rule," *ACT,* 14 September 1889, 2.

68. "A Piece of Meanness," *ACT,* 17 January 1891, 2.

69. *Adam: Catholic Journal of the New South,* quoted in "The Nonsense of It: Adam Again Talks Foolishness," *ACT,* 4 February 1893, 2.

70. "The Congress," *ACT,* 26 July 1890, 1–2.

71. *ACT,* 15 July 1887, 2.

72. "Men and Things," *ACT,* 17 November 1888, 1.

73. *ACT,* 18 November 1887, 2.

74. John Boyle O'Reilly (1844–1890) served as editor/proprietor of the Boston *Pilot* 1876–1890. He was an advocate for African Americans. *Detroit Plaindealer,* 27 January 1893, 4.

75. *ACT,* 18 November 1887, 2. Tanner, who was subsequently elected as a bishop, also edited the *Christian Recorder* 1868–1884.

76. A.M.E. Zion Church's *Star of Zion,* quoted in *ACT,* 2 February 1889, 2. The *Star* was published in Charlotte, North Carolina.

77. *ACT,* 20 January 1888, 2. Rudd seems to have been under the misguided impression Claver was black. In fact, Claver was a Spanish Jesuit who in the seventeenth century served the slave population in what is today Colombia. He was canonized by Pope Leo XIII in 1888. Davis, *The History of Black Catholics,* 23.

78. *ACT,* 4 May 1888, 2.

79. Ochs, *Desegregating the Altar,* 1–8.

80. Ochs, *Desegregating the Altar,* 1–8.

81. Labbe , *Jim Crow Comes to Church,* 17–24.

82. Labbe , *Jim Crow Comes to Church,* 17–24.

83. Labbe, *Jim Crow Comes to Church,* 37; See also Bennett, *Religion,* 168.

84. The Creoles often felt victimized by the American binary form of segregation, which distinguished only racial traits. Before the nineteenth century, the major divide in the city was cultural, French and American. With the Americanization of the city, Creoles, who had prior to this time retained a measure of standing in the city, were increasingly grouped with other nonwhites at the bottom of the social stratum. See Bennett, *Religion,* 164–165, 178–179, 182.

85. *ACT,* 4 May 1888, 2.

86. *ACT,* 9 March 1888, 2.

87. *ACT,* 28 June 1890, 2.

88. *ACT,* 28 June 1890, 2.

89. "Kamloops, B.C.," *ACT,* 27 May 1887, 2.

90. "Kamloops, B.C.," *ACT,* 27 May 1887, 2.

91. *ACT,* 3 June 1887, 2.

92. *ACT,* 3 June 1887, 2.

93. "Mr. Smith Slightly Misinformed," *ACT,* 3 February 1888, 1.

94. "Why Separate Churches," *ACT,* 17 February 1888, 1.

95. "Washington, D.C.," *ACT,* 9 March 1888, 2.

96. "Why Are There Separat [sic] Churchese [sic] for the Colored Race?," *ACT,* 13 April 1888, 1.

97. "A Neat New Church," *ACT,* 24 December 1892, 1.

98. *ACT,* 1 April 1887, 2.

1. *ACT,* 9 August 1890, 2.

2. Vincent Harding, *There Is a River: The Black Struggle for Freedom in America* (New York: Vintage Books, 1983), xxi, 3.

3. *ACT,* 9 March 1888, 2.

4. See Lackner, "Dan A. Rudd," 270.

5. Rabbi Edward N. Calisch, "A Case of Experience with the Negro Problem," *Reform Advocate,* quoted in *ACT,* 5 March 1892, 1.

6. "The Same Old Story," *ACT,* 5 March 1892, 2.

7. "The Same Old Story," *ACT,* 5 March 1892, 2.

8. *Adam: Catholic Journal of the New South,* quoted in "Converting the Negro," *ACT,* 7 February 1891, 2.

9. *Adam: Catholic Journal of the New South,* quoted in "Converting the Negro," *ACT,* 7 February 1891, 2.

10. *ACT,* 11 March 1887, 1; "City and Vicinity," *ACT,* 27 October 1888, 3.

11. "Washington, D.C.," *ACT,* 23 March 1888, 1. Mary Francis began the catering business around 1818. She was the widow of Peter Augustine. One of the offspring of this couple was P. Jerome Augustine, who participated in the Colored Catholic Congress movement. Mary's family name is spelled "Augustin" in this article. It is assumed that the spelling for the family name was later altered given the fact that her son Jerome's name is subsequently spelled "Augustine." See "Items from the Quaker City," *ACT,* 8 March 1890, 2; "Chicago, Ill," *ACT,* 15 November 1890, 1.

12. *ACT,* 11 April 1891, 1; *ACT,* 30 September 1887, 1; "Baltimore," *ACT,* 22 July 1887, 1. The spelling is likely "McGuinn" (*Chicago Conservator,* quoted in "A Colored Inventor," *ACT,* 13 May 1887, 2).

13. *ACT,* 8 December 1888, 2.

14. "City and Vicinity," *ACT,* 13 April 1889, 3.

15. *ACT,* 30 March 1889, 2.

16. See E. B. Jourdain, Boston University Law School, quoted in "Crispus Attucks," *ACT,* 6 July 1888, 1.

17. "Negro in the Dark," *ACT,* 14 March 1891, 4.

18. *ACT,* 27 June 1891, 2.

19. *ACT,* 22 August 1891, 3.

20. "The Sunny South," *ACT,* 13 July 1891, 1.

21. *Afro-American Sentinel,* quoted in "Good Sense," *ACT,* 22 August 1891, 2. This same writer objected to the establishment of race publications. Rudd obviously did not object to the existence of black newspapers and journals.

22. "Some Queer Nonsense," *ACT,* 19 August 1893, 2.

23. "A Man at Last: The Cry of Justice Is Heard," *ACT,* 18 February 1887, 2.

24. Though the sixth article of the Northwest Ordinance of 1787 had forbidden slavery and involuntary servitude in the Northwest Territory, state leaders began placing restrictions on African Americans in 1804, a year after Ohio became a state. Ohio's first Black Law forbade the settlement of African Americans unable to produce a certificate of freedom. In 1807 African Americans were forbidden to settle in the state unless within twenty days of their arrival they could secure a $500 bond, which had to be posted by two whites guaranteeing the good behavior of the individual. Similarly,

laws were drafted that denied blacks the right to testify in court, to be seated on a jury, or to serve in the state militia. In 1829 a law was passed that specifically forbade blacks from attending state common schools or from receiving any portion of the state's school funds. Though this law was repealed in 1849, school districts in Ohio continued to deny blacks entrance into the state's public schools. See Rubin F. Weston, ed., *Blacks in Ohio History: A Conference to Commemorate the Bicentennial of the American Revolution* (Columbus: Ohio Historical Society, 1976), 4–5; Frank Quillin, *The Color Line in Ohio: A History of Race Prejudice in a Typical Northern State* (New York: Negro University Press, 1969), 24; Stephen Middleton, *The Black Laws: Race and the Legal Process in Early Ohio* (Athens: Ohio University Press, 2005), 43–51, 55. House Bill 71, the Ely-Arnett Bill, was introduced to repeal Section 4008 of the Ohio Code. The aim of this historic legislation, sponsored by the assembly's African American delegation, was to erase all remaining vestiges of the state's Black Laws, including the provision prohibiting interracial marriage. The most important practical component of the Ely-Arnett legislation was the outlawing of racial segregation in Ohio's schools. See Quillin, *The Color Line*, 33.

25. *ACT,* 9 March 1888, 2.

26. *ACT,* 18 March 1887, 2; *ACT,* 24 June 1887, 2. Rudd reported that Parham served as the principal of Gaines High School in Cincinnati for the school year ending June 1887. This educator was born in Virginia in 1839 of free parents and migrated to Ohio via Philadelphia. Parham taught in Cincinnati's black schools prior to his elevation to the position of principal. See Gerber, *Black Ohio*, 41–43; *ACT,* 1 July 1887, 2.

27. Gilbert Anthony Williams, *The Christian Recorder, Newspaper of the African Methodist Episcopal Church: History of a Forum for Ideas, 1854–1902* (Jefferson, NC: McFarland & Co., 1996), 77–78.

28. Williams, *The Christian Recorder;* F. L. Cardozo, "Shall Our Schools Be Mixed or Separated," in *Social Protest Thought in the African Methodist Episcopal Church, 1862–1939,* ed. Stephen W. Angell and Anthony B. Pinn (Knoxville: University of Tennessee Press, 2000), 114.

29. *ACT,* 10 June 1887, 2. Rudd regularly reported on the struggle to have black teachers appointed to Baltimore's schools. See "Baltimore, MD," *ACT,* 22 April 1887, 1; "Baltimore," *ACT,* 3 June 1887, 1.

30. "Gaines High School Commence," *ACT,* 22 June 1889, 2.

31. *ACT,* 13 September 1890, 2; *ACT,* 5 September 1891, 2; *ACT ,*10 October 1891, 2. Following the passage of the Ely-Arnett Bill in 1887, integration was "quickly" and "peacefully" accomplished in the majority of school districts in the state. Uproar, however, was caused by this same legislative action in cities like Felicity, Oxford, New Richmond, and Xenia. It took a number of years to desegregate Cincinnati's schools. After the desegregation of the city's schools, a decision was made to keep Gaines High School open for blacks. Black teachers continued to teach in this institution. After the passage of the Ely-Arnett Bill, however, the "superintendency" of the school was abolished. Over the next three years the school declined in attendance as the city's black students moved into racially integrated schools. Gaines was closed in about 1890. As some African American leaders had warned, the board refused to hire black teachers in the city's integrated schools. Repeated attempts to have qualified black teachers appointed to these schools proved unsuccessful. By 1897 the campaign had been given up. See Gerber, *Black Ohio*, 264–265; Quillin, *The Color Line*, 94–97; "City and Vicinity," *ACT,* 24 June 1887, 3; *ACT,* 22 June 1889, 2.

32. Gerber, *Black Ohio*, 258–260.

33. Davison M. Douglas, *Jim Crow Moves North: The Battle over Northern School Segregation, 1865–1954* (New York: Cambridge University Press, 2005), 90–91.

34. Gerber, *Black Ohio*, 58–59.

35. *ACT*, 18 January 1890, 2.

36. "City and Vicinity," *ACT*, 20 July 1888, 3.

37. "A Card," *ACT*, 26 July 1890, 2.

38. *ACT*, 19 April 1890, 2.

39. The reason for the passage of this subsequent bill is unclear. Stanley J. Folmsbee suggests the legislature may have been unaware that the state had already passed such a law. See "The Origin of the First 'Jim Crow' Law," quoted in Gilbert Thomas Stephenson, "The Separation of the Races in Public Conveyances," in *The Age of Jim Crow: Segregation from the End of Reconstruction to the Great Depression, Race, Law and American History 1700–1990 African-American Experience,* ed. Paul Finkelman (New York: Garland, 1992), 4:190–191, 245.

40. *ACT*, 7 October 1887, 2.

41. "'Tis Done at Last," *ACT*, 21 May 1892, 2.

42. Logan, *The Betrayal of the Negro*, 161.

43. "No Colored Men Admitted," *ACT*, 2 September 1887, 2.

44. *ACT*, 31 May 1890, 2.

45. *ACT*, 6 December 1890, 2.

46. *ACT*, 5 August 1887, 2.

47. *ACT*, 13 April 1888, 2.

48. Franklin and Moss, *From Slavery to Freedom*, 168–169.

49. Meier, *Negro Thought in America*, 59–61.

50. Williams, *The Christian Recorder*, 102.

51. *ACT*, 10 February 1888, 2.

52. *New Orleans Pelican*, quoted in "The Proposed Exodus," *ACT*, 10 February 1888, 1.

53. *New Orleans Pelican*, quoted in "The Proposed Exodus," *ACT*, 10 February 1888, 1.

54. See Angell and Pinn, *Social Protest Thought*, 237.

55. Robert P. Weiss, ed., *Social History of Crime, Policing and Punishment* (Aldershot, UK: Ashgate, 1999), 493–495, 510–511.

56. Christopher R. Adamson, "Punishment after Slavery: Southern State Penal Systems, 1865–1900," in Weiss, *Social History*, 566.

57. David M. Oshinsky, *"Worse than Slavery": Parchman Farm and the Ordeal of Jim Crow Justice* (New York: Free Press, 1996), 46–47; Zieger, *For Jobs and Freedom*, 48.

58. "The Afro-American League," *ACT*, 16 September 1887, 1.

59. *ACT*, 7 October 1887, 2.

60. *ACT*, 31 October 1891, 2. According to Rudd, the "sad fruit" being produced by the continuance of such an unjust system was "oppression" and "anarchy."

61. *ACT*, 31 October 1891, 2.

62. Howard Kester, *Revolt among the Sharecroppers* (Knoxville: University of Tennessee Press, 1997), 20–21; Franklin and Moss, *From Slavery to Freedom*, 234.

63. *ACT*, 9 March 1888, 2.

64. *Chicago Times*, quoted in "Sugar Plantation Laborers," *ACT*, 25 November 1887, 1.

65. *St. Louis Post-Dispatch*, quoted in "Credit System," *ACT,* 24 February 1888, 1.

66. *ACT,* 22 June 1888, 2.

67. "The Southern Farmer," *ACT,* 18 August 1894, 2.

68. In the last sixteen years of the nineteenth century, as many as 2,500 blacks were lynched. Mississippi, Alabama, Georgia, and Louisiana were the states where most of these crimes occurred (see Franklin and Moss, *From Slavery to Freedom*, 312). Vigilante murders peaked in 1892. Julius Thompson has claimed 262 people were lynched during this year; of this number, 162 were African Americans (see Julius E. Thompson, *Lynchings in Mississippi: A History, 1865–1965* [Jefferson, NC: McFarland & Co., 2007], 35).

69. Linda O. McMurry, *To Keep the Waters Troubled: The Life of Ida B. Wells* (New York: Oxford University Press, 1998), 143.

70. Dray, *At the Hands of Persons Unknown*, 18.

71. "Bad Man Lynched," *ACT,* 11 May 1888, 2.

72. *ACT,* 20 July 1888, 2.

73. "A Wretch Lynched," *ACT,* 17 November 1888, 4.

74. See Gerber, *Black Ohio*, 249–250.

75. "One Woman's Work," *ACT,* 25 August 1894, 2.

76. McMurry, *To Keep the Waters Troubled*, 143.

77. *St. Joseph's Advocate* (April 1892), quoted in "A Human-Being Holocaust," *ACT,* 26 March 1892, 2.

78. "A Cry from St. Louis," *ACT,* 2 April 1892, 2.

79. "Think! Consolidate! Agitate!," *ACT,* 9 April 1892, 2.

80. "Think! Consolidate! Agitate!," *ACT,* 9 April 1892, 2.

81. "The Negroes Condition," *ACT,* 23 April 1892, 2; Spalding, "The Negro Catholic Congresses," 348.

82. "Danger Ahead," *ACT,* 14 May 1892, 2.

83. "Memorial Mtg.," *ACT,* 4 June 1892, 3.

84. "Colored National Convention," *ACT,* 9 July 1892, 2.

85. "Colored National Convention," *ACT,* 9 July 1892, 2.

86. *ACT,* 25 March 1893, 2.

87. "The Cholera," *ACT,* 24 September 1892, 4.

88. "One Woman's Work," *ACT,* 25 August 1894, 2.

89. Meier, *Negro Thought in America*, 72–73.

90. *Gazette*, 19 August 1893, 2.

91. *Gazette*, 14 October 1893, 2.

92. "Hurt, the Hunter," *ACT,* 28 October 1887, 1.

93. "A Victim to Soap and Water," *ACT,* 22 October 1892, 3.

94. "Father Burke Wants Help," *ACT,* 21 December 1889, 1.

95. *Church News,* quoted in "The Teacher of Nations," *ACT,* 15 June 1889, 1.

96. "Slaves in New York," *ACT,* 20 May 1887, 2.

5 • BEYOND CONCERNS OF RACE

1. James J. Kenneally, *The History of American Catholic Women* (New York: Crossroad, 1990), 13. In Penny Edgell's Becker's study of gender ideology in the *Ave Maria*, 1865–1889, she has pointed out that about one-third of the articles on women produce "alternative interpretations" critical of the "official ideology" of the "True Catholic Woman." Despite this fact, more traditional views of the place of the woman

in society can be found in church writings of the period, including Cardinal Gibbons's *Our Christian Heritage,* published in 1889, a book reported to have sold over 170,000 copies. See Penny Edgell Becker, "Rational Amusement and Sound Instruction": Constructing the True Catholic Woman in the Ave Maria, 1865–1889," *Religion and American Culture: A Journal of Interpretation* 8, no. 1 (Winter 1998): 55–90; James Cardinal Gibbons, *Our Christian Heritage* (Baltimore: John Murphy & Co., 1889); Jay P. Dolan, *In Search of an American Catholicism: A History of Religion and Culture in Tension* (New York: Oxford University Press, 2002), 124; Barbara Welter, "The Cult of True Womanhood: 1820–1860," *American Quarterly* 18, no. 2, pt. 1 (Summer 1966): 151–174.

2. Kenneally, "American Catholic Women," 3–4.

3. Gibbons, *Our Christian Heritage,* 363; Kenneally, "American Catholic Women," in the *Encyclopedia of American Catholic History,* ed. Michael Glazier and Thomas J. Shelley (Collegeville, MN: Liturgical Press, 1997), 53–65.

4. The "True Catholic Woman" ideology made a place for women in the convent. It was assumed, however, these same pious women would submit to male superiors with the same respect and deference a woman was to give her spouse. Religious women, however, did not always aspire to this.

5. Gibbons, *Our Christian Heritage,* 360–361.

6. Gibbons, *Our Christian Heritage,* 361–371.

7. William P. Cantwell, "Woman in Early Christianity and during the Middle Ages," *Catholic World* 45, no. 270 (September 1887): 821.

8. Dolan, *In Search,* 117; Angell and Pinn, *Social Protest Thought,* 266.

9. Evelyn Brooks Higginbotham, *Righteous Discontent: The Women's Movement in the Black Baptist Church, 1880–1920* (Cambridge: Harvard University Press, 1993), 2, 42, 67, 149.

10. Angell and Pinn, *Social Protest Thought,* 267–268.

11. Dolan, *In Search,* 123.

12. "Current Topics," *ACT,* 13 May 1887, 1; "Current Topics," *ACT,* 1 July 1887, 1; "Current Topics," *ACT,* 26 October 1889, 1; "Women Professors," *ACT,* 19 September 1891, 2; "France for Active Women," *ACT,* 8 March 1894, 4.

13. "Woman's Suffrage," *ACT,* 22 July 1887, 1. In 1902 Britton received a license to practice medicine in Lexington after graduating from the American Missionary College in Chicago. She was the first African American physician to practice medicine in Kentucky.

14. "Woman's Suffrage," *ACT,* 22 July 1887, 1.

15. This well-known civil rights advocate and publisher of *Women's Era,* a paper published on behalf of African American women, was the wife of Judge George L. Ruffin (1834–1886). George Ruffin was Harvard Law School's first black graduate. He subsequently became a judge. The Ruffin Club, the Republican political organization to which Rudd belonged, was named after this African American justice from Massachusetts. See Darryl Lyman, *Great African-American Women* (New York: Gramercy Books, 2000), 199.

16. *ACT,* 30 March 1888, 2.

17. J. M. Craig, "Women's Suffrage Movement," in *Dictionary of Christianity in America,* ed. Daniel G. Reid, Robert D. Linder, Bruce L. Shelley, Harry S. Stout, and Craig A. Noll (Downer's Grove, IL: Intervarsity Press, 1990), 1267–1268.

18. *ACT,* 6 December 1890, 2.

19. "Sex Prejudice," *ACT,* 22 February 1890, 3.

20. *Plaindealer,* 24 March 1893, 4.

21. "In Woman's Behalf," *ACT,* 22 February 1890, 3; *Queen Bee;* quoted in "Notes for Woman Readers," *ACT,* 22 February 1890, 3.

22. "How to Cure Social Ills," *ACT,* 23 August 1890, 2.

23. "The Public Rights of Women," *Catholic World* 59, no. 351 (June 1894): 305, 314–315.

24. *ACT,* 24 November 1888, 2.

25. Philip Gleason, *The Conservative Reformers: German American Catholics and the Social Order* (South Bend, IN: University of Notre Dame Press, 1968), 23, 183. The name of this women's organization was the National Catholic Women's Union. *Souvenir Volume of Three Great Events in the History of the Catholic Church in the United States* (New York: Arno Press, 1978); Higginbotham, *Righteous Discontent,* 6–8.

26. O'Connell, *John Ireland,* 291.

27. McGreevy, *Catholicism and American Freedom,* 112–114.

28. Morgan M. Sheedy, "The School Question: A Plea for Justice," *Catholic World* 49, no. 293 (August 1889): 649–655.

29. W. L. Portier, "Americanism," in *Dictionary of Christianity in America,* 53–56.

30. Gleason, *The Conservative Reformers,* 78, 97; David O'Brien, "Americanism," in *The Encyclopedia of American Catholic History,* 97–99.

31. O'Connell, *John Ireland,* 299; Gerald P. Fogarty, S.J., *The Vatican and the American Hierarchy from 1870 to 1965* (Wilmington, DE: Michael Glazier, 1985), 65–66; Gleason, *The Conservative Reformers,* 36.

32. Subsequently, in 1891 Ireland instituted a similar plan in the communities of Faribault and Stillwater, Minnesota. The plan was known as the "Faribault Plan." Robert Leckie, *American and Catholic* (Garden City, NY: Doubleday & Co., 1970), 240; O'Connell, *John Ireland,* 291.

33. O'Connell, *John Ireland,* 298.

34. *ACT,* 23 August 1890, 2.

35. "Moral Education," *ACT,* 8 March 1890, 1.

36. O'Connell, *John Ireland,* 292.

37. *ACT,* 20 September 1890, 2.

38. *ACT,* 23 August 1890, 2.

39. See O'Connell, *John Ireland,* 292; "The School Question," *ACT,* 8 December 1888, 1.

40. "Corner Stone Blessing," *ACT,* 25 July 1891, 1.

41. "A Grand Speech," *ACT,* 25 July 1891, 2.

42. *ACT,* 13 April 1888, 2.

43. *ACT,* 31 August 1888, 2.

44. "The Parochial School," *ACT,* 22 August 1891, 2.

45. *ACT,* 4 April 1891, 2.

46. *ACT,* 20 September 1890, 2.

47. *ACT,* 22 August 1891, 2.

48. Meier, *Negro Thought in America,* 22.

49. *Gazette,* 30 November 1889, 2.

50. "The National Press Association," *ACT,* 12 August 1887, 3.

51. McGreevy, *Catholicism and American Freedom*, 123.

52. See Dolan, *In Search*, 73.

53. Ellis, *American Catholicism*, 106.

54. McGreevy, *Catholicism and American Freedom*, 127–138.

55. Martin E. Marty, *A Short History of American Catholicism* (Allen, TX: Thomas More, 1995), 144.

56. McGreevy, *Catholicism and American Freedom*, 137; Marty, *A Short History*, 147–148.

57. "Pope and Kaiser," *ACT*, 12 April 1890, 1.

58. "Pope Leo's Advice," *ACT*, 29 March 1890, 1.

59. "Labor Problem," *ACT*, 29 March 1890, 1.

60. Fr. Edward McGlynn (1837–1900), like Rudd, centered his controversial social justice campaign on the fundamental unity of the human family expressed in the "Fatherhood of God and Brotherhood of Man" phrase. Whereas Rudd's campaign primarily opposed the divisiveness of racism, McGlynn's commitment to the fundamental unity of the human family challenged the class divisions disadvantaging the impoverished. Despite the similarities in the two theological approaches, Rudd opposed McGlynn's socialist economic policies. See Carey, *American Catholic*, 220–241.

61. "Catholic Congress," *ACT*, 16 November 1889, 1.

62. "League Reading Circle," *ACT*, 8 November 1890, 2.

63. *ACT*, 4 April 1891, 2. Similarly, Rudd was concerned that the railroad industry might gouge its customers. In the same issue of the *ACT*, Rudd urged state authorities to maintain Ohio's canal system in order to prevent such an outcome.

64. McGreevy, *Catholicism and American Freedom*, 130–131.

65. An awareness of the systemic barriers blocking the pathway to progress for blacks seems less recognizable in Rudd's 1917 biography of Scott Bond.

66. *ACT*, 1 August 1891, 2.

67. "Henry George's Theories," *ACT*, 11 March 1887, 2.

68. "All the Same," *ACT*, 19 August 1887, 2.

69. Gibbons, *Our Christian Heritage*, 443.

70. Gibbons, *Our Christian Heritage*, 441.

71. Rudd, *Three Catholic Afro-American Congresses*, 70; "City and Vicinity," *ACT*, 14 May 1892, 3.

72. *ACT*, 16 June 1894, 3.

73. "A Ray of Sunlight," *ACT*, 25 July 1891, 2.

74. *ACT*, 22 July 1887, 2.

75. George's single tax proposal provided for a tax on rent that would have essentially transferred profits from the landlord to the community, though George stopped short of actually nationalizing private property. See Carey, *American Catholic*, 220–221. McGlynn was reinstated into the church in 1892 and died in 1900.

76. "The Same Old Falsehood," *ACT*, 22 July 1887, 2.

77. Alan O'Day, *The English Face of Irish Nationalism* (Dublin: Gill & Macmillan, 1977), 1–2. This legislation marked an important milestone in Ireland's move toward self-government. The subsequent passage of additional legislation over the next few decades increased the sovereignty of the citizens of Ireland.

78. Conor Cruise O'Brien, *Parnell and His Party, 1880–1890* (Oxford: Clarendon Press, 1957), 184.

79. O'Day, *The English Face*, 1. The Home Government Association was formed in 1870 with Isaac Butt as its leader. Not until 1881, when Charles Stewart Parnell, leader of the Irish Land League, began to emerge as the voice of the Home Rule Party, did the petitions begin to carry weight with Gladstone and the English government. During this period, the dependence of Britain's Liberal Government on Parnell's Irish Nationalist Party was a critical factor in winning these gains. See Dr. Michael Hopkinson, "Irish Home Rule," in *Oxford Companion to British History*, 1st edition.

80. S. B. Gorman, "Ireland Again under Coercion," *Catholic World* 45, no. 269 (August 1887): 664–671.

81. *ACT*, 29 April 1887, 2.

82. "Washington D.C.," *ACT*, 23 December 1887, 1.

83. "The National Press Association," *ACT*, 12 August 1887, 3.

84. Davis, *The History of Black Catholics*, 62–63.

85. *ACT*, 7 October 1887, 2.

86. "Shots from Gotham," *ACT*, 16 May 1891, 1.

87. *Baptist Tribune*, quoted in "Same Old Falsehood," *ACT*, 22 July 1887, 2.

88. *ACT*, 4 April 1891, 2.

89. "Nine Thousand Evictions," *ACT*, 22 July 1887, 3; "Ireland's Chances," *ACT*, 23 February 1889, 2.

90. *ACT*, 25 June 1892, 2.

91. Wells's fiery editorials published after the infamous March 1892 Memphis lynchings led to the forced shutdown of the *Free Speech*. Since Wells's life had been threatened, she decided not to return to Memphis. See McMurry, *To Keep the Waters Troubled*, 148–149.

92. R. Aubert, "Pius IX, Pope, BL," in *New Catholic Encyclopedia*, 2nd ed.

93. "Pontiff and Pagan," *ACT*, 17 November 1888, 3.

94. "Pastoral Letter," *ACT*, 8 June 1889, 1.

95. "Malignant Hatred," *ACT*, 10 May 1890, 1. Rudd apparently is referring to Umberto I (1844–1900).

96. McGreevy, *Catholicism and American Freedom*, 21, 45–48.

97. "Catholic Congress," *ACT*, 16 November 1889, 1.

98. *ACT*, 6 June 1891, 2.

99. *ACT*, 26 September 1891, 2.

100. Davis, *The History of Black Catholics*, 39–40, 121, 132.

101. "St. Louis, Mo.," *ACT*, 12 October 1889, 3.

102. Jose de Arteche, *The Cardinal of Africa: Charles Lavigerie: Founder of the White Fathers*, trans. Mairin Mitchell (London: Sands & Co., 1964), 162; *St. Joseph's Advocate*, quoted in "Child Martyrs in Africa," *ACT*, 15 July 1887, 1. Rudd reported Lavigerie was born in Esprit, France, in 1825. He was appointed to the see of Carthage in 1867 and raised to the dignity of cardinalate in 1884. See "The Pope on Slavery," *ACT*, 24 November 1888, 1; *Ave Maria*, quoted in "The Spirit of Cardinal Lavigerie," *ACT*, 9 February 1889, 2.

103. *ACT*, 15 June 1889, 2.

104. "Cardinal Lavigerie to Archbishop Janssens," *ACT*, 27 July 1889, 2.

105. "D.A.R. in Hamburg," *ACT*, 17 August 1889, 1.

106. "The Congress," *ACT*, 26 July 1890, 1.

107. "The Abolition of Slavery," *ACT*, 24 August 1889, 1.

108. "Cardinal Lavigerie," *ACT,* 14 September 1889, 3.

109. "St. Louis, Mo.," *ACT,* 12 October 1889, 3.

110. *ACT,* 9 November 1889, 1.

111. "A Call for a Congress of Colored Catholics," *ACT,* 21 June 1890, 3.

112. "The Congress," *ACT,* 26 July 1890, 1.

113. "Resolutions," *ACT,* 30 August 1890, 1.

114. "Current Topics," *ACT,* 8 July 1887, 1; "Current Topics," *ACT,* 20 January 1888, 1; *Boston Pilot,* quoted in "1,500,000 Slaves Set Free," *ACT,* 1 June 1888, 1; Dale Torston Graden, *From Slavery to Freedom in Brazil: Bahia, 1835–1900* (Albuquerque: University of New Mexico Press, 2006), 199; Arteche, *The Cardinal of Africa,* 159. I have found various reports of the number of slaves residing in Brazil at the time of their emancipation. Some reports are as low as 700,000, some as high as 2 million.

115. "Slavery in Mexico," *ACT,* 25 May 1888, 1.

116. Rudd here appears to be referring to what is today the Dominican Republic.

117. "The Same Old Story," *ACT,* 23 May 1891, 3.

6 • THE COLORED CATHOLIC CONGRESS MOVEMENT, 1889–1894

1. *ACT,* 1 April 1887, 1.

2. "The Colored Man in the Popular Magazines," *ACT,* 6 April 1889, 2.

3. *Three Afro-American Congresses* was published by Rudd in 1893.

4. Both David Spalding and Cyprian Davis identify Rudd as the founder of this movement. Spalding, "The Negro Catholic Congresses," 337; Davis, *The History of Black Catholics,* 164, 187.

5. The date for the establishment of the African American convention movement was 1830. The convention movement was begun by Northern blacks seeking to fight for their civil rights. See Franklin and Moss, *From Slavery to Freedom,* 166–167; Meier, *Negro Thought in America,* 4–10. Fortune's NAAL movement was founded in 1887. See Joseph W. Scott, *The Black Revolts: Racial Stratification in the U.S.A: The Politics of Estate, Caste, and Class in the American Society* (Cambridge, MA: Schenkman, 1976), 116.

6. "Mosaics," *ACT,* 4 May 1889, 2.

7. European Congresses were being held as early as 1848. See "Shall We Have a Congress," *Catholic World* 8, no. 44 (November 1868): 225. The Central-Verein was founded in 1855 in Baltimore. It was a national federation made up of local German benevolent societies. This same organization served as a "symbol" or "primary reference group" of German American Catholics. See Gleason, *The Conservative Reformers,* 9, 12; "Speech of Mr. Dan A. Rudd," *ACT,* 14 September 1888, 2.

8. At the time Tappert was the pastor of the Church of the Mother of God in Covington and chairman of arrangements for the 1887 Chicago meeting that Rudd attended. Rudd printed an exchange that sought to dispel the idea that the purpose for the German Congress was to influence the "Episcopacy" with regard to appointments of German clergy and bishops. Instead, the article suggested the Chicago Convention would follow the "programme of similar meetings in Europe." The issues to be addressed were "the labor question, parochial schools, the German Catholic press, societies, benevolent and otherwise." See "The German Catholic Convention," *ACT,* 12 August 1887, 1.

9. *ACT,* 20 May 1887, 2.

10. "Business and Business," *ACT,* 10 June 1887, 2.

11. "The Afro American League," *ACT,* 17 June 1887, 2.

12. *ACT,* 8 July 1887, 2.

13. *American Baptist,* quoted in "Iola on Race Pride," *ACT,* 11 March 1887, 1.

14. *ACT,* 8 July 1887, 2.

15. *ACT,* 9 September 1887, 2.

16. *ACT,* 16 September 1887, 2.

17. "Congress of Colored Catholics," *ACT,* 4 May 1888, 2.

18. *ACT,* 11 May 1888, 2. Some individuals, though supportive of the idea of discussing issues pertaining to the race, were afraid that such a meeting would institute a "color line" into the Catholic Church. One writer argued the meeting should be neither black nor white but rather "Catholic." See *New Record,* quoted in "A Colored Catholic Congress," *ACT,* 25 May 1888, 2.

19. *ACT,* 18 May 1888, 2. Despite the initial emphasis Rudd placed on the importance of accessing the size and condition of the nation's black Catholic population, there is no evidence in the *ACT* to support a claim that establishing the "exact" number of black Catholics in the country or their condition "intellectually," "morally," and "materially" remained a priority. Slattery did deliver the committee on resolutions report citing the number of black churches, schools and orphanages. See "Reports of &ommittees, [*sic*] Etc.," *ACT,* 12 January 1889, 1, 4. Milton E. Smith, editor of the *Church News,* lamented that of the seven million blacks living in the United States there were but a "few thousand Catholics." See "Fourth Day's Proceedings," *ACT,* 12 January 1889, 4. Throughout the life of the newspaper, Rudd challenged those he believed were underreporting the number of black Catholics in the country. For example, in July 1889 he took issue with a report given at the A.M.E. Sunday School convention in Cincinnati because it estimated there were only 50,000 black Catholics in the United States. Rudd replied, "50,000 is not one fourth of the number of Colored Catholics in the United States." See *ACT,* 20 July 1889, 2; *ACT,* 18 May 1888, 2.

20. *ACT,* 8 June 1888, 2.

21. "The Proposed Congress of Colored Catholics. What Can It Do?," *ACT,* 8 June 1888, 2.

22. "The Proposed Congress of Colored Catholics. What Can It Do?," *ACT,* 8 June 1888, 2. No copy of this memorial has been to date located.

23. "The Proposed Congress of Colored Catholics. What Can It Do?," *ACT,* 8 June 1888, 2.

24. *ACT,* 22 June 1888, 2.

25. *ACT,* 22 June 1888, 2.

26. *ACT,* 21 September 1888, 2.

27. In the extant copy of this edition of Rudd's newspaper, an article on page 1 has been removed. It is presumed this missing article is the official call for the congress. In the October 13, 1888, issue of the *ACT,* Rudd again printed the official call for the Colored Catholic Congress. "A Call," *ACT,* 13 October 1888, 1; Davis has questioned whether such local elections were ever held. Evidence from the *ACT,* however, indicates a local delegate election was held in Rudd's home parish, St. Ann's. See Davis, *The History of Black Catholics,* 172–173. "The Congress of Colored Catholics," *ACT,* 21 September 1888, 1.

28. "Washington D.C. Catholic Congress," *ACT,* 12 January 1889, 1.

29. "Washington D.C. Catholic Congress," *ACT,* 12 January 1889, 1.

30. See Spalding, "The Negro Catholic Congresses," 342.

31. *ACT,* 13 October 1888, 2.

32. Spalding, "The Negro Catholic Congresses," 330. Davis estimates the number of delegates was about 100. See Davis, *The History of Black Catholics,* 163; "Washington D.C.," *ACT,* 12 January 1889, 1; MacGregor, *The Emergence of a Black Catholic Community,* 131–132.

33. "Washington D.C.," *ACT,* 12 January 1889, 1.

34. "Washington D.C.," *ACT,* 12 January 1889, 1.

35. Rudd, *Three Catholic Afro-American Congresses,* 24–25. It appears this speech was not initially published in the *ACT.*

36. Davis, *The History of Black Catholics,* 173; Spalding, "The Negro Catholic Congresses," 341–342; Rudd, *Three Catholic Afro-American Congresses,* 66–72.

37. Rudd, *Three Catholic Afro-American Congresses,* 66–72. Another important resolution was passed that had a marked impact on the life of the American Catholic Church. It was a resolution passed by Rudd and the executive committee of the congress authorizing the sending of a delegation to the German Verein in order to explore the possibility of holding a "general Catholic Congress." This resolution appears to have set in motion a meeting that culminated in the assembly of the first lay Catholic congress in November 1889.

38. *ACT,* 26 January 1889, 2.

39. *Standard,* quoted in "The Congress of Colored Catholics," *ACT,* 26 January 1889, 1. The *Standard* appears to be a Catholic publication, perhaps the *Catholic Standard* of Philadelphia.

40. *Standard,* quoted in *ACT,* 26 January 1889, 2. Most delegates for the meeting appeared to come from Maryland and the Washington, D.C., area. Only a handful of delegates attended the congress from the other southern states, including Virginia, Kentucky, Georgia, South Carolina, Missouri, and Louisiana.

41. "The Catholic Church," *ACT,* 26 January 1889, 1.

42. *ACT,* 2 February 1889, 2.

43. Davis, *The History of Black Catholics,* 175.

44. John Slattery, "The Congress of Negro Catholics," *Donahoe's Magazine* 24 (1890): 269. Cyprian Davis, relying on a *Cleveland Gazette* report, however, estimates only about forty-eight attended. See Davis, *The History of Black Catholics,* 175; Slattery, "The Congress of Negro Catholics," 269; *ACT,* 20 August 1889, 2.

45. For Archbishop Ireland's sermon, see "There Is No Color Line," *Catholic Mirror,* 10 May 1890, 5.

46. "The Congress Proceedings," *ACT,* 19 July 1890, 1.

47. "Mr. Butler's Address," *ACT,* 26 July 1890, 2; "Dr. Lofton's Address," *ACT,* 26 July 1890, 1; "Delegates to the Congress Banqueted," *ACT,* 19 July 1890, 3.

48. Rudd, *Three Catholic Afro-American Congresses,* 94; Slattery, "The Congress of Negro Catholics," 270–271.

49. "Dr. Lofton's Address," *ACT,* 26 July 1890, 1.

50. "Mr. Butler's Address," *ACT,* 26 July 1890, 2.

51. Presumably this is Fr. John T. Harrison, previously discussed. Rudd may have invited Harrison because Archbishop Ireland was unable to attend. Rudd, *Three*

Catholic Afro-American Congresses, 112. Rudd did not publish Harrison's sermon in the *ACT.* Doing so might have caused friction between him and Mackey, his coeditor.

52. *ACT,* 26 July 1890, 2; Slattery, "The Congress of Negro Catholics," 270.

53. Rudd, *Three Catholic Afro-American Congresses,* 124–126.

54. "City and Vicinity," *ACT,* 26 July 1890, 3.

55. "Resolutions," *ACT,* 30 August 1890, 1.

56. "Resolutions," *ACT,* 30 August 1890, 1.

57. Slattery, "The Congress of Negro Catholics," 271.

58. "The Address," *ACT,* 12 January 1889, 4.

59. Lackner, "The *American Catholic Tribune* and the Puzzle of Its Finances," 34.

60. "Washington, D.C.," *ACT,* 2 August 1890, 2.

61. "Washington, D.C.," *ACT,* 23 August 1890, 1.

62. Editors of the *Journal* included such important individuals as Martin J. Lehman and Arthur Arnott of Pennsylvania's delegation to the third congress.

63. *ACT,* 8 August 1891, 2.

64. *ACT,* 25 July 1891, 2.

65. *ACT,* 8 August 1891, 2.

66. *New Orleans Morning Star and Catholic Messenger,* quoted in "Mr. Rudd in New Orleans," *ACT,* 15 August 1891, 2.

67. *New Orleans Morning Star and Catholic Messenger,* quoted in "Mr. Rudd in New Orleans," *ACT,* 15 August 1891, 2; *ACT,* 22 August 1891, 2. There is no evidence to suggest Rudd ever returned to New Orleans, nor does the *ACT* say anything about additional recruiting visits to southern cities. Rudd was, however, partially successful in his delegated duties. For example, W. Edgar Easton, secretary of the Executive Committee of the Republican Party in Texas and a Colored Catholic Congressional delegate from Galveston, revealed that Rudd had invited him via a letter to "attend the Congress." See "From Galveston, Texas, to Cincinnati, O.," *ACT,* 2 January 1892, 1.

68. "Colored Catholic Congress United States Headquarters Executive Committee," *ACT,* 28 November 1891, 1.

69. *ACT,* 19 December 1891, 2.

70. "Washington, D.C.," *ACT,* 19 December 1891, 2.

71. It will be recalled Ryan believed Ireland had gone too far in his proposal to immediately remove the color line. "The Third Congress," *ACT,* 16 January 1892, 1.

72. "Resolutions Adopted," *ACT,* 16 January 1892, 1.

73. "Afternoon Session," *ACT,* 16 January 1892, 1.

74. Davis, *The History of Black Catholics,* 178. For more on McGhee, see a biographical sketch of McGhee in "Candidate for Delegate Honors," *ACT,* 7 May 1892, 1. Davis, *The History of Black Catholics,* 180–181; "Second Day's Session," *ACT,* 16 January 1892, 1; "Third Day's Session," *ACT,* 16 January 1892, 1.

75. "Resolutions Adopted," *ACT,* 16 January 1892, 1; "Second Day's Session," *ACT,* 16 January 1892, 1; "Third Day's Session," *ACT,* 16 January 1892, 1.

76. "The Third Congress," *ACT,* 16 January 1892, 1; Rudd, *Three Catholic Afro-American Congresses,* 148–153.

77. "Third Colored Congress," *ACT,* 16 January 1892, 3; "Proposed Permanent Organization and Building Fund," *ACT,* 16 January 1892, 1. Following the third Colored Catholic Congress, Rudd put his efforts into completing his book on the first three meetings of this body. The bulk of the material for the book had been previously

published in the pages of the *ACT.* Rudd, however, did include some additional speeches and notes on the meeting not initially published in newspaper. On 1 June 1892 James A. Spencer, acting president of the congress movement, chided the delegates for their "slow" and "indifferent" response in forwarding their financial pledges for the project. See "President Spencer's Appeal," *ACT,* 4 June 1892, 1. On 21 January 1893 Spencer informed the delegates the book was at the press and would be available about 1 February. In this same issue, Rudd printed a large advertisement offering the publication for one dollar per copy. The paper version was listed at seventy-five cents per copy. See "Colored Catholic Congress," *ACT,* 28 January 1893, 1. In late February, Rudd announced a delay in the production of the book. He stated, however, it would be delivered on 1 March. See *ACT,* 25 February 1893, 2.

78. The last extant issue of the *Journal* is dated 24 September 1892. This appears to have been the final issue of the publication.

79. W. J. Onahan to John R. Slattery, 30 March 1893; Slattery to W. J. Onahan, Easter Sunday [1893], both in Saint Joseph Society of the Sacred Heart Josephite Archives, Baltimore; Davis, *The History of Black Catholics,* 187.

80. See Davis, *The History of Black Catholics,* 182.

81. "The Catholic Congress," *ACT,* 12 August 1893, 2.

82. Davis, *The History of Black Catholics,* 182–184.

83. Davis, *The History of Black Catholics,* 185–187.

84. "The Colored Catholic Memorial: The Eloquent Expression of Their Fourth Congress," *Boston Pilot,* 23 September 1893, Papers of William J. Onahan, box IX-1-O, University of Notre Dame Archives, South Bend, IN; quoted in Davis, *The History of Black Catholics,* 187–188.

85. Uncles failed to meet Slattery's expectation as to the kind of work the former would do after his ordination. Slattery wanted Uncles to go on speaking tours throughout the North and Midwest in order to raise awareness of the mission. Uncles did not want to play the role of "show priest," a role he was convinced Tolton was forced to fill before him. See Ochs, *Desegregating the Altar,* 90.

86. Davis, *The History of Black Catholics,* 192.

87. *Church News,* 13 October 1894; quoted in Davis, *The History of Black Catholics,* 192.

88. The *Catholic Mirror,* quoted in Davis, *The History of Black Catholics,* 192.

89. Spalding, "The Negro Catholic Congresses," 352; *Catholic Mirror,* quoted in Davis, *The History of Black Catholics,* 192.

90. Spalding, "The Negro Catholic Congresses," 352.

91. Spalding, "The Negro Catholic Congresses," 352.

92. Spalding, "The Negro Catholic Congresses," 353–355; Davis, *The History of Black Catholics,* 192–193.

93. In 1900 McGhee and Lofton wrote Slattery in the hopes of convincing him to support another meeting of the Colored Catholic Congress. There is no record of a reply. Davis, *The History of Black Catholics,* 193; Daniel Rudd to John Slattery, 2 July 1888, transcript in the hand of Daniel Rudd, Saint Joseph Society of the Sacred Heart Josephite Archives, Baltimore; *ACT,* 3 November 1888, 2.

94. Davis, *The History of Black Catholics,* 193–194.

95. *ACT,* 17 December 1892, 2.

7 • DANIEL RUDD'S POST-*ACT* YEARS IN THE SOUTH

1. Rudd wrote, "*The Afro-American News,* published by Messrs. Clark and Vena, at St. Louis, was burned out last week. We sympathize with the gentlemen. We have unfortunately been there ourselves." See *ACT,* 25 February 1893, 2.

2. Willging and Hatzfeld, *Catholic Serials of the Nineteenth Century in the United States: A Descriptive Bibliography and Union List,* 80. This source further reports the *ACT's* subscription list at its zenith may have numbered only 8,000. One source cited in this publication labeled the *ACT* a "regional paper," though, as the editor pointed out, this claim is inaccurate.

3. By 1880 the newspaper claimed not more than 5,400 subscribers. See William Seraile, *Fire in His Heart: Bishop Benjamin Tucker Tanner and the A.M.E. Church* (Knoxville: University of Tennessee Press, 1998), 73.

4. Juliet E. K. Walker, "The Promised Land: The Chicago Defender and the Black Press in Illinois: 1862–1970," in Suggs, *The Black Press in the Middle West,* 20.

5. Eugene Robinson "Gray's Atlas, City of Detroit, Wayne County, Michigan, 1873," Burton Historical Collection, Detroit Public Library.

6. See "The American Catholic Tribune," *ACT,* 18 August 1894, 1.

7. Dorothy (Penny) Arble, "The Catholic Church in the City of Detroit and Its Immediate Vicinity before Nineteen and Ten," Burton Historical Collection, Detroit Public Library.

8. *Detroit City Directory* (Detroit: R. L. Polk & Co., 1897), 1233.

9. *ACT,* 6 June 1891, 2.

10. *ACT,* 13 July 1891, 2.

11. *ACT,* 23 April 1892, 2. William H. Anderson, editor of the *Detroit Plaindealer,* visited Rudd in his Cincinnati office on a number of occasions. Rudd may have met Anderson through Fortune's NAAL movement. Anderson served as the secretary of this organization.

12. *ACT,* 24 September 1892, 4.

13. Eugene P. Willging and Herta Hatzfeld, *Catholic Serials of the Nineteenth Century in the United States Part XV: A Statistical Analysis of the First Series, Parts 1+2 and of the Second Series, Part I–XIV (1+2)* (Washington, DC: Catholic University Press, 1968), 138. This source lists only two newspapers printed on behalf of black Catholics and published by black proprietors, the *ACT* and the *Journal. The Colored American Catholic* was published in New York City by one R. D. Dumas. This publication appears to have had some connection to St. Benedict's Mission in New York City, though Fr. John E. Burke did not endorse it. See "The Colored American Catholic," *ACT,* 31 August 1888, 1.

14. *Journal,* 28 May 1892, 1; See Willging and Hatzfeld, *Catholic Serials,* 80.

15. Willging and Hatzfeld, *Catholic Serials,* 80.

16. "City and Vicinity," *ACT,* 21 October, 1887, 3.

17. *ACT,* 1 June 1889, 2.

18. *ACT,* 8 June 1889, 2.

19. Leslie Woodcock Tentler, *Seasons of Grace: A History of the Catholic Archdiocese of Detroit* (Detroit: Wayne State University Press, 1990), 494–495.

20. See *Statistical Abstract of the United States* (Washington, DC: Government Printing Office, 1915), 52. Though correspondence exits between Rudd and Detroit's

own Henry F. Brownson (1835–1913), who worked with Rudd on organizing the first Catholic lay congress, it offers no clue as to why Rudd chose Detroit as the new home for the *ACT.*

21. Julius Thompson, "An Urban Voice of the People: The Black Press in Michigan, 1865–1985," in *The Black Press in the Middle West, 1865–1985,* 136.

22. Julius Thompson, "An Urban Voice of the People: The Black Press in Michigan, 1865–1985," in *The Black Press in the Middle West, 1865–1985,* 136.

23. Simmons, *The African American Press,* 6.

24. The *Plaindealer* was published up to the spring of 1893.

25. Willging and Hatzfeld, *Catholic Serials,* 80.

26. *ACT,* 8 September 1894, 2; *ACT,* 6 February 1892, 2. The last extent issue of the *ACT* does, however, list an associate city editor, Jul. P. Hoeffel, working alongside city editor John R. Rudd.

27. David J. Maurer, *"Depression in the 1890s": Historical Dictionary of the Progressive Era, 1890–1920* (Westport, CT: Greenwood Press, 1988).

28. Thompson ,"An Urban Voice of the People: The Black Press in Michigan, 1865–1895," 136.

29. Allison Davis , Burleigh B. Gardner, and Mary R. Gardner, *Deep South: A Social Anthropological Study of Caste and Class* (Chicago: Center of Afro-American Studies, 1988), 15–16, 22–26.

30. David E. Weaver, *Black Diva of the Thirties: The Life of Ruby Elzy* (Jackson: University Press of Mississippi, 2004), 11–12.

31. David R. Collins, Rich J. Johnson, and Bessie J. Pierce, *Moline: City of Mills* (Charleston, SC: Arcadia, 1998), 12.

32. Weaver, *Black Diva of the Thirties,* 11–12.

33. John C. Willis, *Forgotten Time: The Yazoo-Mississippi Delta after the Civil War* (Charlottesville: University of Virginia Press, 2000), 155.

34. Louis R. Harlan, *Booker T. Washington: The Wizard of Tuskegee,* 1901 1915 (New York: Oxford University Press, 1983), 219–220.

35. Florence Warfield Sillers, ed., *History of Bolivar County, Mississippi* (Jackson: Mississippi Delta Chapter of the Daughters of the American Revolution, 1948), 64; Dr. Luther Brown, director of the Delta Center for Culture and Learning, phone interview by author, 21 May 2007, Cleveland, MS.

36. See Federal Census of 1910, Bolivar County, Mississippi; Sillers, *History of Bolivar County,* 280.

37. Daniel A. Rudd and Theophilus Bond, *From Slavery to Wealth: The Life of Scott Bond: The Rewards of Honesty, Industry, Economy and Perseverance* (Madison, AR: Journal Printing Co., 1917), 324. This same flood also impacted the Mississippi Delta region near Boyle. Many of the laborers in this region were forced out by the rising waters and were unable to return. See Sillers, *History of Bolivar County,* 297.

38. Fon Louise Gordon, "From Slavery to Uncertain Freedom: Blacks in the Delta," in *The Arkansas Delta: Land of Paradox,* ed. Jeannie Whayne and Willard B. Gatewood (Fayetteville: University of Arkansas Press, 1993), 98, 111–112.

39. Byrd Gibbens, "Strangers in the Arkansas Delta: Ethnic Groups and Nationalities," in Whayne and Gatewood, *The Arkansas Delta: Land of Paradox,* 150, 156–157.

40. Rudd and Bond, *From Slavery to Wealth,* 345–351.

41. James M. Woods, *Mission and Memory: A History of the Catholic Church in Arkansas* (Little Rock: Catholic Diocese of Little Rock, 1993), 195.

42. Rudd and Bond, *From Slavery to Wealth*, 327.

43. Woods, *Mission and Memory*, 196.

44. A photo of this loading device can be found on page 277 of Rudd's biography of Bond. Rudd and Bond, *From Slavery to Wealth*, 284–289.

45. Rudd and Bond, *From Slavery to Wealth*, 332.

46. It is unclear if Rudd knew Bond prior to going to work for him in 1912. Rudd, however, claimed he had known Scott Bond "quite intimately for a number of years." See Rudd and Bond, *From Slavery to Wealth*, 141, 260.

47. Harlan, *Booker T. Washington*, vii–ix.

48. For a good treatment of the structure and function of the jeremiad in African American appeals for justice, see David Howard-Pitney, *The African American Jeremiad: Appeals for Justice in America*, rev. ed. (Philadelphia: Temple University Press, 2005). See also Sacvan Bercovitch, *The American Jeremiad* (Madison: University of Wisconsin Press, 1978); Pitney, *The African American Jeremiad*, 69.

49. Harlan, *Booker T. Washington*, vii–viii.

50. According to Joseph Lackner, Rudd's civil rights campaign bears little resemblance to Washington's accommodationist approach. There is little question, however, the later Rudd was more closely aligned to Washington's platform. This apparent change in philosophy may have been the result of development in Rudd's thinking necessitated by worsening racial relations. See Lackner, "Dan A. Rudd," 272.

51. Rudd and Bond, *From Slavery to Wealth*, 133, 358–359, 367.

52. Rudd and Bond, *From Slavery to Wealth*, 330, 359.

53. Rudd and Bond, *From Slavery to Wealth*, 359.

54. *ACT*, 9 March 1888, 2.

55. Rudd and Bond, *From Slavery to Wealth*, 373–375.

56. Rudd and Bond, *From Slavery to Wealth*, 373–375.

57. Rudd and Bond, *From Slavery to Wealth*, 374–375.

58. Rudd and Bond, *From Slavery to Wealth*, 372.

59. Rudd and Bond, *From Slavery to Wealth*, 368.

60. *ACT*, 7 June 1890, 2; *ACT*, 17 November 1888, 2.

61. Rudd and Bond, *From Slavery to Wealth*, 376–377.

62. Rudd and Bond, *From Slavery to Wealth*, 373.

63. Meier, "Booker T. Washington and the Rise of the *NAACP*," 93.

64. Franklin and Moss, *From Slavery to Freedom*, 319; Dray, *At the Hands of Persons Unknown*, 172, 177.

65. Dray, *At the Hands of Persons Unknown*, 245, 257.

66. Woods, *Mission and Memory*, 196.

67. Charles Flint Kellogg, *NAACP: A History of the National Association for the Advancement of Colored People* (Baltimore: Johns Hopkins University Press, 1967), 236.

68. Kellogg, *NAACP*, 236. See also Mary White Ovington, *The Walls Came Tumbling Down* (New York: Harcourt Brace, 1947), 167–168, 171.

69. Woods, *Mission and Memory*, 196; Davis, *The History of Black Catholics*, 213–214.

70. Rudd and Bond, *From Slavery to Wealth*, 248; For details on the NAACP meeting, see "Fought for the Right to Fight," *Cleveland Gazette*, 28 June 1919, 1.

71. Dray, *At the Hands of Persons Unknown*, 248.

72. This term was coined by James Weldon Johnson and used to describe the period of racial rioting and violence that took place from June 1919 to the end of this same year. See Franklin and Moss, *From Slavery to Freedom*, 349–350.

73. *Historic Arkansas* (Little Rock: Arkansas History Commission, 1966), 243–244; Willie Gammon, interview by author, 3 November 2009, Crittenden County Public Library, Marion, AR.

74. M. Bennett Hooper, "Some Bright Morning: The Tales and Anecdotes of John Gammon, Jr.," 1984, Marion, AR, 2; Davis, *The History of Black Catholics*, 311.

75. Woods, *Mission and Memory*, 196.

76. Daniel A. Rudd Death Certificate, December 4, 1933, file no. 30311, Commonwealth of Kentucky, State Board of Health, Bureau of Vital Statistics, Nelson County Public Library, Genealogy Room, Bardstown, KY, microfilm 7019801.

77. This historic school was added to the National Register of Historic Places in 1995.

78. Woods, *Mission and Memory*, 197.

79. Davis, *The History of Black Catholics*, 214, 312.

80. Daniel A. Rudd Death Certificate.

SELECTED BIBLIOGRAPHY

PRIMARY SOURCES

American Theological Library Association, Chicago

American Catholic Tribune, 1887–1894. Microfilm.

Clark County Historical Society, Springfield, OH

Fisher Family Library and Archives. *The Heart of Springfield 1873–1974*. A promotional brochure authored by the Springfield Bank.

Commonwealth of Kentucky, State Board of Health, Bureau of Vital Statistics

Rudd, Daniel A. Death Certificate. 4 December 1933, file no. 30311. Photocopy in possession of author.

Detroit Public Library, Burton Historical Collection

Arble, Dorothy Penny. "The Catholic Church in the City of Detroit and Its Immediate Vicinity before Nineteen and Ten."

Historical Archives of the Chancery, Cincinnati

Daniel Rudd to Archbishop Henry Elder, 3 May 1888. Elder Collection, 1888. Transcript in the hand of Daniel Rudd.

Daniel Rudd to John Slattery, 2 July 1888. Transcript in the hand of Daniel Rudd.

Nelson County Court, Bardstown, KY

Commissioner's Report of the Slaves of R. Rudd Appraisement & Allotments.

Inventory and Appraisement of the Estate of Richard Rudd.

Nelson County Deed Book, vol. 21.

Record of the Personal Property of Charles Haydon. Will Book, vol. 9, 494.

Nelson County Public Library, Genealogy Room, Bardstown, KY

Charles Haydon Family Chart.

Nelson County Black Baptisms.

Nelson County, Kentucky, Cemeteries, vol. 4.

Slave Data Base for Nelson County.

Saint Joseph Seminary, Yonkers, NY

Archdiocese of New York Archives. Papers. Patrick J. Ryan to Michael Augustine Corrigan, 20 May 1890. Transcript in the hand of Patrick J. Ryan. Special Collections.

Saint Joseph Society of the Sacred Heart Josephite Archives, Baltimore

William J. Onahan to John R. Slattery, 30 March 1893. Slattery Collection.

John R. Slattery to William J. Onahan, Easter Sunday, 1893. Slattery Collection.

University of Notre Dame Archives, South Bend, IN

Hudson Papers. M. Torrensdale to Fr. Hudson, 11 January 1887. Transcript in the hand of M. Torrensdale.

SECONDARY SOURCES

Adamson, Christopher R. "Punishment after Slavery: Southern State Penal Systems, 1865–1900." *Social Problems* 30, no. 5 (June 1983): 555–569. Quoted in *Social History of Crime, Policing and Punishment,* ed. Robert P. Weiss, 566. Aldershot, UK: Ashgate, 1999.

Agee, Gary B. "The Reverend John M. Mackey and Daniel A. Rudd in the Second Colored Catholic Congress." Research Paper, University of Dayton, 2003.

Allbeck, Willard D. *Springfield in the 1870's.* Springfield, OH: Clark County Historical Society, 1977.

Arteche, Jose de. *The Cardinal of Africa: Charles Lavigerie: Founder of the White Fathers.* Translated by Mairin Mitchell. London: Sands & Co., 1964.

Balmes, Jamie Luciano. *Protestantism and Catholicity Compared in Their Effects on the Civilization of Europe.* Baltimore: John Murphy, 1861.

Bercovitch, Sacvan. *The American Jeremiad.* Madison: University of Wisconsin Press, 1978.

Becker, Penny Edgell. "Rational Amusement and Sound Instruction": Constructing the True Catholic Woman in the Ave Maria, 1865–1889." *Religion and American Culture: A Journal of Interpretation* 8, no. 1 (Winter 1998): 55–90.

Bennett, James B. *Religion and the Rise of Jim Crow in New Orleans.* Princeton: Princeton University Press, 2005.

"Bishop Benedict Joseph Flaget." *Bicentennial Celebration of the Diocese of Bardstown 1808–2008* (2008): 6.

Blackmon, Douglas A. *Slavery by Another Name: The Re-Enslavement of Black Americans from the Civil War to World War II.* New York: Doubleday, 2008.

Blocker, Jack S. *A Little More Freedom: African Americans Enter the Urban Midwest, 1860–1930*. Columbus: Ohio State University Press, 2008.

Bronner, Simon J., ed. *Lafcadio Hearn's America: Ethnographic Sketches and Editorials*. Lexington: University Press of Kentucky, 2002.

Cantwell , William P. "Woman in Early Christianity and during the Middle Ages." *Catholic World* 45, no. 270 (September 1887): 816–821.

Cardozo, F. L. "Shall Our Schools Be Mixed or Separated." Quoted in *Social Protest Thought in the African Methodist Episcopal Church, 1862–1939*, ed. Stephen W. Angell and Anthony B. Pinn, 114–117. Knoxville: University of Tennessee Press, 2000.

Carey, Patrick W., ed. *American Catholic Religious Thought: The Shaping of a Theological and Social Tradition*. New York: Paulist Press, 1987.

Carroll, Charles. *The Negro a Beast*. St. Louis: American Book and Bible House, 1900. Reprint, Salem, NH: Ayer Co., 1991.

Coleman, Winston J., Jr. *Slavery Times in Kentucky*. Chapel Hill: University of North Carolina Press, 1940. Reprint, New York: Johnson Reprint Corp., 1970.

Collins, David R., Rich J. Johnson, and Bessie J. Pierce. *Moline: City of Mills*. Charleston, SC: Arcadia, 1998.

Craven, Patricia, and Richard Pangburn. *From Out of the Dark Past: Their Eyes Implore Us: The Black Roots of Nelson County Kentucky*. Bardstown: Nelson County Genealogical Roundtable, 2009.

Dabney, Wendell Phillips. *Cincinnati's Colored Citizens, Historical, Sociological and Biographical*. Cincinnati: Dabney Publishing Co., 1926. Reprint, New York: Negro Universities Press, 1970.

Davis, Allison, Burleigh B. Gardner, and Mary R. Gardner. *Deep South: A Social Anthropological Study of Caste and Class*. Chicago: University of Chicago Press, 1941. Reprint, Los Angeles: Center of Afro-American Studies, 1988.

Davis, Cyprian. *The History of Black Catholics in the United States*. New York: Crossroads Publication Co., 1990.

Dolan, Jay P. *In Search of an American Catholicism: A History of Religion and Culture in Tension*. New York: Oxford University Press, 2002.

Douglas, Davison M. *Jim Crow Moves North: The Battle over Northern School Segregation, 1865–1954*. New York: Cambridge University Press, 2005.

Dray, Philip. *At the Hands of Persons Unknown: The Lynching of Black America*. New York: Random House, 2002.

Ellis, John Tracy. *American Catholicism*. 2d ed. Chicago: University of Chicago Press, 1969.

Fogarty, Gerald P., S.J. *The Vatican and the American Hierarchy from 1870 to 1965*. Wilmington, DE: Michael Glazier, 1985.

Folmsbee, Stanley J. "The Origin of the First 'Jim Crow' Law." *Journal of Southern History* 15 (1949): 235–247.

Franklin, John Hope, and Alfred A. Moss Jr. *From Slavery to Freedom: A History of African Americans.* 7th ed. New York: McGraw-Hill, 1994.

Garraghan, Gilbert J. *The Jesuits of the Middle United States.* Vol. 2. New York: American Press, 1938. Reprint, Chicago: Loyola University Press, 1984.

Gerber, David A. *Black Ohio and the Color Line, 1860–1915.* Urbana: University of Illinois Press, 1976.

Gibbens, Byrd. "Strangers in the Arkansas Delta: Ethnic Groups and Nationalities." In *The Arkansas Delta: Land of Paradox,* ed. Jeannie Whayne and Willard B. Gatewood, 150–183. Fayetteville: University of Arkansas Press, 1993.

Gibbons, James Cardinal. *Our Christian Heritage.* Baltimore: John Murphy & Co., 1889.

Gleason, Philip. *The Conservative Reformers: German American Catholics and the Social Order.* South Bend, IN: University of Notre Dame Press, 1968.

Gollar, Walker C. "Catholic Slaves and Slaveholders in Kentucky." *Catholic Historical Review* 84, no. 1 (January 1998): 42–62.

Gorman, S. B. "Ireland Again Under Coercion." *Catholic World* 45, no. 269 (August 1887): 664–671.

Gordon, Fon Louise. "From Slavery to Uncertain Freedom: Blacks in the Delta." In *The Arkansas Delta: Land of Paradox,* ed. Jeannie Whayne and Willard B. Gatewood, 98–127. Fayetteville: University of Arkansas Press, 1993.

Graden, Dale Torston. *From Slavery to Freedom in Brazil: Bahia, 1835–1900.* Albuquerque: University of New Mexico Press, 2006.

Guizot, François Pierre Guillaume. *The History of Civilization in Europe: From the Fall of the Roman Empire to the French Revolution.* Translated by William Hazlitt. New York: A. L. Burt, n.d. Reprint, New York: J. B. Alden, 1893.

Hahn, Stephen. *A Nation under Our Feet: Black Political Struggles in the Rural South from Slavery to the Great Migration.* Cambridge: Harvard University Press, 2003.

Harding, Vincent. *There Is a River: The Black Struggle for Freedom in America.* New York: Harcourt Brace Jovanovich, 1981.

Harlan, Louis R. *Booker T. Washington: The Wizard of Tuskegee, 1901–1915.* New York: Oxford University Press, 1983.

Hecker, Isaac. *The Church and the Age.* New York: H. J. Hewitt, 1887.

Higginbotham, Evelyn Brooks. *Righteous Discontent: The Women's Movement in the Black Baptist Church, 1880–1920.* Cambridge: Harvard University Press, 1993.

Hooper, M. Bennett. *Some Bright Morning: The Tales and Anecdotes of John Gammon, Jr.* Marion, AR: By author, 1984.

Hoxie, Frederick E. *A Final Promise: The Campaign to Assimilate the Indians, 1880–1920.* Lincoln: University of Nebraska Press, 1984.

Hussey, Edmund M. *1999 Sesquicentennial Directory St. Raphael Catholic Church.* Springfield, OH: St. Raphael Catholic Church, 1999.

Jewett, Clayton E., and John O. Allen. *Slavery in the South: A State-by-State History.* Westport, CT: Greenwood Press, 2004.

Joseph, Satish, C. Ss. R. "Long Live the Republic; Fr. Edward Purcell and the Slavery Controversy: 1861–1865." *American Catholic Studies Journal of the Catholic Historical Society* 116, no. 4 (Winter 2005): 25–54.

Kellogg, Charles Flint. *NAACP: A History of the National Association for the Advancement of Colored People.* Baltimore: Johns Hopkins University Press, 1967.

Kenneally, James J. *The History of American Catholic Women.* New York: Crossroad, 1990.

Kenrick, Francis Patrick. "On Slavery" (1841). Quoted in *Creative Fidelity American Catholic Intellectual Traditions,* ed. Scott Appleby, Patricia Byrne, and William L. Portier, 167–170. Maryknoll, NY: Orbis Books, 2004.

Kester, Howard. *Revolt among the Sharecroppers.* New York: Covici Friede, 1936. Reprint, Knoxville: University of Tennessee Press, 1997.

Koehler, Lyle. *Cincinnati's Black Peoples: A Chronology and Bibliography, 1787–1982.* Cincinnati: University of Cincinnati, 1986.

Labbe , Dolores Egger. *Jim Crow Comes to Church: The Establishment of Segregated Catholic Parishes in South Louisiana.* Lafayette: University of Southwestern Louisiana, 1971. Reprint, New York: Arno Press, 1978.

Lackner, Joseph H., S.M. "The *American Catholic Tribune*: No Other Like It." Paper presented at the American Catholic Historical Association Meeting at University of Dayton, April 23, 2005, Dayton, OH.

———. "*The American Catholic Tribune:* No Other Like It." *U.S. Catholic Historian* 25, no. 3 (Summer 2007): 1–24.

———. "The *American Catholic Tribune* and the Puzzle of Its Finances." *Records of the American Catholic Historical Society of Philadelphia* (Spring/Summer 1995): 25–38.

———. "Dan A. Rudd, Editor of the *American Catholic Tribune:* From Bardstown to Cincinnati." *Catholic Historical Review* 80, no. 2 (April 1994): 258–81.

———. "The Foundation of St. Ann's Parish, 1866–1870: The African-American Experience in Cincinnati." *U.S. Catholic Historian* 14, no. 2 (Spring 1996): 13–36.

Leckie, Robert. *American and Catholic.* Garden City, NY: Doubleday & Co., 1970.

Logan, Rayford W. *The Betrayal of the Negro from Rutherford B. Hayes to Woodrow Wilson.* Originally published as *The Negro in American Life and Thought: The Nadir, 1877–1901.* New York: Dial Press, 1954. Reprint, New York: Collier Books, 1965.

Lucas, Marion B. *A History of Blacks in Kentucky: From Slavery to Segregation, 1760–1891.* 2nd ed. Frankfort: Kentucky Historical Society, 2003.

Lyman, Darryl. *Great African-American Women.* Middle Village NY: J. David, 1999. Reprint, New York: Gramercy Books, 2000.

MacGregor, Morris J. *The Emergence of a Black Catholic Community: St. Augustine's in Washington.* Washington, DC: Catholic University of America Press, 1999.

Manufacturers and Merchants of Ohio. New York: International Publishing Co., 1886.

Marty, Martin E. *A Short History of American Catholicism.* Allen, TX: Thomas More, 1995.

McGreevy, John T. *Catholicism and American Freedom: A History.* New York: W. W. Norton & Co., 2003.

McMurry, Linda O. *To Keep the Waters Troubled: The Life of Ida B. Wells.* New York: Oxford University Press, 1998.

Meier, August. "Frederick Douglass's Vision for America: A Case Study in Nineteenth-Century Negro Protest," in *Along the Color Line: Explorations in the Black Experience,* ed. August Meier and Elliott Rudwick, 4–27. Urbana: University of Illinois Press, 2002.

———. *Negro Thought in America, 1880–1915: Racial Ideologies in the Age of Booker T. Washington.* Ann Arbor: University of Michigan Press, 1963.

Middleton, Stephen. *The Black Laws: Race and the Legal Process in Early Ohio.* Athens: Ohio University Press, 2005.

Moynihan, James H. *The Life of Archbishop John Ireland.* New York: Harper & Brothers, 1953.

"The Negro Planter in the Common School." *Southern Planter and Farmer* 37 (April 1876). Quoted in *In His Image, but . . . Racism in Southern Religion, 1780–1910,* ed. H. Shelton Smith, 267. Durham: Duke University Press, 1972.

O'Brien, Conor Cruise. *Parnell and His Party, 1880–1890.* Oxford: Clarendon Press, 1957.

Ochs, Stephen J. *Desegregating the Altar: The Josephites and the Struggle for Black Priests, 1871–1960.* Baton Rouge: Louisiana State University Press, 1990.

O'Connell, Marvin, R. *John Ireland and the American Catholic Church.* St. Paul: Minnesota Historical Society Press, 1988.

O'Day, Alan. *The English Face of Irish Nationalism.* Dublin: Gill & Macmillan Ltd., 1977.

One Hundred Seventy Five Years of Struggle: A History of Black People in Springfield, Ohio. Springfield, OH: n.p., n.d.

Oshinsky, David M. *"Worse Than Slavery": Parchman Farm and the Ordeal of Jim Crow Justice.* New York: Free Press, 1996.

Ovington, Mary White. *The Walls Came Tumbling Down.* New York: Harcourt Brace, 1947.

Pitney, David Howard. *The African American Jeremiad: Appeals for Justice in America,* Rev. ed. Philadelphia: Temple University Press, 2005.

Portier, William L. "John R. Slattery's Vision for the Evangelization of American Blacks." *U.S. Catholic Historian* 5, no. 1 (1986): 19–44.

Pride, Armistead S, and Clint C. Wilson. *The History of the Black Press.* Washington, DC: Howard University Press, 1997.

"The Public Rights of Women." *Catholic World* 59, no. 351 (June 1894): 299–320.

Quillin, Frank. *The Color Line in Ohio: A History of Race Prejudice in a Typical Northern State.* Ann Arbor, MI: G. Wahr, 1913. Reprint, New York: Negro University Press, 1969.

Rawick, George P., ed. *The American Slave: A Composite Autobiography.* Westport, CT: Greenwood, 1972.

Rockel, William M. *20th Century History of Springfield and Clark Co. Ohio and Representative Citizens.* Chicago: Biographical Publishing Co., 1908.

Ross, Felecia G. Jones. "Democracy's Textbook: A History of the Black Press in Ohio, 1865–1985." In *The Black Press in the Middle West 1865–1985,* ed. Henry Lewis Suggs, 243–266. Westport, CT: Greenwood Press, 1996.

Rudd, Daniel A., and Theophilus Bond. *From Slavery to Wealth: The Life of Scott Bond: The Rewards of Honesty, Industry, Economy and Perseverance.* Madison, AR: Journal Printing Co., 1917.

———. *Three Catholic Afro-American Congresses.* Cincinnati, OH: American Catholic Tribune, 1893. Reprint, New York: Arno Press, 1978.

Scott, Joseph W. *The Black Revolts: Racial Stratification in the U.S.A: The Politics of Estate, Caste, and Class in the American Society.* Cambridge, MA: Schenkman, 1976.

Seraile, William. *Fire in His Heart: Bishop Benjamin Tucker Tanner and the A.M.E. Church.* Knoxville: University of Tennessee Press, 1998.

"Shall We Have a Congress." *Catholic World* 8, no. 44 (November 1868): 224–228.

Sheedy, Morgan M. "The School Question: A Plea for Justice." *Catholic World* 49, no. 293 (August 1889): 649–655.

Sillers, Florence Warfield, ed. *History of Bolivar County, Mississippi.* Jackson: Mississippi Delta Chapter of the Daughters of the American Revolution, 1948.

Simmons, Charles A. *The African American Press: A History of News Coverage during National Crises, with Special Reference to Four Newspapers, 1827–1965.* Jefferson, NC: McFarland & Co., 1998.

Slattery, John R. "The Congress of Negro Catholics." *Donahoe's Magazine* 24 (1890): 269–271.

Souvenir Volume of Three Great Events in the History of the Catholic Church in the United States. Detroit: n.p., 1889. Reprint, New York: Arno Press, 1978.

Spalding, David, C.F.X. "The Negro Catholic Congresses, 1889–1894." *Catholic Historical Review* 55, no. 3 (October 1969): 337–357.

Stedman, Edmund Clarence. "Christophe." *Century* 23 (November 1881): 34–35.

Taylor, Nikki. *Frontiers of Freedom: Cincinnati's Black Community, 1802–1868.* Athens: Ohio University Press, 2005.

Tentler, Leslie Woodcock. *Seasons of Grace: A History of the Catholic Archdiocese of Detroit.* Detroit: Wayne State University Press, 1990.

Thompson, Julius E. *Lynchings in Mississippi: A History, 1865–1965.* Jefferson, NC: McFarland & Co., 2007.

———. "An Urban Voice of the People: The Black Press in Michigan, 1865–1985." In *The Black Press in the Middle West, 1865–1985,* ed. Henry Lewis Suggs, 135–164. Westport, CT: Greenwood Press, 1996.

Walker, Juliet E. K. "The Promised Land: The *Chicago Defender* and the Black Press in Illinois: 1862–1970." In *The Black Press in the Middle West, 1865–1985,* ed. Henry Lewis Suggs, 9–50. Westport, CT: Greenwood Press, 1996.

Wangler, Thomas E. "John Ireland's Emergence as a Liberal Catholic and Americanist: 1875–1887." *Records of the American Historical Society of Philadelphia* 81 (June 1971): 67–82.

Weaver, David E. *Black Diva of the Thirties: The Life of Ruby Elzy.* Jackson: University Press of Mississippi, 2004.

Weiss, Robert P., ed. *Social History of Crime, Policing and Punishment.* Aldershot, UK: Ashgate, 1999.

Welter, Barbara. "The Cult of True Womanhood: 1820–1860." *American Quarterly* 18, no. 2, part 1 (Summer 1966): 151–174.

Weston, Rubin F., ed. *Blacks in Ohio History: A Conference to Commemorate the Bicentennial of the American Revolution.* Columbus: Ohio Historical Society, 1976.

Williams, Gilbert Anthony. *The Christian Recorder, Newspaper of the African Methodist Episcopal Church: History of a Forum for Ideas, 1854–1902.* Jefferson, NC: McFarland & Co., 1996.

Willging, Eugene P., and Herta Hatzfeld. *Catholic Serials of the Nineteenth Century in the United States: A Descriptive Bibliography and Union List.* 2nd ser., pt. 12. Washington, DC: Catholic University Press, 1966.

———. *Catholic Serials of the Nineteenth Century in the United States Part XV: A Statistical Analysis of the First Series, Parts 1+2 and of the Second Series, Part I—XIV (1+2).* Washington, DC: Catholic University Press, 1968.

Willis, John C. *Forgotten Time: The Yazoo-Mississippi Delta after the Civil War.* Charlottesville: University of Virginia Press, 2000.

Woods, James M. *Mission and Memory: A History of the Catholic Church in Arkansas.* Little Rock: Catholic Diocese of Little Rock, 1993.

Woodstock Letters: A Historical Journal of Jesuit Missionary and Educational Activities 46, no. 2 (1917).

Zieger, Robert H. *For Jobs and Freedom: Race and Labor in America since 1865.* Lexington: University Press of Kentucky, 2007.

INDEX

Acton, Lord, 134

Adam, The Catholic Journal of the New South (Memphis), 74, 75, 86, 120

Advocate, 31

Afro-American League, 98

Afro-American News, 217n1

Agassiz, Louis, 44

Alexander, James, 4

Alexander, John, 4

Alexander, Margaret Rudd, 4

Alexander, Mary, 113

American (Cincinnati), 169, 197n92

American Colonization Society, 95–96

American School of Ethnology, 44

Anatok (Bardstown), 2–3

Anderson, William F., 169

Anderson, William H., 169, 217n11

Armstrong, James, 86

Arnott, Arthur, 162, 215n62

Arthur, Chester A. (President), 23

Attucks, Crispus, 88

Augustin, Mary Frances, 86, 204n11

Augustine, P. Jerome, 147, 158, 204n11

Augustine, Peter, 204n11

Ave Maria, 31, 57, 136, 207n1

Badin, Stephen T., 12

Balmes, Jamie, 48, 50–51

Baptist Tribune, 132

Basilica of St. Joseph's Proto-Cathedral, 2, 5–6, 8, 11–13, 80, 187

Becker, Penny Edgell, 207n1

Bell, Charles W., 29, 169, 197n92

Bennett, James B., 196n80

Benoit, Peter L., 78

Berger, Geza, 60

black press. *See* colored press

Blackstone, William E., 147

Blaine Club (Cincinnati), 35

Blair, Henry W., 124, 125

Bond, Scott, xv, 174–78, 180–83, 185–87, 190, 210n65, 219n46

Bond, Theophilus, 175–76

Bond, Viola, 175

Boogie, Dan, 11, 14

Boyle, John, 33

Bragg, Braxton, 13

Britton, Mary E., 113–15, 208n13

Brown, John, 87

Brown, Luther, 218n35

Brownson, Henry F., 217–18n20

Brownson, Orestes, 134, 192n16

Brownson's Quarterly Review, 192n16

Buell, Don Carlos, 12

Burke, John E., 33, 56, 217n13

Burke, Thomas, 56

Butler, Charles H., 75, 81, 147, 153–54, 157, 160, 162–63, 165

Butt, Isaac, 211n79

Cafin, Mr., 173

Calisch, Edward N., 85

Cantwell, William P., 112

Capuchins, 134

Cardozo, F. L., 90

Carpenter, J. A., 87

Carroll, Charles, 44

cathedral (St. Paul, Minnesota), 65, 72, 154

Cathedral of St. Peter in Chains (Cincinnati), 39, 57, 69–70, 145, 152

Catholic Columbian, 67

Catholic Knights of America (Kentucky), 60

Catholic Mirror, 65–67

Catholic Telegraph, 193n17

Catholic Universe (Cleveland), 74

Catholic World, 119, 131

Charles V (Holy Roman Emperor), 52
Chattanooga Justice, 41
Chicago Conservator, 67, 151, 167
Chicago Tribune, 114
Chinese Americans, 38, 84, 108
Christian Recorder (A.M.E.), 48, 65, 75,
    90, 96, 106, 167
Church of the Mother of God
    (Covington, Kentucky), 212n8
Church News, 108,
Church Review (A.M.E.), 75, 90, 106
Cincinnati: black neighborhoods in,
    20–21; Rudd's move to, 20
Cincinnati Catholic Telegraph, 192n16,
Cincinnati Post, 42
Cincinnati Times-Star, 30
Clark, Consuela, 87,
Claver, Peter (Saint), 76, 203n77
Clay, Henry, 95,
Cleveland, Grover (President), xiii, 23
Cleveland Gazette, 28, 29, 31, 34, 106,
    124, 185
Cochin, Pierre S. A., 134
Cole, Sarah, 88
Colored American Catholic (New York
    City), 169, 217n13
Colored Catholic Congress ix, xiii, 17,
    33, 56, 86, 190, 200n46, 204n11,
    213n19, 213n27, 216n93; establish-
    ment of, 141–48; success of, 165–66;
    first gathering of, xiii, 51–52, 99, 117–
    18, 129, 142–43, 147–51, 200n46,
    214n32, 214n40; second gathering of,
    30, 39, 69–71, 120, 137, 142, 152–57,
    197n92, 214n44, 214–15n51; third
    gathering of, 56, 73, 142, 155, 157–59,
    162–64, 215n62, 215–16n77; fourth
    gathering of, 142, 161–63; fifth gath-
    ering of, 142, 164–65
Colored Citizen (Cincinnati), 29
Colored Harvest (Josephite Publication),
    157
Colored Patriot (Cincinnati), 29
colored press, 87, 88; newspapers, xiii,
    18, 27–29, 30–31, 34, 37, 41, 65, 67–
    68, 75–76, 106, 151, 168–69, 171–72,

    189, 198n1, 204n21; Rudd's leader-
    ship in, 28
Columbus, Ohio: Rudd's residence in,
    16
Commercial Gazette (Cincinnati), 34–35,
    53, 144, 197n92
Congregation of the Holy Ghost
    (Spiritans), 197n99
Connecticut Catholic, 50
convention movement (African
    American), 142, 212n5
Convent of the Sisters of the Holy
    Family (New Orleans), 47
Corbin, Henry, 101
Cornish, Samuel Eli, 27
Corrigan, Michael Augustine, 69, 119
Corrigan, Patrick, 33, 56
Coy, Ned, 102
Crisis (NAACP), 185
crop mortgage system, 38, 84, 99–100,
    127–28, 132, 146, 181
Cuffee, Paul, 84, 95

Dabney, Wendell P., 35
Dahlgren, John, 110
Dahlgren, Madeleine Vinton, 110
Darwin, Charles, 196n83,
Davis, Cyprian, ix, 152, 163, 165, 166
Davis, Jefferson, 23
Davis, Stephen, 162
Declaration (Cincinnati), 29
DeGruyter, Henry, 60
Delille, Henriette, 197n99
Democratic Party, 35
De Ruyter, John, 164
Detroit Advocate, 172
Detroit Plaindealer, 75, 88, 116, 123,
    168–69, 171, 217n11
Donahoe's Magazine, 153
Dorsey, John H., 77
Douglass, Frederick, xv, 6, 17, 18, 84, 131,
    147, 177, 178–79, 189, 194n59
Douglass League (Cincinnati), 35
Dowd, Mary A., 117
Drexel, Katharine (Saint), 31, 74, 78, 86,
    197n98

Driessen, John, 22
Du Bois, W. E. B., 100
Duckworth Club (Cincinnati), 35
Dumas, R. D., 217n13
Dupanloup, Felix, 134

Easton, William Edgar, 161, 215n67
economic justice, 109, 125–30, 146, 150,
    154–56, 163–64, 181–82, 186, 210n60;
    relations of labor and capital, 125–30
Ecton, William, 33
Elder, William Henry, 20, 21, 33, 56, 117,
    142, 148, 152–53, 198n110, 200n46
Elliot Club (Cincinnati), 35
Ely-Arnett Bill, 89–90, 91, 205n24,
    205n31
emigration from the South (black):
    Rudd's opposition to, 84, 95–97
England, John, 135
Ervin, William, 171

Farinholt, F. C., 117; "Fatherhood of
    God, Brotherhood of Man" ix, 36,
    42–48, 62, 67, 70, 107–8, 118, 126,
    149–50, 152, 166, 190, 210n60
Faust, A. J., 51–52
Flaget, Benedict J., 2
Flasch, Kilian, 121
Foley, Bishop (Detroit), 170
Foos, Gustavus S., 16
Foos, William, 16
Foraker, J. R., 93
Foraker, Joseph B., 35, 131
Fortune, T. Thomas, 6, 54, 68, 84, 98,
    132, 144, 189, 212n5
Freedom's Journal, 27, 37
Freeman (New York), 75,
Free Speech, 101, 211n91

Gammon, Ambrose, 186,
Gammon, John, 186–87
Gammon, John, Jr., 186
Garfield, James (President), 23
Gazaway, Eva, 19
Gazaway, J. W., 19
George, Henry, 128, 130, 210n75

German Central Verein, 46, 142–44,
    212nn7–8, 214n37,
Gibbons, James (Cardinal), xiii, 111–12,
    117, 125, 129, 148–49, 208n1
Gladstone, William E., 131, 211n79
Globe Republic, 35
Gmeiner, John, 63, 65
Gollar, Walker, 12
Gorman, S. B., 131
Grant Club (Cincinnati), 35
Green, John, 92
Gregory XVI (Pope), 135
Gregory the Great (Pope), 52
Guadin, Juliette, 197n99
Guizot, François, 50

Harding, Vincent, 84
Harlan, John Marshall, 24
Harrison, Benjamin (President), 23
Harrison, John T., 63, 65, 154–55,
    214–15n51
Hart, Sam B., 162, 169
Hayden, Basil, 1
Haydon, Charles, 2–4, 36, 191n2
Haydon, John Polin, 2
Haydon, Maria, 2, 12
Haydon, Matilda Rose Smith, 2, 3, 36,
    191n2
Hayes, Rutherford B. (President), 23
Healy, James A., 58
Hecker, Isaac, 51, 62, 202n62
Heider, John, 92
Heiss, Michael, 121
Henderson, George, 11, 14
Higginbotham, Evelyn Brooks, 112
Higgins Father, 128
Hoecken, Adrian, 22
Hoeffel, Jul. P., 218n26
Holy Trinity Parish (Cincinnati), 22
Howard University, 86
Hudson, Daniel E., 31
Hughes, William H., 170–71
Humbert, King, 134
Humphreys, John, 101
Hunter, S. J., 104
Hurst, John, 185

Hurt, Joe, 107

In Plurimis (encyclical), 138
Ireland (nation): campaign for the home
  rule of, 109, 131–33, 139, 210n77,
  211n79
Ireland, John: promotion of the rights
  of women, 113, 117; on the public
  school question, 119–21, 209n32;
  racial justice, views on, 41–42, 44, 51,
  55, 60–73, 75, 77, 82, 152–57, 160–61,
  163, 201n26, 202n54, 214n51, 215n71;
  treatment of Native Americans and
  Ruthenian Uniates, 201n32

Janssens, Francis, 25, 75, 78–79, 136
Jesuits: in Bardstown, 12–14; in
  Cincinnati, 22
Johnson, James Weldon, 220n72
Jones, Henry L., 147
Joseph, Satish, 192–93n17
Josephites (St. Joseph's Society of the
  Sacred Heart), 26, 31, 77–78, 149,
  153, 156–57, 164
Jourbert, Jacques Hector Nicolas,
  197n99
Journal, xv, 73, 156–58, 162, 168–70, 172,
  215n62, 216n78, 217n13
justice: church-centered, ix, 14, 18, 35,
  45–53, 55, 82, 84, 108, 149, 166, 182,
  189–90; racial, ix, xiv–xv, 17, 27, 30,
  34, 36, 38, 41–42, 44, 52–53, 55, 62–
  64, 67–69, 71–72, 74–76, 80, 82–85,
  88–89, 91–93, 98, 100, 104, 105, 112,
  124, 132, 139, 141, 145–51, 153–56, 160,
  166, 172, 181–83, 189–90

Katzer, Frederick, 121
Keane, John J., 62, 77, 119, 121
Kenneally, James J., 110
Kenrick, Francis P., 8
King, Martin Luther, Jr., 84
KKK (Ku Klux Klan), 174
Knights of St. Augustine Commandery
  No. 2, 73
Koehler, Lyle, 195n60

Labbe, Dolores Egger, 25, 78
Lackner, Joseph H., ix, 70, 219n50
Lacordaire, Henri-Dominique, 134
Lange, Mary Elizabeth, 197n99
Lavigerie, Charles (Cardinal), xiii, 32–33,
  57, 75, 97, 135–37, 156, 211n102
lay Catholic congress movement,
  xiii–xiv, 57, 59, 107, 117, 126, 134, 162,
  170, 190, 191n1, 214n37, 21718n20
Lee, Benjamin F., 96
Lehman, Martin J., 162, 215n62
Leo XIII (Pope), 52, 56, 65, 126, 128, 129,
  136, 138, 201n26, 203n77
Liberatore, Matteo, 127
Lincoln, Abraham, 24, 87
Lofton, William S., 73, 75, 86, 147,
  153–54, 159, 163–65, 216n93
Logan, Rayford, 23
Louisville Courier Journal, 53
Lynch, John R., 65
lynching, 38, 84, 89, 100–106, 133, 171,
  174, 178, 184, 186, 207n68, 211n91;
  national convention opposing in
  Cincinnati, 104–5

Maceo Club (Cincinnati), 35
Mackey, John M., 38–39, 62, 69–71,
  122–23, 145, 152–54, 167, 202n46,
  202n54, 215n51
Maes, Paul Camillus, 153
Malcolm X, 84
Manning, Henry E. (Cardinal), xiii, 129
Mayfield, Bert, 10–11
McDermott, Patrick, 156–57
McDowell, Calvin, 84, 101–2
McGhee, Fredrick, 160–61, 165, 216n93
McGlynn, Edward, 130, 210n60, 210n75
McGreevy, John T., 118, 125
McGwinn, W., 87
McKinley, William (President), 23
McNeal, Henry, 189
McQuaid, Bernard, 119
Meier, August, 96
Memphis Free Speech, 88
Merryweather, Mr., 105
Mexican Americans, 38, 84, 108

Mexico's agriculture workers, 138
Michigan Catholic, 170
Mill Hill Fathers, 78, 197n99
Mitchell, John, Jr., 87
Montalembert, Charles de, 50, 134
Morgan, Lewis Henry, 196n83
Morgan, W. H., 91
Morris, John B., 185, 187
Morton, Samuel G., 44
Moss, Thomas, 84, 101–2
Moten, Isaac, 147, 171
Moynihan, James H., 201n26
Mullaney, Katherine, 117
Mullheron, William, 122
Murray, John, 113

National Afro-American League,
    142–44, 212n5, 217n11
National Association for the
    Advancement of Colored People
    (NAACP), 18, 184–87
National Catholic Women's Union,
    209n25
National Independent (Detroit), 172
National Negro Business League, 174
Native Americans, 31, 38, 49–50, 57, 84,
    107–8, 132, 201n32
Negro American, 46
Nelson, Ida Gray, 87
Nerinckx, Charles, 12
Newman, John Henry, 134
New Orleans Crusader, 89
New Orleans Pelican, 67, 97
New Orleans Times Democrat, 68, 70,
    196n90
New York Age, 68, 75
New York Tribune, 68
Nichols, Clifton, 19,
Northwestern Chronicle, 62–63

Oats, Will, 10
Oblate Sisters of Providence, 47, 87, 147,
    197n99
Observer, 29
O'Brien, W. M., 170
O'Connell, C. J., 15

O'Connell, Daniel, 132
O'Connell, Denis J., 62
Ohio Republican (Cincinnati), 169
Ohio State Tribune, 18, 29–30, 83, 85, 99,
    194–95n60
Onahan, William J., xiv, 162
O'Reilly, Bernard, 110
O'Reilly, John Boyle, 75, 81, 203n74

Page, John, 147
papacy. *See* Vatican
Parham, William H., 90, 205n26
Parnell, Charles Stewart, 131, 133, 211n79
Paulists, 51
People's Advocate, 67
Philadelphia Sentinel, 76
Philadelphia Standard, 151
Phillips, Wendell, 87
Pilot (Boston), 203n74
Pinchback, Pickney Benton Stewart, 23
Pius, VII (Pope), 1
Pius, IX (Pope), 133
Plantevigne, John J., 77
Porter, W. B., 104
Portier, William L., 199n46
Powers, Senator (Minnesota), 65
printing school, 14, 22, 32, 189
prisons (southern), 38, 84, 97–99, 129,
    132, 146–47
public school question, 109, 118–25, 139
Puller, A. W., 102
Purcell, Edward, 62, 192–93nn16–17
Purcell, John Baptist, 62, 192–93nn16–17
Pye, Felix, 147

Queen Bee, 116

race pride, 38, 85–88, 146–47, 161, 181
racial equality, ix–x, xiv–xv, 17–18, 27,
    30, 34–36, 38, 40–46, 48, 52, 54–57,
    60–64, 66–69, 71–73, 75–77, 79–80,
    82–84, 89, 92, 100, 105, 108–9, 129,
    135, 141, 145–49, 152–55, 157, 160–61,
    166, 170, 172, 176, 180, 182, 184,
    194n59
Randolph, John, 95

Reed, Edward, 88, 101
Republican Party 16, 18–19, 24, 29,
    34–35, 62, 131–32, 190, 208n15
Rerum Novarum (encyclical), 126,
    127–29
Revels, Hiram R., 23
Review (Springfield, Ohio), 18
Reynolds, George, 19
Robinson, Belle, 11
Romantic Apologetic for Catholicism
    (Romantic Theology), 45, 47, 49–52,
    62, 108, 111–12, 199–200n46
Roosevelt, Theodore (President), 173
Rosecrans, Sylvester H., 192nn16–17
Ross, Felecia Jones, 29, 195n60, 197n92
Rudd, Anice, 192n11
Rudd, Catherine, 192n11,
Rudd, Charles, 192n11
Rudd, Charles Henry, 15–17, 192n11
Rudd, Christopher, 4
Rudd, Daniel (elder), 3–4
Rudd, Elizabeth (Eliza), 2, 6, 8, 15,
    192n2
Rudd, Frank, 192n11
Rudd, Isabella, 192n11
Rudd, James, 4
Rudd, Jemimah, 15, 194n45
Rudd, John R., 192n11, 218n26
Rudd, Josephine, 192n11
Rudd, Madison, 192n11
Rudd, Richard, 2–4, 9
Rudd, Robert, 2–4, 6, 192n2
Rudd, Robert (sibling), 16
Rudd, Sarah, 192n11
Rudd, William, 4, 6, 16, 192n11
Ruffin, George L., 35, 208n15
Ruffin, Josephine St. Pierre, 114
Ruffin, Robert L., 136–37, 147, 200n46
Ruffin Club (Cincinnati), 35, 208n15
Russwurm, John Brown, 27
Ruthenian Uniates, 201n32
Ryan, Patrick J., 33, 56, 69, 107, 159, 160,
    215n71

Sacred Heart Mission Church
    (Crawfordsville, Arkansas), 187

Scovel, S. F., 122
Second Plenary Council (Baltimore II),
    31, 135
Seward, William H., 87
sharecropping. *See* crop mortgage system
Sheedy, Morgan, 119, 122
Sherman, Ellen Ewing, 110
Sherman, William T., 110
Shillady, John, 184
Sidley, William H., 17
Simmons, Charles A., 28
Simpson, Richard, 134
Sisters of Mercy, 75
Sisters of the Blessed Sacrament for
    Indians and Colored People, 78,
    197n98
Sisters of the Holy Family (New
    Orleans) 47, 87, 197n99
Slattery, John R., 25–26, 62, 31, 77,
    81–82, 148, 152–53, 155–57, 162,
    164–65, 199n46, 202n54, 213n19,
    216n85, 216n93
slavery: African slave trade, 52, 56–57,
    90, 99, 107, 109, 135–37, 155–56;
    in Brazil, 138, 212n114; Catholic
    views on, 7–8, 52, 192nn16–17; in
    Kentucky, 1–3, 6–12, 14–15, 139,
    193n39; Protestant and Catholic
    treatment compared, 8–9; Roman,
    51; in the U.S., 2, 6–8, 15, 37, 64, 66,
    71, 78, 90, 99, 107, 132, 135, 139, 174,
    181, 189, 191n2, 204–5n24
Smith, Aaron, 173
Smith, Amanda Berry, 113
Smith, Ann, 191n2
Smith, Edward, 191n2
Smith, Harry C., 28, 34, 106, 124
Smith, John F., 80–82
Smith, Katie, 173
Smith, W. H., 149
Smith, W. J., 157
Smythe, John H., 40
Socrates, 186
Soto, Dominic, 52
Spalding, David, ix, 70, 104, 149, 165
Spalding, John Lancaster, 113

Spalding, John Martin, 7–8, 13
Spaunhorst, Henry J., xiv
Spellissy, Mary A., 117
Spencer, James A., 161, 163, 165, 216n77
Spencer, Herbert, 196n83
Springfield: Rudd's life in, 16–19
Springfield Globe-Republic, 34–35
Springfield State Capital, 123
St. Aloysius Parish (Detroit), 168
St. Ann's Parish (Cincinnati), 22
Star of Zion (A.M.E. Zion), 76, 151
St. Augustine Church (Washington,
   D.C.), 65, 67, 73, 75, 149, 201n26
St. Benedict the Moor Parish (New York
   City), 33, 217n13
St. Bernard Parish (Springfield, Ohio),
   16
St. Elizabeth Parish (St. Louis), 137
Stewart, Mr., 174–75
Stewart, William H., 84, 87, 101–2
St. Francis of Assisi Parish (Marion,
   Arkansas), 187
St. Francis Xavier's Church (Baltimore),
   164
St. Joseph Advocate, 101, 157
St. Joseph's College (Bardstown,
   Kentucky) 12, 13
St. Mary's Parish (Detroit), 168
St. Patrick Parish, (Cincinnati), 22
St. Peter Claver Church (St. Paul,
   Minnesota), 63, 65, 201n19
St. Peter and Paul Parish (Detroit), 168
St. Pius Parish (Scott County,
   Kentucky), 12
St. Raphael Parish (Springfield, Ohio),
   16–17
Strauss Brothers, 93
St. Rose Church (Washington County,
   Kentucky), 12
St. Stephen's Parish (New York City),
   130
St. Xavier's College (Cincinnati), 22
Sumner, Charles, 87
Sunday News, 18
Supremo Apostolatus (encyclical), 135
Swann, Thomas W., 162, 169

Tanner, Benjamin Tucker, 75, 96, 189
Tappert, William, 143, 212n8
temporal authority for the pope. *See*
   Vatican
Tentler, Leslie Woodcock, 170
Third Plenary Council (Baltimore III),
   30–31, 119, 135, 150, 160
Thompson, Julius, 207n68
Tisdale, W. S., 169
Tolton, Augustus, 56, 57, 59, 76, 86, 147,
   149, 162, 216n85
Torrensdale, M., 31
Towns, George A., 185–86
Truth, Sojourner, 6
Turner, Cora, 21
Turner, Nat, 84,

Umberto I (1844–1900), 211n95
Uncles, Charles Randolf, 77, 164, 216n85

Valle, Lincoln, 17, 56, 135
Vanbansher, Vintrolia, 75
Vardaman, James Kimble, 172–73
Vatican (Holy See), 31, 50, 77, 109, 127,
   133–35
Vaughan, Cardinal Herbert, 197n99
Verdin, John S., 1, 13–14
Victor Emmanuel II, 133
Volksfreund, (Cincinnati), 60

Walsh, Michael, J., 65
Wangler, Thomas E., 198n15
Washburn, William D., 65
Washington, Booker T., xv, 18, 84, 166,
   173–80, 182–85, 189, 219n50
Washington, Bushrod, 95
Washington Bee, 31, 68,
Watson, D. K., 35
Watterson, John Ambrose, 153
Wells-Barnett, Ida B., 6, 84, 88–89, 100–
   101, 106, 133, 144, 178, 189, 211n91
Welter, Barbara, 110
Wenniger, Francis Xavier, 22
Western Appeal, 75
Whig Party, 16
White, E. E., 91

White, Robert, 147
Whitely, William, 16
Whitman, Albert, 55
Whitson, James Theodore, xiii, 19–20
Willging and Hatzfeld, 170
Williams, George Washington, 18
Windon, William, 65
Wood, Robert N., 161

women: rights and equality for, 49, 51, 87, 109–18, 207–8n1
Women's Era, 208n15
World War II, 84

Yale University, 87

GARY B. AGEE is adjunct professor of church history at Anderson School of Theology, Anderson University.